THE TIMELINE HISTORY OF
LONDON

THE TIMELINE HISTORY OF
LONDON

PEOPLE PLACES PAGEANTRY

GILL DAVIES

INTRODUCTION BY GAVIN WEIGHTMAN

WORTH
PRESS

This page: Nelson's Column in Trafalgar Square.
**Page 1: London's famous clock, Big Ben, reflected in
wet pavement.**
**Page 2: Troops from the Household Division march in
front of Buckingham Palace during the Trooping the
Colour ceremony.**
Page 3: Her Majesty Queen Elizabeth II.

First published in 2005
by Worth Press Ltd and Playne Books Ltd
This revised edition first published in 2012
by Worth Press Ltd, Cambridge, England
info@worthpress.co.uk

British Library Cataloguing in Publication Data
A catalogue record for this book is available from the British
Library

ISBN: 978-1-84931-063-5

10 9 8 7 6 5 4 3 2 1

Design and layout: Arati Devasher, www.aratidevasher.com

Printed and bound in China

CONTENTS

INTRODUCTION

In the reign of Queen Victoria London became the wealthiest city in the world, and the heart of the greatest Empire in history. Yet, the very first London, buried deep beneath the mountainous tower blocks of the commercial square mile of the City, was founded by an imperialist invader. This military encampment, defending a wooden bridge on the north bank of the Thames, was established by the Romans to cross more easily into hostile territory. In time Roman Londinium became a thriving port and a bustling provincial town with an amphitheatre, a forum and a basilica. Then all this fell into ruin when the Western Empire of Rome collapsed and Londinium was no longer defended.

For many years there was a mystery about what happened to London after the Romans abandoned it in AD 410. Ancient texts still referred to it as a centre of trade. The answer turned out to be quite simple: after Londinium came Lundenwic, an Anglo-Saxon settlement just to the west of the Roman town. These invaders had no taste for Roman architecture and laid out their streets and houses on the shore of the Thames roughly where Covent Garden Opera House is now. However, when Viking invaders sailed up the river to pillage and burn, the Saxon King Alfred retreated to the safety of the old Roman town after the undefended Lundenwic had been torched. From that time on, around AD 880, London's position on the north of the Thames was firmly established.

With charts, maps, illustrations and hundreds of key facts, *The Timeline History of London* sets out the growth of this great city from that time on, and provides many details of its colourful, teeming life right up to the Olympic year of 2012. The book explores every aspect of how London developed over 20 dramatic centuries.

Successive invaders battled the Anglo-Saxons after they retreated to the surviving Roman defences of the City. But none had such a lasting impact as the Normans. After his victory at the Battle of Hastings in 1066, William the Conqueror marched on London proclaiming himself king. To secure the town and to provide a haven against a hostile population, he built castles, the most important of which was the White Tower, still standing in the centre of the Tower of London fortress. The stone was shipped across the Channel from Caen in

The River Thames has historically been the heart of London.

The Houses of Parliament, housed in the old Palace of Westminster, and London's most famous clock, Big Ben.

Northern France. In 1176, work began on the edifice which was to define London from the Middle Ages to the eighteenth century: the first stone bridge. It took 33 years to complete, spanning the river on 19 arches which slowed the tides and acted as a barrier against hostile invasions of the river. Houses and shops built across it narrowed the roadway but provided much needed income for the upkeep of the bridge.

Old London Bridge was one of the wonders of medieval Europe and was like an arm of the City reaching out across the river. As it was the only bridge in the area of what is now central London, there was little development south of the Thames except in the region of Southwark, the southern side of the bridge. The City opposed the building of rival river crossings which it feared would weaken its hold on commerce. London was still a compact town which had not spread very far beyond the old Roman wall, then, over five days in 1666, it was devastated by fire. About 80 per cent of the largely timber-built city was destroyed: more than 13,000 houses and 87 churches. Old St Paul's Cathedral was badly damaged.

Two miles to the west, the seat of political power was untouched. Westminster, the home of royalty and government, was then a place quite distinct from London itself.

The City raised money, and royalty spent it — never an easy relationship. In the days when carriages were a novelty and roads narrow and muddy, the main highway between the two was the Thames. The seventeenth-century diarist, Samuel Pepys, records taking a boat from the City to Westminster 'for speed'. In the days of sailing ships, and before the cutting of canals or building of railways, that tidal power was how London was supplied with all of its building materials and coal for its fires, and much of its food. About every six hours the tide races inland far beyond London Bridge, steadies for about 20 minutes, and then flows out again giving ships a free ride downstream.

As Westminster grew, the demand for a bridge to replace the old horse ferry became irresistible, and finally, in 1750, the monopoly of Old London Bridge was broken. London was now growing fast, outstripping its old rival Paris in terms of population and wealth. Westminster Bridge was opened just as Britain's spectacular industrialisation began, and the wealth generated by this produced, in time, sprawling suburbs, particularly south of the river which pushed the boundaries of London way out across the Thames valley. In the centre, new prosperity produced many of its most venerable monuments, such as Big Ben, built in 1859, and Tower Bridge, first opened in 1894.

By the time of the first national census in 1801 the built-up area of London housed more than a million people. This had risen to six million a century later. Between the two world wars, in the years 1918–39, the population rose by a further two million, and the built-up area doubled as miles and miles of semi-detached houses arose beyond the limits of the Victorian suburbs. The destruction of much of London's fabric in the Second World War left it with a shrunken population in 1945, but it has risen again and is now home to more than eight million people.

No world city has a biography which quite rivals that of London as it grew from Roman outpost to capital of the British Empire. This *Timeline History* gives you some highlights of the story at a glance as well as providing an up-to-date guide to museums, events, festivals and street markets.

Gavin Weightman,
London 2012

The firework display at the Opening Ceremony of the 2012 London Olympics.

THE GREAT FIRE AND ITS LEGACY
Medieval London burns down

Children are handed down to the river to escape the flames.

- The Great Fire spread from Pudding Lane in the City towards the Tower of London in the east and Whitehall in the west. In its aftermath, there was a vast rebuilding of London, largely inspired by Sir Christopher Wren's vision of a new, more open city.

On Sunday, 2 September, 1666, the Great Fire began in King Charles II's own bakery in Pudding Lane, where a maid had failed to extinguish the ovens that night. To begin with, it was largely ignored by the authorities, fires being a fairly common event in the timber-built town. In fact, the Lord Mayor, displeased at being woken, commented that 'a woman might piss it out'. Not so – fanned by a stiff wind, it spread rapidly through the old wooden buildings that were built closely together in narrow streets, with overhanging eaves that almost touched each other.

When the fire reached the Thames,

The city burns during the Great Fire of 1666.

it was further fuelled by the stores and warehouses containing highly flammable pitch, tar, timber and brandy.

There was no organised fire brigade, water sources and wells were low after a hot, dry summer, and access to much of the Thames water was cut off by the raging combustion.

Local people, armed with leather buckets, tried to douse the flames or to beat them out with staves but it was a futile attempt. When that failed, they then tried to create windbreaks by demolishing buildings that lay in the path of the inferno. At first, the Lord Mayor gave orders to stop this because the owners' consents were

needed, but many ignored him – and later, under the king's orders, he encouraged the tearing down of structures in the path of the fire. Had he permitted this in the first instance, perhaps the fire might have been contained.

As it was, the flames spread. King Charles detailed his brother, the Duke

A MAP OF LONDON

I n any map of the London the blue flow of the River Thames stands out, dividing the city into the busy, central areas of the north, and the slightly more peripheral regions of the south. The other colour that stands out is green: apart from the old, cramped streets of the City of London (the 'Square Mile'), there are small green squares or large, welcoming parks to be found at regular intervals.

Hand-drawn, pictorial maps such as this also show the comparative size of roads and buildings. The grandeur of monumental edifices such as Buckingham Palace and the Houses of Parliament can be clearly seen, while in contrast most streets contain rows of terraced buildings pressed together. Only a few roads qualify as wide boulevards, for, as a city that grew and developed naturally over time instead of being planned, most streets are relatively narrow, winding and twisting.

This is particularly evident in the oldest part of London, the City, where roads are often no more than narrow, short alleyways. Incidentally, there are no roads in the City of London – the streets are all called 'street', 'alley', 'way', or other words. They were named before the word 'road' became a common part of the English language. (William Shakespeare probably popularised the word, along with many others.)

of York, to organise guards to prevent looting as terrified Londoners deserted their burning homes and premises. Some paused to bury their valuables under the ground or hide them in the sewers. Others snatched them up to carry with them. The cost of cart hire suddenly rocketed from £3 to £30. Where the Thames was accessible, refugees packed into boats. Many others camped on high ground or in the parks.

Diarist John Evelyn described how molten lead from St. Paul's Cathedral ran down into the streets, stones flew like hot grenades and the pavements glowed a fiery red. Burning pigeons plummeted down.

After hurrying to Whitehall to report to the king, Samuel Pepys wrote:

… poor people staying in their houses till the very fire touched them, and then running into boats or clambering from one pair of stairs by the waterside to another.

The fire lasted for almost five days. At last it was checked in the east by gunpowder explosions that cleared a vast area and so saved the Tower of London.

The flames still spread westwards, however, leaping over the River Fleet and raging on until the Wednesday morning. Then, at last, the wind changed direction and the fire weakened sufficiently for its flames to be doused. It was finally extinguished by Thursday night.

The fire virtually destroyed the old city at a cost of some £11 million and burned almost all of the remaining medieval parts of London.

The losses included:

- 13,200 houses
- 87 churches
- 52 Company Halls
- 3 city gates
- St. Paul's Cathedral
- The Guildhall
- The Royal Exchange
- The Custom House
- The Session House
- Bridewell Palace
- Many other palaces and mansions
- Prisons

Amazingly, only a few people died – various accounts say 5, 9 or 16 perished,

A rebuilt London in 1740. The city has spread much further north.

although the deaths of poor people may not have been recorded. Notwithstanding this, one sixth of the population, some 100,000 people, were left homeless.

Within the city walls, five-sixths of London had vanished. Beyond the city walls, there was also fierce destruction. In total, 1.8 square kilometres (436 acres) of the city was in ruins.

However, by destroying buildings, materials, clothing and countless rats, the Great Fire did put a final stamp on the plague that had killed 68,950 people in 1665. Moreover, the dreadful slums had been burned away and the noxious waters of the Fleet were sterilised by the heat.

SUMMARY OF THE FIRE

- **Sunday, 2 September** Early hours the fire begins in Pudding Lane, spreads to Thames Street, St. Botolph's Street and Fish Street Hill. Soon, 300 buildings burn and fire reaches Thames.
- **Monday, 3 September** Southern half of city burns. Mass exodus of Londoners.
- **Tuesday, 4 September** The Guildhall and St. Paul's Cathedral

burn. Fire heads west and south. Planned explosions in east create firebreaks that stall fire. In west, fire spreads across Fleet River towards Whitehall.

- **Wednesday, 5 September** Wind drops, and the fire lessens; flames can now be doused.
- **Thursday, 6 September** All fires finally extinguished by nightfall.

LONDON'S REGROWTH

It took only five years for 70 percent of the houses to be rebuilt in London's new, wider streets.

From 1666 to 1711, Sir Christopher Wren played a large role in rebuilding the city. He designed more than 51 churches, including the new St. Paul's Cathedral which was completed by 1710 and was, at the time, the largest cathedral in Europe. The great spurt of rebuilding created a labour shortage and many migrant workers arrived. The populations of many European cities were falling at this time, but London's rose – by 1700 it could claim to be the largest city in northern Europe.

The Monument, designed by Christopher Wren and Robert Hooke,

Looking towards the west facade of old St. Paul's Cathedral, seen from Blackfriars, slightly south of Ludgate. On the right are the ruins of St. Anne's, Blackfriars.

stands near the place where the fire began, and the Golden Boy of Pye Corner is a small statue that marks where the fire ended.

Gradually the areas of London became more distinct in style. In the West End, shops and wealthy houses sprang up; the City became the centre for business and banking; and the East End was where the labourers, immigrants and those who worked on the nearby docks took lodgings.

The new city had wider and more elegant streets. The buildings were no longer timber but were built in solid stone or brick. A coal tax raised £736,000 for the rebuilding and public works programme.

In the wake of the financial crisis the fire had caused, insurance companies and fire brigades sprang up. Each had its own 'fire mark' on a lead plaque placed high on the front of a building. Whichever brigades could get there first would deal

with the fire and would then be paid back by the house-owner's brigade. It would be another 200 years before London's Metropolitan Fire Brigade was formed.

From 1700 to 1750 the many hospitals built included Westminster (1719), Guy's (1725), St. Bartholomew's (rebuilt 1730–33), St. Thomas's (1732), the London Hospital (1741), and the Middlesex (1745).

LONDON IN THE NEW MILLENNIUM

Greater London is now the largest urban zone in Western Europe, with an area of 607 square miles (1,572 sq km) and a population of more than 8 million residents. About 40 percent of London is green space or parks, making it one of the 'greenest' cities of its size in the world.

London has more than 150 ancient monuments and historic buildings and four world heritage sites: Maritime Greenwich; Westminster Abbey, Westminster Palace and St. Margaret's Church; the Tower of London, and the Royal Botanic Gardens at Kew.

The new Globe Theatre is the first London building since medieval times to be permitted a thatched roof.

AD 50　　　200　　　400　600

ROMAN LONDON: LONDINIUM　**ANGLO-SAXON LONDON**

BUILDINGS AND INSTITUTIONS

AD 50 Londinium is founded by the Romans. The main settlement is on the north bank of the Thames, a smaller one on the south side.

60 Queen Boudicca with Iceni warriors attacks London. The Romans and other inhabitants flee and the first Londinium is razed to the ground.

70–100 Londinium is rebuilt with the first forum, basilica and amphitheatre. A bridge, probably the second, is built over the Thames.

120 A new forum and basilica are completed. There are two public bath houses, shops and workshops.

c.200 A wall is built enclosing Londinium. It is at least 6 metres high (20 feet) surrounded by a wide ditch. Gatehouses are built into the wall: Ludgate to the west, Bishopsgate to the north, and Aldgate to the east.

c.250 The Temple of Mithras, the eastern God of Heavenly Light, is built.

c.275 A riverside wall is built connecting the eastern and western ends of the existing wall around London.

c.300 Britain is divided into four provinces, reducing the importance and wealth of London. Major public buildings are demolished.

c.350 Around 20 defensive towers are built on the eastern side of London wall.

c.368 London is given the title Augusta (Imperial). But it is still in decline.

410 Romans no longer defend London: their rule is finished.

410–50 People leave the town and it is finally deserted.

604 Christian missionaries convert some pagan Saxons and, according to the monk Bede, Ethelbert of Kent builds a church in London dedicated to St. Paul.

670 A Royal Charter refers to the port of London, and later archaeological evidence confirms that, just north of where the Strand runs now, there were wooden buildings which were perhaps Saxon warehouses.

THE RIVER, PORT AND TRANSPORT

125–30 Archaeological evidence that much of the town was burned down. No historical records.

140 Roman London at its population peak, perhaps 50–60,000.

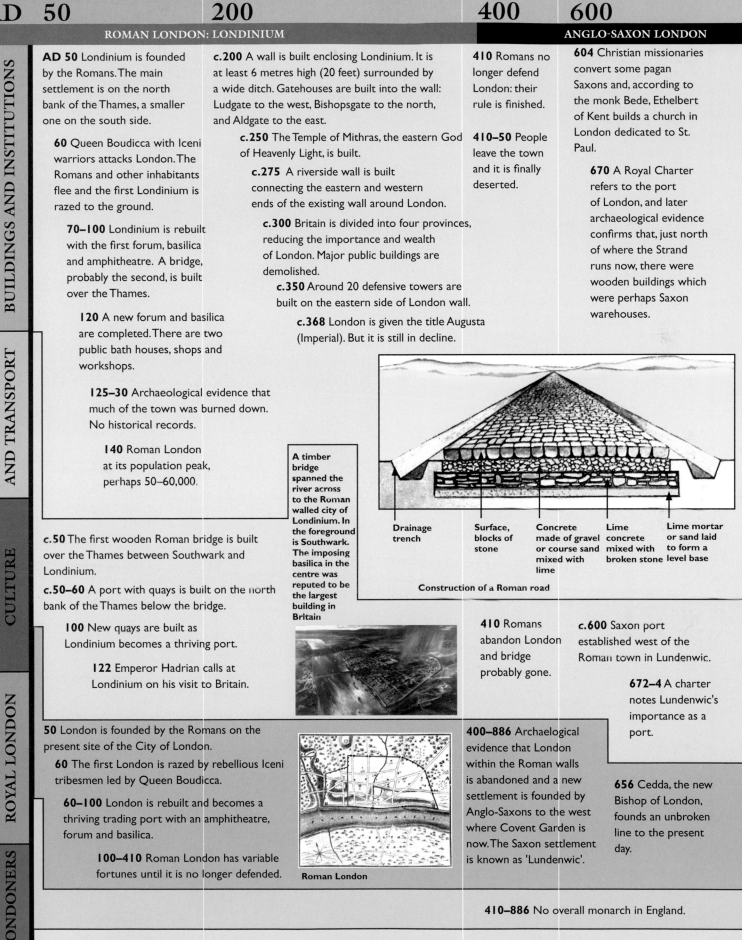

A timber bridge spanned the river across to the Roman walled city of Londinium. In the foreground is Southwark. The imposing basilica in the centre was reputed to be the largest building in Britain

Drainage trench

Surface, blocks of stone

Concrete made of gravel or course sand mixed with lime

Lime concrete mixed with broken stone

Lime mortar or sand laid to form a level base

Construction of a Roman road

SOCIETY AND CULTURE

c.50 The first wooden Roman bridge is built over the Thames between Southwark and Londinium.

c.50–60 A port with quays is built on the north bank of the Thames below the bridge.

100 New quays are built as Londinium becomes a thriving port.

122 Emperor Hadrian calls at Londinium on his visit to Britain.

410 Romans abandon London and bridge probably gone.

c.600 Saxon port established west of the Roman town in Lundenwic.

672–4 A charter notes Lundenwic's importance as a port.

ROYAL LONDON

50 London is founded by the Romans on the present site of the City of London.

60 The first London is razed by rebellious Iceni tribesmen led by Queen Boudicca.

60–100 London is rebuilt and becomes a thriving trading port with an amphitheatre, forum and basilica.

100–410 Roman London has variable fortunes until it is no longer defended.

Roman London

400–886 Archaeological evidence that London within the Roman walls is abandoned and a new settlement is founded by Anglo-Saxons to the west where Covent Garden is now. The Saxon settlement is known as 'Lundenwic'.

656 Cedda, the new Bishop of London, founds an unbroken line to the present day.

FAMOUS LONDONERS

410–886 No overall monarch in England.

LONDON'S POPULATION

	60 30,000.	**100–200** 60,000.	**250** 15,000.	**410** 10,000.	**600+** Lundenwic 10–12,000.

Note: Population figures are for the built up area of London. Estimates to 1801, then Census figures.

ANGLO-SAXON **LATE SAXON/DANISH**

BUILDINGS AND INSTITUTIONS

c.800 All Hallows-by-the-Tower built.

842 Lundenwic is attacked and probably destroyed by Viking invaders from Denmark.

c.960 A Benedictine monastery dedicated to St. Peter is founded on Thorney Island to the west of the City. It becomes known as the West Minister as opposed to the East Minister of St. Paul's.

Location of Westminster

1018 The Danish King Cnut has London pay 10,500 pounds of silver to prevent his fleet from attacking, and settles in the town beginning 25 years of Scandanavian rule in which several churches are built. He builds a palace on Thorney Island.

1042 Edward the Confessor becomes king and work begins rebuilding St. Peter's Abbey, which is consecrated in 1065 before it is finished and just before he dies. It is thought he also builds a palace next to the Abbey.

Edward the Confessor's Tomb, Westminster Abbey

THE RIVER, PORT AND TRANSPORT

886 The Saxon King Alfred pushes back the Danish invaders and begins to rebuild London inside the old Roman walls.

851 Viking ships sail up the Thames and attack London.

c.900 Lundenwic becomes the 'Old Town' or Aldwych. London is called Lundenburg.

994 A Viking armada of 94 ships attacks London but is driven back.

886 Saxon King Alfred abandons Lundenwic and moves back inside Roman London and its defensive wall.

1000 Lundenburg described as centre for international trade with duties paid at Billingsgate wharf.

1009 The Danes again sail up the Thames to attack London, but are repulsed.

1014 According to the *Olaf Sagas* the Norwegian King Olaf Haraldsson pulls down the wooden London bridge with his boats, throwing the defending Danes into the river.

Viking longships terrorised London for centuries

SOCIETY AND CULTURE

886 King Alfred re-occupies the old Roman London as a defensive move. New streets are laid out.

c.990 Aelfric lists the goods a London merchant might have: silks, precious stones, gold, wine, olive oil, ivory, bronze, and glass among the luxuries.

994 Vikings begin a major assault on London but are beaten back.

c.1000 Customs duties at Billingsgate paid on timber, fish, chickens, eggs, and butter. Merchants come from France, Flanders and Germany.

1016 Cnut, son of Swein Forkbeard of Denmark, becomes King of England. He charges London merchants 10,500 pounds in silver to pay off his seamen.

1016–1042 Cnut's family rule England. Their reign comes to an end when his son King Harthacnut dies suddenly at a wedding feast in Lambeth, south of the Thames.

1042–1065 Edward does not have a royal residence in London but settles at Westminster where he builds a church and a royal hall. A week later, his church is dedicated at Christmas.

ROYAL LONDON

886 Alfred the Great (king from 871 to 889) makes London one of his fortresses or "boroughs" to defend against the Danes.

889–1042 London has no significant royal connections.

Alfred the Great: according to legend he took shelter with a humble housewife and was so absorbed in thoughts of the Danish invasion that he let the cakes burn

Edward the Confessor as shown on the Bayeux Tapestry

1042 Edward III, nicknamed 'The Confessor', who had been brought up in Normandy, founds the Royal connection with Westminster, building the first Abbey.

FAMOUS LONDONERS

LONDON'S POPULATION

1066 The crowning of William the Conqueror in Westminster Abbey begins the reign of the Normans and a new phase of building in London.

1078 The White Tower, originally a wooden fort on an earth mound, is rebuilt in Caen limestone by Bishop Gundulf of Rochester. It remains as the keep of the Tower of London.

1087 The Anglo-Saxon church of St. Paul's burns down. Rebuilding takes 200 years, with another fire in 1136.

1097–9 William II, the Conqueror's son, rebuilds Westminster Palace. The Hall, much of which survives today, is believed to be the biggest in Europe.

1106 A new church, St. Mary Overie (or Ovary, meaning 'over the river'), is built on an ancient site in Southwark on the banks of the Thames.

1107–8 Holy Trinity Priory, Aldgate, is the first religious house to be built inside the walls of London.

1123 Land granted at Smithfield for the building of St. Bartholomew's Priory, a medieval hospital and the oldest in Britain which is known affectionately today as Barts Hospital. Also the Priory Church of St. Bartholomew.

c.1128 Some evidence that a guildhall was built here on the site of the former Roman amphitheatre.

1066 Edward has no heir and both the Norman duke William, son of his cousin Robert, and the English Earl Harold of Wessex think they have been promised the Crown. Harold beats off a Norwegian force in Yorkshire only to be defeated by William at Hastings. ¤ William the Conqueror is crowned King of England in Westminster Abbey on Christmas Day having placated the powerful citizens of London.

1066–1215 William is wary of Londoners and what was described as 'the restlessness of its large and fierce populace' so he builds fortresses within the city. One is Baynard's Castle on the west side of town, and another the Tower of Montfichet by St. Paul's Cathedral. The work on the White Tower begins around 1080. ¤ London is governed locally by a 'portreeve' chosen by William.

1091 A great storm on 16 November destroys many buildings in London and another wooden London bridge is swept away.

1085 William orders a survey of his new kingdom, the Domesday Book. There is little mention of London but information on farming villages such as Stepney and Kensington, as well as Fulham, a noted fishing village.

1109 The Bishop of Winchester builds a palace, Winchester House, near Southwark Bridge.

c.1120 Queen Matilda, wife of Henry I, founds the Hospital of St. Giles to care for lepers. Leprosy is a feared disease which has taken the lives of two bishops of London.

1130 Among the immigrants to London are Jews from France who settle in Jews' Street, named Old Jewry, and are led by Rabbi Joseph.

1130–40 Suburbs are growing in Southwark and out towards Westminster. These are mostly inhabited by poorer people. William Fitz Stephen remarks 'almost all the bishops, abbots and nobles of England are, as it were, citizens and townsmen of London, having their fine houses there'.

c.1133 A fire destroys much of the timber-built City from Aldgate to St. Paul's.

1130–33 Henry I recognises the importance of London as a source of wealth and, according to legend (the document has never been found), gives the city a charter which permits some self-government and a right to trade freely.

1066 Harold II is the first king to be crowned in Westminster Abbey. When Harold is killed in the Battle of Hastings Edgar Atheling claims the crown. No record of a coronation. ¤ The crowning of William I in Westminster Abbey on Christmas Day begins the hugely influential Norman development of London. Claiming that he had been promised the crown by Edward III, William made sure of seizing it with 600 transport ships and an army of 7,000, including 2–3,000 cavalrymen.

1087 William II (William Rufus) the Conqueror's son is crowned. He builds Westminster Hall.

1100 Henry I marries Matilda in Westminster Abbey, the first Royal Wedding to take place there.

William the Conqueror greeting English leaders after he is crowned king

c.1118 Thomas Becket is born in Cheapside, City of London. Becomes Archbishop of Canterbury and is murdered in the Cathedral. Venerated as a saint and martyr.

1135 The last of the Norman Kings, Stephen, a nephew of Henry I is crowned in Westminster Abbey. His wife, Matilda, is crowned Queen Consort.

1139 Henry I's daughter, Matilda, claims she is the rightful heir to the throne and civil war breaks out. After Stephen is captured Londoners prevent Matilda being crowned, invading her pre-coronation feast.

c.1135 Birth of Henry Fitz Ailwin de Londonestone, first Mayor of London.

NORMAN LONDON

BUILDINGS AND INSTITUTIONS

1155 A Royal Charter granted to the Weavers' Company, one of the early trade associations known as guilds. ¤ The Fleet Prison is built close to the Ludgate entrance to the City. The keeper is especially privileged with housing and income and is also the keeper of Westminster Palace. It is known as the king's Fleet Prison, a royal keep like the Tower of London.

1197 Foundation stone laid for the Augustinian priory St. Mary without Bishopsgate is laid. This is later known as St. Mary's Spital.

c.1207 The earliest buildings on the site of Lambeth Palace, originally known as Lambeth Manor or Lambeth House.

1183 In his description of London, the monk William Fitz-Stephen claims there are thirteen great Conventual Churches (those established by orders of nuns or monks) and 126 parish churches.

1150: The Thames freezes for 3 months.

1185 The round Temple Church built by the Knights Templar is consecrated. It is modelled on the Church of the Holy Sepulchre in Jerusalem and survives today among the buildings of the Inner Temple off Fleet Street.

London's first Lord Mayor, Henry Fitz Ailwyn is elected

THE RIVER, PORT AND TRANSPORT

1189 Tradition has it that Henry Fitz Ailwin de Londonestone becomes the first Mayor of London. It is a title borrowed from French towns such as Rouen which have some independence from royal government. As well as the mayor, London has aldermen from the Anglo-Saxon tradition, guilds whose members pay a subscription, and hustings derived from Viking laws. The future structure of City rule is already taking shape.

1209 Stone London Bridge is completed.

1170 Archbishop Thomas Becket, the son of a Rouen merchant Gilbert Becket, is murdered in Canterbury Cathedral by knights who believe Henry II wanted him killed. He is adopted as Patron Saint of London. A hospital in Southwark is named after him – St. Thomas's – as is, later, the chapel on the new, stone London Bridge.

1144 The Clink Prison is built in Winchester House, Southwark.

SOCIETY AND CULTURE

1196 A rare uprising of London's poor is led by the scholarly Fitz Osbert, nicknamed 'The Bearded', who assembles a raggle-taggle army with which to rob the rich. He is defeated by the Archbishop of Canterbury's forces, pulled apart by horses and hanged along with some of his supporters.

1148 The Royal Hospital and Collegiate Church of St. Katharine by the Tower is founded by Queen Matilda.

1170s William Fitz-Stephen writes that there are 123 monastic churches and 126 parish churches in London. An exaggeration, but a measure of London's importance and wealth.

1189–99 London begins to claw back some of its freedoms under the rule of Richard I called Coeur de Lion (the Lionheart) who is absent for many years fighting in the crusades, and as a prisoner in Austria.

1200 London's population is perhaps 30,000 with many immigrants from Europe and frequent visitors. Merchants from Rouen and Caen in northern France favour London for its lively trade. Germans, settle in London too, including 'Men of Cologne' who have a house near the Thames.

ROYAL LONDON

1207 Lambeth Palace becomes the official residence of the Archbishop of Canterbury.

1154 The age of Norman rule comes to an end with the death of Stephen.

1154–1189 The first of the Plantagenets, Henry II, is crowned in Westminster Abbey. He is the ruler not just of England but of a large part of France down to the Pyrenees. In his long reign he spends only 13 years in England. He takes away the right of the City to elect its own sheriffs.

King Henry II

King John signs the Magna Carta

1199–1216 John 'Lackland' is king. Falling out with the most powerful men in England, the barons, he is forced in 1215 to agree to a charter limiting the power of the monarchy. It is later known as Magna Carta and also confirms ancient privileges of the City of London.

FAMOUS LONDONERS

LONDON'S POPULATION

1210 St. Helen's Bishopsgate, a priory of Benedictine nuns, is founded. It becomes William Shakespeare's parish church when he lives in London. It survives the Great Fire and the Blitz but is badly damaged in the early 1990s by IRA bombs which explode nearby. Much of the original remains in the restored building.

1212 After a serious fire, the first mayor, Henry Fitz Ailwin, bans new thatched roofs. ¤ Church of St. Mary Overie at Southwark is rebuilt after extensive fire damage.

1216 King Henry III ascends the throne at the age of nine, the first in a line of Plantagenet monarchs who would rule for more than three turbulent centuries.

1224 A group of Dominicans, reforming monks from Europe, build on the sites of the Norman fortresses Baynard's Castle and Montfichet in the area now known as Blackfriars. (Dominicans wear dark habits and are known as the Black Friars, while the Franciscans are known as the Grey Friars.)

1234 King Henry III bans legal education in the City, while a Papal bull forbids the clergy to teach common law. Lawyers migrate to Holborn and in time found the Inns of Court.

c.1237 What becomes known as York House is built on the Strand as a London home for the Bishops of Norwich. It is later the home of the Archbishop of York which gives its name.

1240 The Archbishop of York buys a property in London near Westminster and calls it York Place. This will later grow to be Whitehall Palace. ¤ The rebuilt St. Paul's Cathedral is consecrated.

1241 Carmelite friars arrive in London and are in time given a site near the river in the area of what is now Fleet Street.

1245 Placed strategically between the City of London and Westminster, the Savoy Palace is built on the Strand.

1212 A fire in Southwark spreads to houses on London Bridge and flying embers set houses on the north side of the bridge alight trapping people in the middle. Many killed, but the death toll is unknown.

King John's Charter

1236 In his *Chronicles of England*, Stow says the Thames overflowed its banks and 'in the Palace of Westminster men did row with wherries in the midst of the hall'. ¤ A lead pipe, or conduit, brings water from the river Tyburn, which runs into the Thames at Westminster, into the City of London.

1242 A great flood spreads out from Lambeth on the south bank for six miles, once again engulfing Westminster.

1249 King Henry III takes over control of London Bridge to use the revenues from rents to pay for his wars.

1214 Prince Louis, son of the King of France, is invited by English barons to usurp the throne of King John who is accused of failing to honour the agreements of Magna Carta. He enters London and is crowned in St. Paul's Cathedral as Louis VIII.

1216 King John dies and his nine-year-old son Henry is crowned in Gloucester Abbey, bringing to an end support for Prince Louis.

1217 Louis gives up his claim to the English throne by signing the Treaty of Lambeth.

1216–72 Henry III raises taxes and angers the barons and the Church, but gives to charity and starts the rebuilding of Westminster Abbey. In his battles with the barons led by Simon de Montfort, a Great Parliament is called in 1256 and, for the first time, representatives from cities and burghs are called to Westminster.

Crusaders bring leprosy back to London

1235 A menagerie is set up in the Tower of London with the gift of three leopards from Holy Roman Emperor Frederick to Henry III.

The Tower of London today: it housed a menagerie until the 1830s

1250	1260	1270	1280	1290

BUILDINGS AND INSTITUTIONS

1256 Work begins to enlarge St. Paul's Cathedral.

Old St. Paul's Cathedral

1275 A Custom House is built on Wool Quay near Billingsgate to collect tax on exported goods, the most valuable of which is wool.

The 'Eleanor Cross' at Charing Cross station

1294 When his Queen Eleanor of Castile dies in Nottinghamshire in 1290, Edward I has crosses erected at each of the places the funeral cortege stops on its way to Westminster Abbey. The last of these is erected close to Whitehall at the hamlet of Charing. Initially carved from wood, it was replaced by one of carved Caen stone and becomes known as Charing Cross. A replica stands in the forecourt of the railway station of that name.

THE RIVER, PORT AND TRANSPORT

1269 King Henry gives custody of the bridge to Queen Eleanor who allows it to fall into disrepair.

1275 The First Custom House is built to oversee the collection of duties on imports.

1263 Anger at Henry III's tax demands, and his staging of fairs in Westminster to rival those of the City, leads to rebellion and a short-lived civil war. Henry's wife Queen Eleanor is pelted and abused by a London crowd as she goes from the Tower to Windsor. Simon de Montfort challenges Henry's troops and is supported by London. Violence gets out of hand and many Jews, perhaps 500, are killed, before Henry reasserts his power and takes away property from the rebellious Londoners.

1294 A tidal surge floods Bermondsey Priory, breaching a river wall, and causes some damage to St. Thomas's Hospital in Southwark.

1281 King Edward I gives ownership of London Bridge back to the City of London. But it is in bad condition and five arches collapse following the break-up of ice on the Thames.

SOCIETY AND CULTURE

1252 Street lighting is introduced as small, carefully managed bonfires.

1275 Edward I introduces the first official customs duties to be paid on goods coming in and out of London as a way of raising funds for his military campaigns. Wool is the most important commodity.

1297 Pigsties are banned from the streets.

1266 Henry III gives the Hansa merchants a charter for trading in London. Known as the Hanseatic League, they in time build an enclosed courtyard by the Thames called The Steelyard.

1281–84 King Edward I uses his influence to get Henry le Waleys elected Mayor of London so that he can clamp down on rowdiness, crime and those who break the nightly curfew when the City is shut down. Violence continues and a leading goldsmith is lynched in St. Mary-le-Bow Church.

1285 A riot in Newgate Jail is followed by a further clamp-down by King Edward who favours foreign merchants and has a new prison, the Tun, built on Cornhill.

ROYAL LONDON

King Edward I

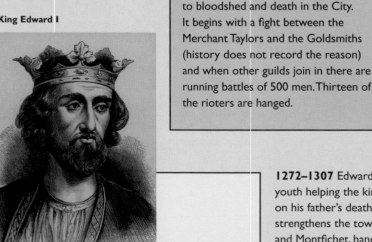

1267 Fighting between guilds leads to bloodshed and death in the City. It begins with a fight between the Merchant Taylors and the Goldsmiths (history does not record the reason) and when other guilds join in there are running battles of 500 men. Thirteen of the rioters are hanged.

1290 As resident aliens in London, the Jewish community has no legal rights and relies on protection of the monar. They are often persecuted, with 300 p to death on a charge of 'coin clipping', but provide money for the Crown. The fate is sealed when Italian bankers mo in and they are all expelled unless they convert to Christianity. Old Jewry is taken by Christians.

FAMOUS LONDONERS

1272–1307 Edward I 'Longshanks', son of Henry III, spends much of his youth helping the king in his battles with the barons. When he becomes king on his father's death he seeks to impose more regal control on London. He strengthens the tower and gets rid of the two other Norman castles, Baynard's and Montfichet, handing them over to religious orders. He encourages foreign merchants to settle in the City, which is not a popular move.

LONDON'S POPULATION

PLANTAGENATE LONDON

1300 Enlarged St. Paul's is consecrated

1310 Thought to be the date that Lincoln's Inn formally becomes one of the four Inns of Court to which barristers belong.

1337 Middle Temple established about this time.

1344 Carpenters' Guild incorporated.

1345 Durham House, home to the Bishop of Durham, is built on the Strand. It later becomes a royal residence and home to Henry VIII's second wife Anne Boleyn.

1307 Bakers' Guild gets its charter of incorporation: Master and Wardens of the Mystery or Art of Baking of the City of London.

1314 The Cathedral that becomes known as Old St. Paul's is finally completed. It still has a timber roof, but one of Europe's tallest spires at 489 feet high (149 m).

1327 The Goldsmiths' Company gets its first Royal Charter. ¤ Billingsgate Market gets a charter to trade in corn, coal, iron, wine, salt, pottery, and seafood.

1339 The first Goldsmith's Hall is built on the site of several later halls.

1351 Temple Bar, a wooden structure marking the boundary between Westminster and the City of London, is erected on the site of an older barrier or chain. It is here that a ritual exchange of swords confirms the loyalty of the City to the Crown and gives the monarch access to the City.

1305 The head of the Scot, William Wallace, who had been hanged, drawn and quartered for treason, is put on the Drawbridge Gate of London Bridge, the start of a gruesome ritual which lasts more than three centuries.

William Wallace

1358 The warden's accounts show that there are 138 rent-paying shops on London Bridge.

1315 Across northern Europe, harvests are ruined by bad weather and famine is widespread. London does not escape and a chronicle records that two small onions were worth a day's wage.

Patients suffering from the Black Death

1348 The 'sweating disease' which has been spreading across Europe hits London in the winter and lasts for a year. Nobody knows what the death toll was but the name the 'Black Death' gives some idea of the horror and devastation of the disease. Was it bubonic plague? After years of dispute scientists claim they can prove it was so with DNA testing of victims' remains.

1368–9 Another plague epidemic.

1361 Plague returns, killing many children who had no immunity.

1307–27 Edward II continues to antagonise Londoners who support Isabella of France, his wife, when she invades England. In 1327 Edward is forced to renounce the throne in favour of his 14-year-old son who becomes Edward III.

1337–77 Edward III antagonises London's merchants by allowing in Italians and members of the Hanseatic League to trade freely. He needs money to fight the battles of what becomes known as the Hundred Years' War with France, and there are labour shortages and price rises after the Black Death kills a large part of London's population.

Geoffrey Chaucer

Edward III

c.1343 Geoffrey Chaucer, author of *The Canterbury Tales*, is born in the City, the son of a vintner.

BUILDINGS AND INSTITUTIONS

1370 Records of lawyers being established at Grays Inn from this date. Originally in the family home of Baron Grey of Wilton.

1371 The Charterhouse, the name for this monastery derived from the order of French monks known as *La Grande Chartreuse*, founded in Smithfield.

1373 A permanent prison is built in Southwark for those held prisoner by the Court of Marshalsea, the name derived from Marshal. A second prison close by is built for the Court of King's Bench.

1378 Custom House rebuilt.

1393 Richard II commissions a new roof for Westminster Hall.

1400 King Henry IV gives the City the right to collect tolls and customs at Billingsgate and Smithfield.

1411 Work begins on the building of a new Guildhall which is complete in 1440.

1415 A doorway or postern in the old Roman wall between Bishopsgate and Cripplegate is replaced by a larger structure leading out of the City to Moorfields. It is called Moorgate.

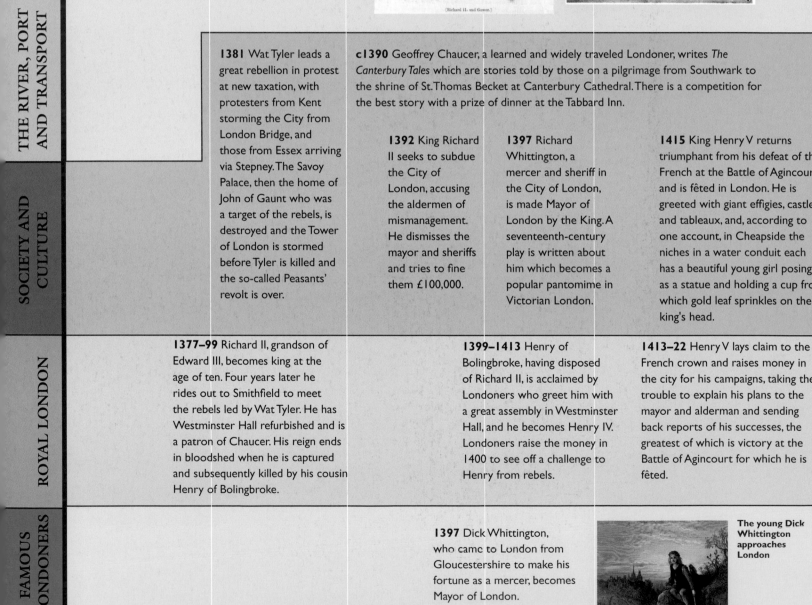

Richard III on the Thames

[Richard II. and Gower.]

Builders at work

THE RIVER, PORT AND TRANSPORT

1381 Wat Tyler leads a great rebellion in protest at new taxation, with protesters from Kent storming the City from London Bridge, and those from Essex arriving via Stepney. The Savoy Palace, then the home of John of Gaunt who was a target of the rebels, is destroyed and the Tower of London is stormed before Tyler is killed and the so-called Peasants' revolt is over.

c1390 Geoffrey Chaucer, a learned and widely traveled Londoner, writes *The Canterbury Tales* which are stories told by those on a pilgrimage from Southwark to the shrine of St. Thomas Becket at Canterbury Cathedral. There is a competition for the best story with a prize of dinner at the Tabbard Inn.

SOCIETY AND CULTURE

1392 King Richard II seeks to subdue the City of London, accusing the aldermen of mismanagement. He dismisses the mayor and sheriffs and tries to fine them £100,000.

1397 Richard Whittington, a mercer and sheriff in the City of London, is made Mayor of London by the King. A seventeenth-century play is written about him which becomes a popular pantomime in Victorian London.

1415 King Henry V returns triumphant from his defeat of the French at the Battle of Agincourt and is fêted in London. He is greeted with giant effigies, castles, and tableaux, and, according to one account, in Cheapside the niches in a water conduit each has a beautiful young girl posing as a statue and holding a cup from which gold leaf sprinkles on the king's head.

ROYAL LONDON

1377–99 Richard II, grandson of Edward III, becomes king at the age of ten. Four years later he rides out to Smithfield to meet the rebels led by Wat Tyler. He has Westminster Hall refurbished and is a patron of Chaucer. His reign ends in bloodshed when he is captured and subsequently killed by his cousin Henry of Bolingbroke.

1399–1413 Henry of Bolingbroke, having disposed of Richard II, is acclaimed by Londoners who greet him with a great assembly in Westminster Hall, and he becomes Henry IV. Londoners raise the money in 1400 to see off a challenge to Henry from rebels.

1413–22 Henry V lays claim to the French crown and raises money in the city for his campaigns, taking the trouble to explain his plans to the mayor and alderman and sending back reports of his successes, the greatest of which is victory at the Battle of Agincourt for which he is fêted.

FAMOUS LONDONERS

1397 Dick Whittington, who came to London from Gloucestershire to make his fortune as a mercer, becomes Mayor of London.

The young Dick Whittington approaches London

LONDON'S POPULATION

1447 Humphrey, Duke of Gloucester, builds a palace that he calls Bella Court at Greenwich on the south bank of the Thames. When he is arrested for treason and dies in prison Bella Court became a royal palace, birth place of Henry VIII and Queen Elizabeth I.

Humphrey, Duke of Gloucester

1476 William Caxton establishes a printing press at Westminster.

William Caxton

1422 The procession for the Lord Mayor's Show goes on the Thames from the City to Westminster for the first time.

1428 Thirty people die when their barge 'shooting' London Bridge hits one of the piers. The Duke of Norfolk is saved when he jumps onto the pier and is pulled on to the bridge by rope.

1450 Anger at rising taxes used to pay for the long war with France gives rise to a rebel army in Kent led by Jack Cade. Several thousand strong, they march on London and are joined by protesters from Essex. Crossing London Bridge, Cade's army executes some prominent members of the Royal Household and loots the houses of the wealthy before retreating to Southwark. The following day the rebels are beaten back on London Bridge. The king pardons Cade and then has him arrested and executed.

1455 Outbreak of the War of the Roses between rival claimants to the English throne, the Lancastrians (Red Rose) and the Yorkists (White Rose). London maintains "self-interested neutrality" favouring one side and then the other.

1471 Henry VI, deposed and then re-crowned, is imprisoned in the Tower of London and dies there, almost certainly murdered. ¤ Richard III has Henry's body buried in a Chapel at Windsor. Henry is venerated as a saintly martyr.

Battle of Agincourt

War of the Roses`

1421–61 Henry VI is born at Windsor Castle and ascends the throne when he is just nine months old, the youngest English monarch. He is crowned King of England in 1429 and King of France in 1431. Though he founds Eton and King's College, Cambridge, he loses a lot of French land and makes life difficult for London merchants by selling off important administrative posts in order to raise money. He becomes a victim of the War of the Roses, is imprisoned in the Tower of London and is probably killed there.

1461–83 Edward IV trades wool in order to bring in independent funds and draws on the profits of the Crown Estates. He is a good financial manager, encourages trade, and is not too lavish with his court at Westminster where his staff numbers around 600: musicians, grooms, knights, clerks, and cooks among them.

Thomas Wolsey

c.1473 Thomas Wolsey is born in Ipswich, the son of a butcher. As a friend of Henry VIII he becomes immensely powerful and wealthy; he transforms Hampton Court Palace and York House, which becomes Whitehall Palace.

1478 Thomas Moore is born in Milk Street, in the City. He is knighted but falls out with Henry VIII over the king's marriage to Anne Boleyn and is executed in 1535.

TUDOR LONDON

BUILDINGS AND INSTITUTIONS

1485 After victory over Richard III at Bosworth Field, Henry VII becomes king and brings in the era of Tudor London.

Battle of Bosworth Field

Crest at Drapers Hall building

1509 The start of the reign of Henry VIII during which London is dramatically transformed by the break with the Catholic Church during the Reformation.

1512 The Palace of Westminster is largely destroyed by fire and it ceases to be the home of royalty.

1515 There are 48 livery companies in the City and the Court of Aldermen draws up an order of precedence based on their relative wealth and power. The top ten Worshipful Companies are Mercers (general merchants), Grocers, Drapers, Fishmongers, Goldsmiths, Merchant Taylors (tailors), Skinners (furs), Haberdashers, Salters, and Ironmongers.

1518 The Royal College of Physicians gets its Royal Charter.

1519 York Place, the home of Cardinal Thomas Wolsey, is described as 'a very fine palace'.

THE RIVER, PORT AND TRANSPORT

1513 Henry VIII establishes the Royal Dockyards at Deptford and Woolwich to build warships.

The Royal Docks at Deptford

SOCIETY AND CULTURE

1485 Henry VII, nephew of Henry VI, defeats Richard III at the Battle of Bosworth and continues the veneration of his uncle so that a Cult of Henry VI arises. Londoners make pilgrimages to his grave at Windsor and souvenirs are mass produced. The saintly Henry is credited with curing all kinds of diseases.

1499–1500 Plague returns with a vengeance, reputedly killing thousands once again. It is never absent for long in the 1500s.

c.1501 Wynkyn de Worde, William Caxton's apprentice, moves away from Westminster and sets up a printing shop near Fleet Street, beginning the long association there with the press.

1517 Rioting by apprentices angry at foreign influences in the City. Henry VIII sends troops to subdue the mob and the ringleaders are hanged, drawn and quartered. A few are pardoned.

1519 Cardinal Thomas Wolsey, still enjoying the patronage of Henry VIII, and a powerful figure in Government, asks for records of deaths from plague, perhaps a forerunner of the London Bills of Mortality which are later collected weekly by parish clerks.

ROYAL LONDON

1483–85 Richard III arrives in London with his nephew Edward, the coronation of the boy fixed for 22 June. In mid-June Edward and his brother Richard are declared illegitimate and imprisoned in the Tower. They are never heard of or seen again.

1485–1509 The reign of the Tudors begins with the victory of Henry Tudor at Bosworth where Richard III is killed. When he comes to London to be crowned as Henry VII he is greeted at Shoreditch with trumpeters and gifts.

1509–47 The reign of Henry VIII changes the entire social structure and ownership of London when the huge amount of land and property owned by the Catholic Church and various monastic orders is confiscated and taken over by wealthy laymen.

FAMOUS LONDONERS

Henry VII

Henry VIII

LONDON'S POPULATION

1500 50–70,000.

1530 Henry VIII takes over York Place where he has often stayed and turns it into Whitehall Palace, his principal residence now that Westminster Palace is being rebuilt after a fire destroyed it.

1531 Henry has a new palace, St. James's, built on the site of the Hospital of St. James in Westminster. Completed four years later, much of the building survives today.

1532 Henry confiscates the land of a former leper colony and creates St. James's Park, the first Royal Park in London.

1536 Large-scale confiscation of religious property begins during the Reformation and many of the finest London properties change hands as the monasteries and nunneries are sold off, filling the coffers of Henry VIII's treasury. ¤ Hyde Park is taken out of the possession of the monks of Westminster Abbey and becomes a private hunting ground for the King.

1540 The Dissolution of the Monasteries is complete, the finest buildings bought by noblemen who turn them into fine town houses.

1546 Henry VIII relents and saves St. Bartholomew's and St. Thomas's hospitals from dissolution.

1547 When Henry VIII dies his Whitehall Palace covers 23 acres and is the largest royal residence in Europe, with a tennis court and a tiltyard for jousting.

1548 The Crown takes over the pasture and gardens of the Convent of St. Peter, Westminster, in the area later known as Covent Garden.

1549 The Duke of Somerset begins the building of his mansion on the Strand which is named Somerset House, on the site of the current and much later building of that name. ¤ A medieval townhouse formerly owned by the Bishop of Bath and Wells is bought by Henry Fitz Alan, twelfth Earl of Arundel, and is named Arundel House where early meetings of the Royal Society would be held.

1536 Henry VIII reported as travelling in a carriage on the frozen Thames from London to Greenwich.

A Tudor explorer's ship

1538 The Common Council of the City decrees that journeymen should work from 6 AM to 6 PM in winter with 90 minutes of breaks for meals for 7 pence, and two hours longer for an extra penny in summer.

1552 The Company of Merchant Adventurers is founded to fund the fitting out of three ships to search for a north-eastern route to Asia. The expedition is led by Richard Chancellor and Sir Hugh Willoughby. Chancellor makes it through to Russia and negotiates a trading deal with Ivan the Terrible which leads to the formation of the Muscovy Company, the first of the great trading companies which helps make London's fortune. Sir Hugh's ships are wrecked on the Lapland coast and he and his crew perish.

The Tudor buildings of the Queen's House, Tower of London. It was built about 1530 by Henry VIII, probably for Anne Boleyn, who was later beheaded at the Tower Green

Anne Boleyn

1547–53 Only nine when he becomes king, Henry VIII's son Edward reigns for only six years before his death from tuberculosis.

Burning at Smithfield

1553 Just before he dies, Edward is persuaded to name Lady Jane Grey as his heir. She is deposed after nine days.

1553–58 London suffers the return of heresy laws under the rule of Mary I, known as 'Bloody Mary' for her brutal treatment of Protestants who refuse to convert to the Catholic faith. Many are burned at the stake in Smithfield.

c.1552 Edmund Spencer, the poet and author of *The Fairie Queene*, is born in East Smithfield.

BUILDINGS AND INSTITUTIONS

1557 The Earl of Leicester builds a mansion on the Strand which becomes Essex House when bought by Robert Devereux, the Earl of Essex. After demolition it becomes Essex Street.

1561 The spire of St. Paul's crashes through the roof when a fire melts the bells and lead on the roof, leaving the Cathedral badly damaged.

1566–7 Sir Thomas Gresham founds the first Royal Exchange. It becomes the city's business centre.

1555 The Company of Watermen and Lightermen (carrying passengers and goods respectively), is established by Act of Parliament to regulate London's chief form of transport.

1576 The theatre is established in Shoreditch after playhouses are banned in the City of London.

1577 The Curtain Theatre opens in Shoreditch.

1580 Because of fears that London is growing too fast, Elizabeth I issues a proclamation that there should be no new building within three miles of the gates of London, and that in the City there should be no more division of houses into tenements. It has little effect.

1581 The first Banqueting House built by Elizabeth I to hold entertainments when she is negotiating to marry the Duke of Alencon. It is made of timber and canvas.

1587 The Rose theatre opens on Bankside, Southwark.

Interior of The Royal Exchange

THE RIVER, PORT AND TRANSPORT

1564–5 Elizabeth I walks on the frozen Thames.

1558 When she becomes queen in 1558 Elizabeth I passes a Royal Act to create legal quays on the north bank of the Thames below London Bridge with rights to handle taxable goods.

1579 Another flood at Westminster leaves fish floundering on the floor of the Hall when the river recedes.

1580 A Dutchman, Peter Morris, establishes a tidal mill on the north side of London Bridge to pump water into the City.

SOCIETY AND CULTURE

1554 Fears that Catholic Queen Mary would marry Philip II of Spain (as she did) lead to an uprising led by Thomas Wyatt. Londoners back Mary and prevent Wyatt and his supporters from crossing London Bridge. The rebel army takes a long way round via Kingston and is defeated at Ludgate. Wyatt and other leaders are executed, most hanged, drawn and quartered.

1555–57 Protestants are burnt at the stake in Smithfield as Queen Mary imposes Catholic religion on the country.

1563 Bubonic plague returns, affecting the parishes in the centre of the City more than the outskirts. It is thought a greater proportion of Londoners lose their lives in this epidemic than in the plague years that followed.

1576 One of London's first purpose-built playhouses is built in Finsbury Fields by the theatrical entrepreneur James Burbage, as the demand for entertainment grows in London.

1580 The Levant Company is formed with a Royal Charter giving it a monopoly of trade with Turkey.

1583 Parishes are charged with carrying out Plague Orders, appointing people to search for the sick and the dead in an attempt to control the spread of the disease. Plague Orders are regularly made after this date, often associating unruly behaviour with the spread of the disease. ¤ The Venice Trading Company formed.

ROYAL LONDON

1558–1603 Queen Elizabeth I, daughter of Henry VIII and Anne Boleyn, is highly cultured, speaks six languages, and encourages exploration. In 1600 she gives the Royal Charter to the East India Company which contributes hugely to London's future wealth. A patron of the theatre, Shakespeare's company put on performances for her at Greenwich.

1564 The Thames freezes over. Queen Elizabeth I 'shoots at marks' on the river and Londoners play on the ice, though there is no Frost Fair as such.

Elizabeth I

FAMOUS LONDONERS

1572 Benjamin Jonson, playwright, is born in or near London and goes to school in St. Martin's Lane. ¤ John Donne, the poet and one-time Dean of St. Paul's Cathedral, is born in London.

1573 Inigo Jones, one of London's greatest architects, is born in Smithfield, the son of a cloth worker.

Inigo Jones

LONDON'S POPULATION

TUDOR LONDON   STUART LONDON

1595 The Swan theatre built in Southwark.

1597 Gresham College is founded with an endowment left by Sir Thomas Gresham, merchant and builder of the Royal Exchange who dies in 1557. It is housed in his former home in Bishopsgate until 1768 when it is relocated several times before settling at its present building in Holborn.

1599 The Globe theatre built by William Shakespeare's playing company The Lord Chamberlain's Men (destroyed 1613, rebuilt 1614).

1611 Thomas Sutton, a coal magnate from Lincolnshire, leaves money to create the Charterhouse hospital and school on the site of the old Carthusian monastery in Smithfield.

1611–12 Robert Baker, a tailor and manufacturer of fashionable stiff-collars or peccadilloes, builds a house which is nicknamed Peccadillo Hall, and in time gives its name to the street Piccadilly.

[The Globe Theatre, Bankside.]

The Globe theatre in the 16th century (above) and its reconstruction today

1600 The Fortune theatre built just to the north of the City.

1604 Red Bull theatre opens in Clerkenwell.

1605 One of the grandest buildings on the western outskirts of London, Holland House, is built by Sir Walter Cope on a 500-acre estate. Parts of it still survive as a theatre, art gallery, youth hostel, and restaurant, though most is destroyed in the Blitz. ¤ The Guild of Butchers is given its Royal Charter.

1613 The New River is finally completed bring fresh water into a reservoir in Clerkenwell from the villages in Hertfordshire. Gravity provides the flow as the river drops five inches every mile. ¤ The Globe theatre burns down when a cannon accidentally goes off and sets the thatched roof alight during a performance of Shakespeare's *King Henry the Eighth*.

1609 Robert Cecil, first Earl of Salisbury, begins London's expansion westwards when he buys plots of open land called St. Martin's Field and lets it out on 31-year building leases. ¤ The Banqueting House in Whitehall is rebuilt in brick and stone and is a place of entertainment.

1588 A great triumphal procession is held by Elizabeth I in celebration of the defeat of the Spanish Armada. The Lord Mayor waits at Temple Bar to present the Queen with the keys of the City, while she presents the Lord Mayor with a pearl-encrusted sword, one of five City swords. This tradition has been preserved for more than 400 years, and the ceremony now is carried out on major state occasions where the Queen halts at Temple Bar to request permission to enter the City of London, and is offered the Lord Mayor's Sword of State as a sign of loyalty.

1593 Bubonic plague returns.

1600 The East India Company gets its Charter.

1603 The civic ceremony to mark the accession to the throne of James I is postponed because of an outbreak of plague. His coronation is put off until the following year.

1608 The Thames freezes over and people play on and ride across it.

1614 The Thames watermen fail to get a Bill passed in Parliament against 'outrageous coaches'. A novelty introduced from Europe, the horse-drawn coach is becoming popular.

1605 Gunpowder Plot. The plot to blow up the House of Lords along with King James I during the State Opening of Parliament on 5 November is foiled at the last minute when the conspirators are betrayed. Guy Fawkes, with cloak and lantern, is found in the basement of the building along with barrels of gunpowder. ¤ The ritual of wealthy landowners leaving their country estates to spend the winter and spring in London is frowned upon. King James I criticises 'swarms of gentry who, through the instigation of their wives and to new-model and fashion their daughters...did neglect their country hospitality and cumber the city...'

1617 The East India Docks are opened at Blackwall to build ships for the East India Company, one of the great merchant-adventurer companies of London.

1609 The Virginia company formed to trade with the American colonies.

Christopher Wright   John Wright   Thomas Percy   Guido Fawkes   Robert Catesby   Thomas Winter
Robert Winter

1603 Elizabeth I dies.

1603–25 James I begins the dynasty of Stuart monarchs. Already king of Scotland for 36 years when he ascends the English throne, James survives the Gunpowder Plot and commissions the architect Inigo Jones to build the Banqueting House in Whitehall.

Guy Fawkes and the Gunpowder Plot

1608 John Milton, the poet and author of *Paradise Lost*, is born in Bread Street.

John Milton

1592 The first definite record that William Shakespeare is working as an actor and playwright in London.

BUILDINGS AND INSTITUTIONS

1615 The livestock market at Smithfield is paved and enclosed with railings.

1616 Work begins on the Queen's House in Greenwich designed by Inigo Jones for Anne of Denmark, wife of King James I. She dies in 1618 while it is being built and the house is not completed until 1629.

1619 The new Banqueting House is destroyed by fire and rebuilt in a much grander style by Inigo Jones who brings back classical influences from Italy.

1630 The 4th Earl of Bedford, owner of the land formerly belonging to the Convent of St. Peter, commissions Inigo Jones to build a square with housing and a church.

1630–41 The first housing is built, with permission of King Charles I, at Lincoln's Inn Fields.

1631 The so-called Dutch House is built at Kew by Samuel Fortrey, a Dutch merchant. It has distinctive carved brickwork and round gables in the Dutch style. In the eighteenth century it is lived in by royalty and becomes known as Kew Palace.

1632–6 Robert Sidney, Earl of Leicester, builds Leicester House in what is still a rural fringe of London. What becomes Leicester Square is ground used for drying clothes.

1642–3 When Civil War breaks out London becomes the headquarters of Oliver Cromwell and the Parliamentarians opposing the Royalist armies of Charles I, who moves to Oxford. At great expense, defensive earthworks with forts at intervals are built around London running from Wapping, through Islington to Tottenham Court Road, across the river to Vauxhall and back along south of the river to Wapping.

1644 The Globe theatre is demolished and tenements built on the site.

1647 Cromwell wins the Civil War. ¤ The original Charing Cross, erected by Edward I in memory of his consort Queen Eleanor, is removed by Puritans.

1645 The Company of Watermen petition King Charles I against the increasing use of Hackney carriages on the streets of London.

THE RIVER, PORT AND TRANSPORT

1621 The first 'Hackney coach', fore-runner of the London taxi, plies for hire.

1633 St. Paul's Church, Covent Garden is completed in Tuscan style by Inigo Jones.

1637 Charles I opens Hyde Park to the public.

1642 The Puritans close down London theatres.

Sedan chairs become available for hire like taxis

1634 Sedan chairs become available for hire and are a popular form of transport for the well-to-do.

1644 A Parliament dominated by Puritans bans the traditional Christmas festivities which involve a great deal of eating and drinking. May Day celebrations are also banned.

SOCIETY AND CULTURE

1625 Plague kills over 41,000 Londoners.

1632 The London Season is becoming popular with the aristocracy who are leasing houses in the new West End developments. But King Charles I does not like the development and 37 noblemen, 147 baronets and knights, and 130 gentlemen appear before the court of Star Chamber for ignoring an order to stay on their country estates instead of enjoying themselves in town.

1636 The City of London refuses to take on responsibility for the slum-like suburbs that have grown up around it. Charles I creates a new authority to provide local government for this growing region but it vanishes at the outbreak of the Civil War.

1642 The outbreak of Civil War between the Royalists, supporting King Charles I, and the Puritans. London is a stronghold for the republican cause. Their Trained Bands of soldiers, funded by the Livery Companies, play a vital role in the defeat of Charles.

1647 A change of heart in London brings about an attempt to support the king, but fear of Cromwell's New Model Army puts an end to it.

ROYAL LONDON

Charles I is beheaded

1625–49 Confrontation between King Charles I and Parliament leads to Civil War in which the king flees to Oxford and the Parliamentarians or Roundheads occupy and govern London, closing the theatres. Charles is beheaded on a scaffold erected by Banqueting House in Whitehall.

Trial of Charles I

1649 The beheading of Charles I on 30 January takes place outside the Banqueting House in Whitehall rather than at the Tower to avoid a procession through the City and to make it easier to control. According to an eye-witness the crowd gives 'a great groan' when the axe comes down.

FAMOUS LONDONERS

1632 Christopher Wren, leading architect of London after the Great Fire, is born in East Noyle, Wiltshire, the son of the rector.

1633 Samuel Pepys, MP, Naval Administrator and author of a famous Diary, is born in Salisbury Court off Fleet Street.

1649–60 The interregnum: the monarchy is abolished.

LONDON'S POPULATION

1620 280,000.   **1630** 200,000.   **1640** 350,000.

1656 Cromwell lifts a ban imposed in 1209 on Jews living in England and the first synagogue is built in Creechurch Lane in the City.

Cromwelll dissolves the Long Parliament

1651 Hay's Wharf, which becomes the largest riverside warehouse in London, is opened by Alexander Hay.

1654 Parliament approves the regulation of Hackney coachmen.

1652 Although the playhouses are shut down, it is not all misery in Cromwellian London. There is opera, public dancing, coach racing in Hyde Park and many other entertainments. ¤ The first of hundreds of coffee houses opens in the City after Daniel Edwards, a member of the Levant Company, brings back from Sicily as a servant Pasqua Rosée who knows how to prepare and brew the unfamiliar beverage. It becomes popular with Edwards' friends and he sets up Rosée in business, first of all in a tent.

1655 Oliver Cromwell lifts the ban on Jews living and working in London.

There are coffee rooms in the City. Cocoa or chocolate houses also appear

1661 An old road between Charing Cross and St. James's Palace is replaced by a new road built on the line of the old Pall Mall Alley where the croquet-like game of pelle melle is played with mallets, hoops and wooden balls. It is developed as Pall Mall.

1662 Charles II gives Henry Jermyn, 1st Earl of St. Albans, a lease of land south of Piccadilly and he begins the building of St. James's Square.

1663 Theatre Royal, Bridges Street, is opened by Thomas Killigrew, theatre manager and playwright. It is a forerunner of the 1663 Theatre Royal Drury Lane.

1662 The first Hackney carriage licenses are issued.

1663 A tidal surge floods Whitehall.

1658 The death of Cromwell leaves London in a lawless state, with shops closing up and trade suspended.

1665 Thomas Wriothesley, Earl of Southampton, builds a square in the district of Bloomsbury and a town mansion, Southampton House.

1666 Great Fire of London. Over five days about 80 per cent of London is razed to the ground as a conflagration, driven by an east wind, leaves 87 parish churches, 44 Guild halls and 13,200 houses smoking ruins. Though it is thought fewer than ten people die in the fire, an estimated 80–100,000 are made homeless. St. Paul's Cathedral is badly damaged. Westminster is spared. ¤ King Charles appoints commissioners to oversee the rebuilding of the city.

1667 The rebuilding of London begins almost immediately. But grand plans drawn up by Christopher Wren and others are rejected. Much of the old street pattern remains, but there are new rules about the width of roads, the height of buildings and the use of brick and stone rather than timber.

1667 Rebuilding of riverside wharfs and quays begins after the Great Fire of 1666.

1669 A new Royal Exchange is opened replacing the early building destroyed in the fire. ¤ The Shadwell Waterworks company is founded to pump water from the Thames to about 8,000 houses in Stepney and east Smithfield. The pump is horse-powered.

1669 A 'flying coach' service is begun between London and Oxford. On a good day the journey is made between sunrise and sunset. Much faster coach services begin to link London with other cities.

1660 General Monck, commander of the British army in Scotland, returns to bring order to London. He finds disillusion with the Puritans and a mood to restore the monarchy. Charles II returns from exile to London to be welcomed with roads strewn with flowers and wine flowing from the fountains. ¤ The theatre returns to London after the Puritan ban. But only two theatre companies are licensed to perform serious drama, the King's Company and the Duke's Company. Other theatres can put on musical shows and pantomimes in which there is no speech.

1660–85 The Restoration of the Monarchy with Charles II enthroned. He extends St. James's Park and opens much of it to the public. Hyde Park, sold off by the Parliamentarians, is returned to the royals and opened again to the public. London comes back to life.

1663 There are 82 coffee houses in the City. Some also begin to sell cocoa and chocolate.

1665 Great Plague. The wealthy flee London when the plague strikes once again. Though funeral processions are banned, Londoners ignore the order and follow coffins. Samuel Pepys records in his Diary how empty the streets are. In September deaths are running at 8,000 a week. By December the plague has abated and shops begin to open again as people return.

1666 Refugees from the Great Fire camp out in Moorfields and other parts of the rural hinterland of London. Some return to their homes in the countryside, others cram into the suburbs that escape the fire. The king orders temporary markets to be opened in Islington and other outlying districts. A nationwide charitable appeal is launched.

1659 The composer Henry Purcell is born St. Ann's Lane, Old Pye Street, Westminster. He becomes organist at Westminster Abbey.

1661 Nicholas Hawksmoor, who works with Wren on St. Paul's Cathedral and builds six of London's finest churches, is born in Nottinghamshire.

1669 The actress Eleanor or 'Nell' Gwyn becomes the mistress of King Charles II. She later lives in a house in Pall Mall.

Nell Gwyn

Sir Christopher Wren

BUILDINGS AND INSTITUTIONS

1670 The Duke of Bedford gets a Royal Charter for Covent Garden market which has grown up without any official licence. It is for the sale of fruit and vegetables and stall holders now have to pay rent to the estate.

1670s The age of housing speculation begins, with its most unscrupulous operator Dr Nicholas Barbon. He devises a way of borrowing money to buy plots of land to the west of the City and selling on to builders who put up rows of terraced houses, a form of mass production. On the Strand he has the old palaces and mansions pulled down and replaced with streets. He develops Rupert Street and Gerrard Street in Soho, Red Lion Square and Bedford Row in Holborn. ¤ Most of the Palaces that line the Strand with a waterfront onto the Thames are demolished as the area is redeveloped.

1672 A new and grander gate to the City, the Temple Bar, is rebuilt in stone reputedly to a design by Christopher Wren. The ornate arch leading out towards Westminster has four statues: Charles I, Charles II, James I and Anne of Denmark.

c.1676 St. James's Square is developed with town houses for the aristocracy, and St. James's Church, designed by Wren, is begun.

1676 Commissioned by Charles II and designed by Christopher Wren, the Royal Observatory is built at Greenwich to improve timekeeping and navigation through astronomy. ¤ A fire destroys 500 houses in Southwark and kills 20 people, more than the death toll in the Great Fire. ¤ Chelsea Physic Garden is founded.

1682 Charles II revives old Spitalfields Market to the east of the City which had been on the site since 1638 but declined. New buildings are put up selling fruit, vegetables and meat.

1683 Sir Thomas Bond with a syndicate of developers buys Clarendon House in Piccadilly, demolishes it and begins the building of Bond Street, the first finished section known as Old Bond Street. They also build Dover Street and Albermarle Street running north from Piccadilly. ¤ The second theatre to open after the Restoration is the Musick House in Clerkenwell run by Richard Sadler. When he finds a well on the site he promotes the waters as a cure-all and Sadler's Wells becomes very popular for a while.

1688 Meeting in a coffee house of that name, Lloyd's is founded for the insurance of shipping.

1689 William III choses not to live in Whitehall, which is damp and run-down, and instead buys a Jacobean mansion built in 1605 in the village of Kensington to the west of London and has it turned into a palace, with the help of Christopher Wren. It is renamed Kensington Palace

THE RIVER, PORT AND TRANSPORT

1673 The Central Criminal Court, known as the 'Old Bailey', replaces the medieval court destroyed in the Great Fire.

1675 A new St. Bride's Church, Fleet Street, is completed to replace the medieval church destroyed in the fire. It is the first of 50 churches to be built to replace the 87 lost in the fire. Christopher Wren is the architect. ¤ York Building Waterworks, a commercial water supply company, begins to supply houses close to where Villiers Street is today. ¤ Foundations laid of the new St. Paul's Cathedral.

1677 The Monument commemorating the rebuilding of the Great Fire is completed to the design of Christopher Wren and Robert Hooke. Its height is the same as the distance of the column from the site of the Great Fire: 212 feet (65m).

1690 There are 420 horse-drawn coach services between London and nearby towns, most within 40 miles.

SOCIETY AND CULTURE

1683–4 A great Frost Fair is held on the Thames with bull baiting on the ice, a printing press set up to sell notes with the names of revelers and the date they stood on the frozen river, and an ox is roasted.

1680 A London Penny Post service is begun for delivery of letters in the City and Westminster.

1690 London gin distillers lose their monopoly as the Governmen encourages the production of cheap, home-produced spirits to compete with foreign brandy.

1685 French protestant refugees, the Hugenots, begin to arrive in London when religious tolerance is revoked by Louis XIV. They bring with them many skills in weaving, hat and instrument making, settling in Spitalfields, Soho and Wandsworth over the next few years.

The Great Fire of London

ROYAL LONDON

Frost Fair on the Thames, 1683

1685–88 The return of a Catholic monarch, James II, divides London once again. His son James Stuart 'The Old Pretender', and grandson Charles Edward Stuart 'The Young Pretender' promise a Catholic dynasty. Anti-Catholicism means that when Protestant William of Orange invades from Holland he is welcomed. He is crowned with his wife Mary (James II's daughter) in Westminster Abbey and for the first time there is a king and a queen. The Act of Settlement ensures that royalty will be Protestant.

FAMOUS LONDONERS

1688 The poet Alexander Pope is born the son of a linen merchant in Plough Court, Lombard Street.

LONDON'S POPULATION

1674 500,000.

1691 Whitehall Palace damaged by fire.

1692 The Chelsea Hospital for old soldiers is opened on a site adjoining the Thames.

1698 A fire much more destructive than that of 1691 destroys nearly all the buildings of Whitehall Palace, sparing only the Banqueting House of Inigo Jones which survives to the present day. ¤ Stockbrokers are expelled from the Royal Exchange for rowdiness and meet in coffee houses, favouring Jonathan's in the City where they later form a new club.

1699 An Act of Parliament makes Billingsgate Market 'free and open for all sorts of fish whatsoever' breaking the monopoly of a few fishmongers. The Dutch eel boats are allowed to keep their monopoly as they had helped feed Londoners after the Great Fire.

1703 A great storm on 7–8 December (26–27 November in the old Calendar) ravages London. The new slate roofs put up in place of thatch after the Great Fire are sent crashing into the street and hundreds of chimneys are blown down. The lead roof comes off Westminster Abbey.

1705 Buckingham House, which will later be remodelled as Buckingham Palace, is built as the home of the 1st Duke of Buckingham partly on land known as the Mulberry Garden after the trees planted as food for silk worms. ¤ The Queen's Theatre is opened in the Haymarket. Rebuilt it becomes the Kings Theatre and, in 1837, Her Majesty's Theatre on the accession of Queen Victoria. Rebuilt again it becomes the Italian Opera House, finally Her Majesty's Theatre again in 1952. ¤ The first buildings of a new Royal Hospital for Seamen are completed on the site of the former Royal Palace at Greenwich. The complex of buildings and courts takes nearly half a century to complete.

1707 Hugh Mason, who has a stall in St. James's Market, and William Fortnum, a footman in the Queen's household, form a trading partnership which will grow into one of the most prestigious stores in London and the world: Fortnum & Mason on Piccadilly.

1711 Marlborough House is completed for Sarah Churchill, Duchess of Marlborough and is the London home of the Marlboroughs for a century before becoming a royal residence. ¤ The newly rebuilt St. Paul's declared officially completed on Christmas Day. ¤ Concerned about the rapidly rising population of London and lack of places of worship, Parliament sets up a commission for building fifty new churches.

1712 A rebuilt York Buildings Waterworks company is the first of its kind to use a steam engine instead of horses to pump water from the River Thames.

Kensington Palace

The Old Billingsgate Fish Market

1699 At Rotherhithe on the south side of the Thames the Howland Great Wet Dock is opened for the refitting of East India Company ships.

1709 London fan makers, now including many French refugees, petition for a Royal Charter so that they become a Worshipful Company which can employ apprentices and oppose foreign competition. It is the newest of the old Livery Companies.

1711 The South Sea Company which, in theory, will make huge profits from trading with Spanish colonies in South America even while Britain remains at war with Spain, is set up with government backing as a way of paying off the National Debt. Shares are issued and become popular with wealthy investors. ¤ Sir Gilbert Heathcote, taking part as Lord Mayor in the annual pageant of the Lord Mayor's Show, is thrown from his horse and breaks a leg. Next year a coach is hired and from then on the Mayor travels in a carriage or on the river.

1702–14 In the brief reign of Queen Anne the Parliaments of Scotland and England are united under a common flag and with common coinage.

Castle Baynard where Charles II died in 1685

1697 William Hogarth, printmaker, satirist and cartoon maker, is born at Bartholomew Close, London, to an improvished school teacher and his wife.

1702 Jack Sheppard is born in Spitalfields to a poor family. He becomes London's most celebrated thief and jail-breaker before being hanged at Tyburn at the age of 22.

1709 Samuel Johnson is born in Lichfield, Staffordshire. He settles in London as a young man where he is known as Dr Johnson and as author of the *Dictionary of the English Language*. He says famously 'A man who is tired of London is tired of life.' He is buried in Westminster Abbey.

1710 George Frederick Handel, composer of *Water Music*, performed on Thames barge for King George I, settles in London.

BUILDINGS AND INSTITUTIONS

1714 George I of the House of Hanover becomes King and London's colourful Georgian era begins.

1714–33 The Commission for new churches provides the funds for some of London's finest surviving places of worship including: Christ Church, Spitalfields; St. John's, Smith Square; St. George's, Hanover Square; St. Mary le Strand, and St. George's, Bloomsbury.

1717 Work begins on laying out Cavendish Square just north of Oxford Street as a speculative housing venture by Edward Harley, Earl of Oxford, who owns the land. The name alludes to his wife Henrietta Cavendish-Holles.

1717–19 The Earl of Scarborough begins development of Mayfair, laying out a square named in honour of the new monarch. Hanover Square is first occupied by aristocrats and leading military men.

1720 First known as the Little Theatre, the Theatre Royal Haymarket is the venture of a carpenter who builds it on the site of the King's Head Inn and a gunsmith's shop. It is the third oldest surviving theatre in London. ¤ The Westminster hospital for the poor opens, the first of a number of famous London voluntary hospitals to be built in Georgian London.

1721 Guy's Hospital is founded by Thomas Guy, a publisher who made a fortune as a speculator, to care for incurable patients from St. Thomas's Hospital.

1722–7 George I has Kensington Palace refurbished with added State rooms.

1726 The old church of St. Martin-in-the-Fields is pulled down and replaced by the building which survives today overlooking Trafalgar Square.

1723 The Chelsea Waterworks Company is founded to supply the area around Hyde Park and Green Park, taking water from the Thames and storing it in reservoirs.

1731–5 A new street of houses is put up on the estate of the 3rd Earl of Burlington and is named Savile Row after his wife Lady Dorothy Savile.

1732 The first Covent Garden Theatre.

1733 St. George's Hospital established by a group of doctors in Lanesburgh House close to Hyde Park. ¤ Queen Caroline, wife of George II, commissions the landscaping of Hyde Park and Kensington Gardens and has the Serpentine created by the damning of the River Westbourne.

THE RIVER, PORT AND TRANSPORT

The Thames freezes again in 1716 and an ox is roasted whole on the ice

1729 A wooden bridge is built across the Thames at Putney, the only permanent crossing between Old London Bridge and Kingston-upon-Thames.

1730 There are around 200 coaching inns in London – the hub of London's transport system until the coming of the railway in the 1830s.

SOCIETY AND CULTURE

1715 The accession of George I of Hanover triggers an uprising among Catholic supporters of James II which leads to violence in London.

1719–20 The so-called Calico Riots are triggered by the importation of cheap Indian cotton goods which threaten the livelihood of Spitalfields silk weavers. Women wearing cotton are attacked and have their clothes ripped off them. The leader of the rioters is put in the stocks, but Parliament bans the wearing of cotton in 1721 to protect the silk weavers.

1720 The Honourable Society of Knights of the Round Table is formed by a group of actors, artists and literary friends, who are concerned that the ideals of chivalry, associated with King Arthur, are almost forgotten by their generation. Later Charles Dickens becomes a member. ¤ The Gin Craze causes great concern as the cheap spirit leads to widespread drunkenness. ¤ In a few months of national madness, share prices in the South Sea Company rise from £100 each to £1,000. Then they plummet leaving many investors impoverished.

1724 The gallows at Tyburn are large enough to hang 21 people at a time. There are galleries for public viewings of the hangings.

ROYAL LONDON

King James I on the Thames

1714–27 The first of the Hanoverians, George I, spends very little time in London. He speaks little English and leaves government up to politicians, notably Robert Walpole.

1727–60 George II also spends much of his time in Hanover. London is threatened by an invasion led by Charles Stuart, or Bonnie Prince Charlie, who believes he has the right to the throne, but his troops turn back before they reach the City. Robert Walpole takes up George II's offer of a house at 10 Downing Street.

FAMOUS LONDONERS

George I

1725 Huge crowds turn out to witness the hanging of the criminal Jonathan Wild at Tyburn. He posed as a thief taker while running a gang of criminals.

Jonathan Wild

LONDON'S POPULATION

1715 630,000.

1734 The Bank of England, founded in 1694, gets its first purpose-built premises in Threadneedle Street in the City of London. ¤ A new building for the Treasury designed by architect William Kent is opened on Horse Guards.

1738 The piecemeal redevelopment on the site of the former London home of Lord Berkeley, which had been sold to the Duke of Grosvenor, is begun. In time it becomes Berkeley Square.

1739 The London Foundling Hospital is built at Lamb's Conduit Field by Thomas Coram to care for abandoned children.

1740 The London Hospital is founded, built on what is then a quiet road leading to the village of Mile End. It is for the poor of Aldgate. ¤ Grosvenor Square is completed, the centrepiece of the Grosvenor estates.

1745 Middlesex Hospital is founded to provide care for the poor of Soho. ¤ The West Towers of Westminster Abbey, designed by Hawksmoor, complete the building.

The Bank of England

1747 The London Lock Hospital is opened in Grosvenor Place for the treatment of syphilis. It is the first of its kind in London.

1749 London's first maternity hospital, the British Lying-in Hospital for Married Women is established in Covent Garden by doctors unhappy with the treatment of pregnant women at the Middlesex Hospital.

1739 Construction starts on Westminster Bridge, hampered by a bitter winter.

1739–40 A Frost Fair begins on Christmas Day and continues until mid-February. On 21 January a temporary thaw piles many of the booths and shops up against London Bridge where they become a frozen mass when the temperature drops again.

1740 The Thames freezes again.

1735 Robert Walpole, as First Lord of the Treasury, moves into a refurbished and enlarged 10 Downing Street. Though it is not an official title, Walpole is generally regarded as the first prime minister.

1743 Riots break out when an attempt to stamp out the gin craze by raising taxes and issuing licences makes the popular spirit unaffordable.

Gin Lane, **William Hogarth's illustration of the evils of cheap gin**

1736 A big improvement in street lighting comes about with a new law making the payment of lamp contractors the responsibility of alderman who charge householders in the City. The lamps burn rapeseed oil and have a reflector to increase their brightness. ¤ Riots in Shoreditch and Spitalfields break out in protest against an influx of Irish workers accused of undercutting the wages of Londoners. Irish inns are smashed up.

1745 Charles Edward Stuart, known as Bonnie Prince Charlie, marches south with an army of 6,000 men in a bid to reclaim the crown for his father. He is expected to head for London, but turns tail in Derbyshire and is defeated at Culloden in 1746.

1748 An Act of Parliament gives power to local parishes and vestries to levy rates for street paving and other improvement works. Also, 100 or so unelected Commissions with the same powers are created.

1738 Spitalfields gets the right to levy a rate for street lighting.

1739 The number of oil lamps lighting the streets is vastly increased to 5,000 provided by 17 contractors. In 1736 there about 1,000 lamps.

Dick Turpin and his exhausted horse

1739 Dick Turpin, butcher turned burglar, horse thief and highwayman who terrorised Londoners north and south of the river, is tried and hanged in York where he had been living under a pseudonym.

1746 The Venetian painter Canaletto comes to London to live for eight years recording (with embellishments) the building of the first Westminster Bridge.

Westminster Bridge

BUILDINGS AND INSTITUTIONS

1750–60 The Horse Guards buildings and parade ground are built on the site of the old tiltyard of Whitehall that had been used for jousting.

1752 Princess Augusta, recently widowed wife of Frederick, Prince of Wales, oversees the development of the gardens around Kew Palace which become in time the celebrated Kew Gardens.

1753 A bequest of the physician Sir John Soane provides the first collection of a new British Museum. To his own collection of 71,000 manuscripts and other objects King George II adds the 'Old Royal Library'.

1759 The British Museum is housed in its first home, Montague House. Admission is free.

Montague House

1760s Four city gates, Moorgate, Ludgate, Bishopsgate and Aldgate are taken down to ease the flow of traffic. Dismantling of the old London Wall begins as the City expands beyond its old boundaries.

1762 King George III acquires Buckingham House as a private residence for Queen Charlotte and it becomes known as The Queens House. ¤ The gentleman's club, Boodles, named after the head waiter, is formed with premises in Pall Mall before a move to its present site in St. James's Street.

1764 Henry William Portman begins to develop an inherited 200 acres of meadowland to the south of the New Road, London's first by-pass. Portman Square, with fine houses designed by Robert Adam and James 'Athenian' Stuart make for very fashionable new addresses. ¤ The gentleman's club Brooks's is founded with four dukes among its 27 members. Originally in Pall Mall, it later moves to its present site in St. James's Street.

THE RIVER, PORT AND TRANSPORT

1750 Westminster Bridge – London's second – is opened as a replacement to the ancient and much hated Lambeth horseferry.

1756–7 London's first by-pass, the New Road, is built for cattle driven from the west country to Smithfield Market, avoiding the centre of town. It is now Euston Road.

1757–62 To ease the flow of traffic the crumbling shops and houses on Old London Bridge are taken down.

1759 The central arch of London Bridge is widened, forming the Great Arch.

SOCIETY AND CULTURE

1750 Sir John Fielding, magistrate at Bow Street, recruits six ex-constables to form a force of thief takers commanded by Saunders Welch, High Constable of Holborn. They are popularly known as Bow Street Runners.

1751 Bethnal Green gets an Act allowing it to raise a street lighting rate. ¤ The Gin Craze is finally suppressed with new legislation on licensing.

1752 The Murder Act passed a year earlier comes into force with the intention of deterring would-be killers. No convicted murderer can be buried but must be either dissected or hung in chains.

1755 A Society of Cogers has its first meeting in a room above a tavern in Bride Lane off Fleet Street to debate and promote free speech and freedom of the press. John Wilkes is a founder member. ¤ Samuel Johnson's *Dictionary of the English Language* is published nine years after he was commissioned to write it by a group of London booksellers who paid him £1,575 (about £230,000 today).

1762 The Westminster Paving Act passed to create commissioners responsible for paving, cleaning and lighting the streets in that part of London. This is the first of many Acts to create bodies responsible for the upkeep and safety of London's streets.

1762 Westminster finally gets an Act enabling it to levy a rate for street lighting.

1763 Southwark Fair in September, one of London's most popular gatherings, is banned because of congestion on Bankside and a rise in crime.

ROYAL LONDON

1752 John Nash, the favourite architect of George IV and designer of Regent Street and Regent's Park, is born in Lambeth, the son of a millwright.

1760–1811 George III, known as 'Mad King George' because of mental illness in his later life, has a great impact on London. He buys for his wife Charlotte the 'Queen's House' which later becomes Buckingham Palace. He starts a new royal collection of books of which 65,000 are later given to the British Museum. He founds and finances the Royal Academy of Arts and his scientific instruments are later preserved in the Science Museum.

FAMOUS LONDONERS

Regent Street

1756 Oliver Goldsmith, poet and novelist, settles in London and is befriended by Samuel Johnson. He works as a hack writer before producing *The Vicar of Wakefield* and *She Stoops to Conquer*.

1757 William Blake, poet and painter, is born in Broad Street, Soho (now Broadwick Street) the son of a hosier. A preface to his *Milton a Poem* becomes the words of the hymn *Jerusalem*.

1760 James Boswell, who is to write the biography of Samuel Johnson, visits London. He is back in 1762 and meets Johnson for the first time in 1763.

LONDON'S POPULATION

1770

1768 The Royal Academy of Arts is founded with the patronage of King George III and a membership of 40 for promotion of painting. Originally housed in Pall Mall, it has several other homes before moving to Burlington House, Piccadilly.

1768–74 An over-ambitious scheme of Robert Adam and his brothers sees the building of the Adelphi Terrace overlooking the Thames at the western end of the Strand with an embankment onto the river.

1769 A breakaway group of insurance underwriters form New Lloyd's Coffee House in Pope's Head Alley in the City. ¤ The rebuilding of Kenwood House for William Murray, the 1st Earl of Mansfield, with design by Robert Adam is completed. The original building dated from the seventeenth century and the Orangery was built around 1700.

1769 Blackfriars Bridge (replaced in 1869) is the third river crossing to open in the centre of London.

1769 The first Royal Academy Exhibition for all artists is held when it is in a wing of Somerset House.

Royal Academy Summer Exhibition, 2008

1773 Stockbrokers and jobbers put up their own building in Sweeting's Alley, calling it New Jonathan's and then the Stock Exchange.

1774 Lloyd's insurance moves into the Royal Exchange. ¤ The Old Bailey is rebuilt to the design of City architect John Dance.

1775–80 The Duke of Bedford offers 200 acres of his Bloomsbury estate for redevelopment and the handsome terraces of Bedford Square arise, put up by builders who lease the land.

Bedford Square

1776 Manchester House is built by the Duke of Manchester forming one side of what becomes Manchester Square in Marylebone.

1776–80 The Tudor palace, Somerset House, is demolished and a new building erected to house the Royal Academy of Arts, the Royal Society, Society of Antiquaries, the Navy Board, government offices and an army of cooks and other servants. The architect is William Chambers.

Somerset House

1776 First Battersea Bridge opens (replaced in 1890).

1770 Poverty-stricken Jews arrive from Poland.

1794 3,663 ships laden with goods from other parts of Britain and from all over the world moor in the Pool of London below London Bridge. The need for 'enclosed' docks where goods can be unloaded safely is recognised.

1796 A House of Commons committee hears that merchants believe they lose between £250,000 and £800,000 worth of goods a year to thieves.

1798 A river police force is set up by Scots merchant Patrick Colquhoun to combat theft in the Pool of London.

1778 The Catholic Relief Act lifts some of the restrictions on Catholics holding property provided they swear an oath of allegiance to the sovereign. It is bitterly opposed by Protestants.

1763 The American painter Benjamin West comes to London and paints portraits of King George III and members of the Royal Family.

Benjamin West

1771 At the age of 21, Philip James de Loutherbourg arrives in London where he impresses the actor-manager David Garrick with his special theatrical effects and set designs.

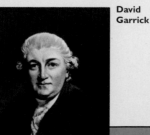

David Garrick

1775 J.M.W. Turner, the landscape painter, is born in Maiden Lane, Covent Garden where his father is a barber and wig maker. ¤ Painter John Constable is born.

1778 Beau Brummell, the London Dandy famed for his dress sense and careful grooming, is born. He flees the fashionable world in 1816 when he falls out of favour with the Prince Regent and cannot pay a gambling debt, and dies in poverty in France in 1840. ¤ William Hazlitt, who begins a distinguished career as a journalist from 1812, is born in Maidstone, Kent. His London home is in Westminster.

BUILDINGS AND INSTITUTIONS

1792 Sir John Soane buys a house on the north side of Lincoln's Inn Fields and demolishes it to build a new house to his own design. He subsequently buys two adjoining houses and redevelops them. One is now the Soane Museum.

1794 The new Theatre Royal, Drury Lane, opens.

1799 Bedford House is demolished to prepare the way for the development of the north side of Bloomsbury Square and the laying out of Russell Square.

1805 A London Dispensary for the Relief of the Poor Afflicted with Diseases of the Eye and Ear is founded, housed in Charterhouse Square. It moves to Moorfields and becomes in time the Royal London Ophthalmic Hospital or just Moorfields Eye Hospital.

Moorfields Eye Hospital

THE RIVER, PORT AND TRANSPORT

1780 A Londoner, Eton scholar and MP, Lord George Gordon, heads a Protestant group demanding the repeal of the Catholic Relief Act and presents a petition to Parliament as his followers harrass the Lords and the Commons. The protest gets out of hand and thousands of rioters go on a rampage breaking open gaols and pulling down Catholic owned houses and places of worship. The riots are stopped after several days by 10,000 troops. No Catholics are killed but 285 rioters die and of those 450 arrested, 25 are hung. Gordon, who gives his name to the Gordon Riots, is found not guilty of treason.

1783 The long tradition of the procession of those condemned to death from Newgate Prison to the Tyburn gallows in Mayfair ceases when the development of the area for fine housing begins. Hangings now take place outside Newgate Prison.

1802 The first of London's enclosed docks is opened despite opposition from the porters and owners of the 'legal quays'. It is funded by the West India merchants and becomes known as the West India Dock. High walls provide security and the docks appoint their own police.

1802 Cornishman Richard Trevithick, inventor of the steam locomotive, runs a steam carriage in London.

1803 The first public railway to require an Act of Parliament is opened between Wandsworth and Croydon to carry goods. Wagons are drawn by horses or mules and customers provide their own wagons. It is known as the Surrey Iron Railway and is a cheaper alternative to a canal.

1805 The London Dock is opened.

1806 Opening of Commercial Road built by a private company to link the East and West India Docks with the City.

1807 The first phase of what is to become the huge Surrey Dock system, the only enclosed dock on the south side of the Thames, is completed.

SOCIETY AND CULTURE

1784 There is a balloon ascent from the Artillery Ground, Finsbury.

1785 The first issue of *The Times* newspaper – then *The Daily Universal Register* – appears.

1787 Marylebone Cricket Club is formed with its first ground at Dorset Square.

1791 *The Observer* is founded as a Sunday newspaper by W.S. Bourne with £100 of borrowed money. He thinks he will make a fortune but loses £1,600 in his first year.

1797 Hatchards, now London's oldest bookshop, opens on Picccadilly.

1798 7,000 watchmakers are listed in Clerkenwell.

ROYAL LONDON

1801 The first National Census of population is conducted and reveals that greater London has a population of 1,096,784.

1805 The first Eton vs. Harrow cricket match played on the Old Lord's Ground in Marylebone.
¤ A Horse Patrol of 60 men, under the Bow Street Magistrates, is created to police the main roads into London which are the haunt of highwaymen.

1784 James Leigh Hunt, the son of an American lawyer, is born in Southgate, north London and becomes a poet and friend of Keats and Shelley.

1792 George Cruikshank, cartoonist who illustrates some early works of Charles Dickens including *Oliver Twist*, is born in London.

1795 John Keats, the romantic poet, is born in London.

FAMOUS LONDONERS

1799 Marc Isambard Brunel comes to London from America and marries his English sweetheart Sophia Kingdom in Holborn. He becomes a successful inventor and engineer who learns how to tunnel through London clay. His son, Isambard Kingdom Brunel, born in 1808, becomes the most celebrated engineer of his day.

1802 Anna Maria Tussaud, a skilled maker of waxworks, having evaded the guillotine in the French Revolution, comes to London and has her first exhibit at the Lyceum Theatre. As Madame Tussaud she establishes her waxworks in Baker Street.

Marc Isambard Brunel

LONDON'S POPULATION

Greater London 1801 1 million.

1810

1810 A new, modernised building for the Royal Mint is opened on Tower Hill.

1812 Mivart's Hotel is established which later becomes Claridges. ¤ A new Theatre Royal, Drury Lane, which survives today, is opened following the complete destruction of the old theatre by fire in 1809.

1814–32 A rare and over ambitious attempt at grand planning in London begins with the laying-out of plans for a new aristocratic suburb of 50 villas on farmland to the north of the New Road to be called the Regent's Park. A shopping street will provide a stately avenue down to Carlton House Terrace. Overseen by the architect John Nash, financial difficulties lead to a curtailing of the plans though Regent Street is built and Regent's Park laid out.

1817 London's first purpose-built picture gallery opens in Dulwich. Designed by Sir John Soane, it houses a private collection bequeathed to Dulwich College by a Swiss businessman and art dealer.

1818 The Royal Coburg theatre opens in Lambeth and is later renamed the Royal Victoria theatre, or affectionately the Old Vic. ¤ The West London Infirmary and Dispensary is opened in Suffolk Street near the Haymarket Theatre by Dr Benjamin Golding to provide care for the poor. It later moves to Villiers Street off the Strand and is renamed Charing Cross Hospital in 1827.

1818–19 The Burlington Arcade of up-market shops is built on the land of Burlington House.

1819 Piccadilly Circus is created as one of three junctions on the new Regent Street road between Regent's Park and Carlton House Terrace.

1813–14 The last of the Frost Fairs is held on the frozen Thames. Ice damages Old London Bridge and the City decides to demolish it. Once this barrier to the flow of the tides is gone the water is never still enough to freeze solid again.

1815 The first steamboat service from Wapping to Gravesend begins with a comical boat, the *Margery*, nicknamed by watermen the 'Yankee torpedo' after an American steamer that exploded.

The last Frost Fair

1816 Originally called Regent Bridge, the first Vauxhall Bridge opens and proves to be very profitable though the owners have to pay compensation to the owners of Battersea Bridge and a ferry. ¤ The first section of the Regent's Canal linking the Grand Junction at Paddington to Limehouse on the Thames is opened as far as Camden.

Regent's Canal entrance gates at Limehouse

1812 The Gas Light and Coke Company is given a charter to light Westminster, Southwark and the City of London from a gasworks in Great Peter Street, Westminster. ¤ The only prime minister to be assassinated, Spencer Perceval, is shot dead in the lobby of the House of Commons.

1815 Soldiers returning from the Napoleonic Wars create fears of a crime wave and an extra 100 men are recruited to form a night time foot patrol.

1817 Planned before Wellington's defeat of Napoleon at Waterloo, a new crossing from Westminster on the north bank to Lambeth in the south was to have been called Strand Bridge. After the victory it becomes Waterloo Bridge and is opened officially on the second anniversary of the battle. It is later rebuilt.

1819 The original Southwark Bridge is opened with a cast iron central span of 240 feet (73m), the largest in the world at the time, to allow ships through. It is later rebuilt.

1811–20 When George III's mental illness makes it impossible for him to rule, his son George, then aged 48, becomes regent until his father's death in 1820. A dandy with a great love of art and ceremony, George has a huge impact on London during the nine years of the Regency, commissioning the building of Regent's Street and the laying-out of Regent's Park. He has his favourite architect John Nash refurbish Buckingham Palace.

Southwark Bridge

1812 Charles Dickens is born in Portsmouth where his father is a clerk in the Navy Pay Office. He becomes a great chronicler of London life in his many novels such as *Bleak House*.

Charles Dickens

1819 Joseph Bazalgette, the great engineer responsible for the building of London's Embankments and sewage system, is born in Enfield, the son of a naval officer.

1811 1.3 million.

1820

BUILDINGS AND INSTITUTIONS

1821 The Theatre Royal, Haymarket, is rebuilt at the instigation of John Nash as part of his plans for improvement. Its position is changed slightly so that its splendid Corinthian columns look directly onto Charles Street.

1824 The Athenaeum Club is founded and a club house built on the corner of Pall Mall and Waterloo Place by the young architect Decimus Burton.
¤ Parliament agrees to buy the art collection of banker John Julius Angerstein and the 38 pictures are put on show for the public in his home at 100 Pall Mall. It is the beginning of the National Gallery collection.

1825 The Marble Arch is built as a ceremonial entrance to the new Buckingham Palace. ¤ Work begins on the British Museum. It will take more than 25 years before it nears completion.

Marble Arch

1826 Work begins on the refurbishment and rebuilding of Buckingham House. The extravagance of the architect John Nash causes problems. It is finally turned into a Palace in the reign of William IV. ¤ An Act of Parliament gives Lord Grosvenor permission to develop a marshy area on the north bank of the Thames which is known as Five Fields, an area notorious for its footpads and robbers. Over the next few years the land is filled in and drained and Belgravia is built with its elegant, white stucco mansions and terraces in Belgrave and Eaton Squares.

1828 Surgeon William Marsden sets up London General Institution for the Gratuitous Care of Malignant Diseases in Hatton Garden, Holborn. It becomes the Royal Free Hospital with new premises in Gray's Inn Road and is now a major London teaching hospital in Hampstead.
¤ London Zoo opens to fellows of the Zoological Society only.

1829 The Travellers' Club opens.
¤ The General Post Office, founded in 1660, is housed in a new headquarters designed by Sir Robert Smirke at St Martin's-le-Grand in the City.

THE RIVER, PORT AND TRANSPORT

1820 The Regent's Canal from Camden to Limehouse is opened.

1821 The Lovegroves, fishermen at Boulter's Lock, catch only two salmon, which is two more than the previous year. These valuable migratory fish have almost disappeared from the river.

1827 The first suspension bridge in London at Hammersmith is opened (later rebuilt).

St. Katharine's Dock

1828 St. Katharine's Dock is carved out of a densely populated district next to the eastern edge of the City. It is named after the ancient St. Katharine's Hospital which is demolished to make way for it. 11,300 Londoners are evicted. Much of the earth is shipped up river to provide foundations for Belgravia. ¤ Work on the Thames Tunnel suspended because of lack of funds.

SOCIETY AND CULTURE

1820 The Cato Street Conspirators, plotters who plan to murder the government, are betrayed and arrested at 6 Cato Street after a fight.

1825 A ceremony takes place to mark the first stone of a new London Bridge. It is built alongside the Old Bridge which remains open. ¤ Work begins on the Thames Tunnel using a new cutting device invented by Marc Isambard Brunel, the French father of Isambard Kingdom Brunel. It is intended to provide a river crossing for carriages as well as pedestrians where a bridge would be impossible because of shipping on the river.

1829 Taking advantage of the New Road, George Shillibeer, a London coach-maker, begins the first horse bus service from a pub, the Yorkshire Stingo in Paddington, to the Bank of England in the City.

ROYAL LONDON

Cato Street Conspiritors

1826 The last draw of the English State Lottery is made at Coopers' Hall on 18 October as this way of raising money for Government projects is abolished.

1827 First issue of the *London Standard* which becomes an evening newspaper in 1859.

1829 Amid great controversy, the Metropolitan Police Force is established at the instigation of Sir Robert Peel.

FAMOUS LONDONERS

1820–30 On the death of George III, the Prince Regent becomes George IV. He takes little interest in government and leaves London to live in seclusion in Windsor.

George IV's Coronation

LONDON'S POPULATION

1821 1.5 million.

1830

1830 The London Geographical Society is founded, later called the Royal Geographical Society.

1833 The London Fire Engine Establishment is formed by an amalgamation of private insurance companies. There are 80 firefighters and 13 fire stations.

1834 The Houses of Commons and Lords are completely destroyed by fire.
¤ University College Hospital is founded.

Buckingham Palace

1835 Madame Tussaud, who has toured Britain with her waxwork models, sets up with her sons in the Baker Street Bazaar.

1836 The University of London is founded.

1837 Rebuilt by architect John Nash, Buckingham Palace becomes the official home of Queen Victoria on her accession to the throne.
¤ The Government School of Design is opened in Somerset House. It later becomes the Royal College of Art.
¤ Brown's Hotel is established in Albemarle Street by James and Sarah Brown.

The National Gallery

1838 The new National Gallery is opened on Trafalgar Square.

1830 The water closet, or flush toilet, becomes popular with the well-to-do replacing the old cesspit latrines. Raw sewage from the closets is flushed straight into the Thames.

1831 The new London Bridge replaces the old one.
¤ Shillibeer's bus service fails as he cannot stop in the City because of the hackney cab monopoly and his buses are too wide for the streets. He goes bankrupt.

1832 The Stage Carriages Act removes the hackney cab monopoly on picking up passengers in the City. Bus services multiply.

1834 Joseph Hansom, an architect from Yorkshire, designs a new kind of horse-drawn cab pulled by a single horse. It is safe and easily manoeverable and becomes very popular in London.

1835 Work starts again on the Thames Tunnel financed partly with Government funds.

1832 The first outbreak of Asiatic cholera kills 5,000. It is not the deadliest disease at the time, but it leads to a horrible death by dehydration and its cause is a mystery.

1835 Once popular pastimes, bull and bear baiting and cock-fighting are banned by the Cruelty to Animals Act. Wild animals are not included. ¤ While the rapidly growing industrial cities in the north of England are granted new local government bodies, London remains without any overall authority.

1830–37 At the age of 64, William, younger brother of George IV, is crowned after a life in which he had little to do with royalty, living for 20 years with the actress Dorothea Jordan. She already has four children by three different fathers, and she and William IV have ten before he is persuaded he needs a legitimate wife and, in 1818, marries Princess Adelaide. William IV's reign begins with rural rioting and he is warned not to enter the City for fear of his life. He oversees tumultuous change but has little impact on London.

1834 Thomas Carlyle, the Scottish writer and satirist, moves to London and becomes known as the 'Sage of Chelsea'. He is a founder member of the London Library in St James's Square, now the world's largest independent lending library. ¤ William Morris, textile designer, socialist and member of the Arts and Crafts movement, is born in Walthamstow, just to the north of London.

1836 London's first steam railway opens between Spa Road, Bermondsey, and Deptford. It competes with the existing stage coach service and the steamboat. It is extended to London Bridge within a year and later to Greenwich.

1837 The first mainline railway into London arrives from Birmingham with the terminus at Euston Station. The first stop out of London is Harrow.

1838 The first section of Isambard Kingdom Brunel's Great Western Railway opens running from Paddington Station to Maidenhead.

1839 The River Police, founded in 1798, become the Thames Division of the Metropolitan Police.

1836 The first Oxford and Cambridge Boat Race in London takes place.

1837–8 An epidemic of typhus fever, also known as gaol fever as it is common in prisons, kills around 6,000 Londoners, mostly the poor. It is spread by a louse that lives on the body of the victim.

1838 Edwin Chadwick, the sanitary reformer, is asked to investigate living conditions among the poor of East London.

1837–1901 Just 18 when she ascends the throne, Victoria's reign sees the spectacular rise of London to the world's largest and wealthiest metropolis. Far from not 'being amused', she loves theatre, and is thrilled by animal tamers at Drury Lane and the horse dramas at Astley's. With her husband Albert (they marry in 1840) she is a patron of the arts, a supporter of the Great Exhibition of 1851. She establishes Buckingham Palace as the London home of royalty. After Albert dies in 1861, Victoria withdraws from public life, but is persuaded back into the public eye for the Jubilees of 1887 and 1897.

Queen Victoria

BUILDINGS AND INSTITUTIONS

1841 The Reform Club moves into its new building at 104 Pall Mall. It is designed by Charles Barry, architect of the new Houses of Parliament.

1844 Hoardings are removed and Trafalgar Square is opened on 1 May. ¤ Queen Victoria opens the new Royal Exchange to replace the last one destroyed by fire in 1838.

1847 London Zoo opens to the public for the first time. ¤ The House of Lords is occupied in the new Houses of Parliament.

1849 Henry Harrod, a draper and retailer, moves his business to Brompton to be near to Hyde Park for the Great Exhibition. It thrives.

1850 The Marble Arch is taken from the entrance to Buckingham Palace and put up the following year as an entrance to Hyde Park by the Cumberland Gate.

1851 The Great Exhibition is staged in Hyde Park in the giant greenhouse that is dubbed the Crystal Palace. It is dismantled and moved to Sydenham in south London.

1852 The House of Commons is occupied in the newly built Houses of Parliament.

1854 Nelson's Column is finally put in place in Trafalgar Square. ¤ Mr and Mrs Claridge buy Mivart's hotel in Mayfair. Its reputation is established when Queen Victoria is entertained there by the French Empress Eugene.

Nelson's Column

THE RIVER, PORT AND TRANSPORT

1841 The first railway station within the City of London opens at Fenchurch Street as the terminus of the London to Blackwall railway.

1843 The Thames Tunnel finally opens. It is wide enough for carriages, but there is no money to create the necessary approach roads so it is for pedestrians only.

1848 The London and South Western Railway opens its terminus in Lambeth calling it Waterloo Bridge Station. It becomes known just as Waterloo.

1851 Tourists visiting the Great Exhibition in Hyde Park make the omnibus very popular and there is fierce competition to provide services. There are already about 1,000 buses in London.

1852 The Great Northern Railway, which has the East Coast mainline, opens its London terminus at King's Cross on the site of an old hospital.

1854 A survey of commuters coming into and going out of the City of London every day finds that 400,000 walk, 88,000 take horse buses, 52,000 take cabs and other vehicles, 30,000 travel on steamers and 54,000 go by rail.

SOCIETY AND CULTURE

1840 Rowland Hill's Penny Post brings about a huge increase in letters posted.

1845 Representatives of Surrey cricket clubs vote to create Surrey County Cricket Club. They lease a market garden at Kennington Oval and create a pitch with 10,000 turfs from Tooting Common. **1845–50** The famine caused by potato blight in Ireland greatly increases immigration and the Irish-born population in London swells to more than 100,000.

1848 The Duke of Wellington organises elaborate defences for the capital as the Chartists, demanding political reform, stage a meeting at Kennington Common hoping to present a petition to Parliament. In the end there is little violence as the troops and thousands of special constables keep order. ¤ The first British Public Health Act is passed creating the General Board of Health and making local authorities responsible for drainage, water supplies and inspection of property. **1848–9** A second outbreak of cholera in London kills 14,000.

The Penny Post

1855 A group of Paris businessmen try to cash in on the London transport scene with *La Compagnie Générale des Omnibus de Londres* which is later renamed the London General Bus Company. They are unable to beat off the competition. ¤ The Victoria Dock opens on Plaistow Marshes. It is the first built to accept steamships, and is given the title 'Royal' in 1880, the first of three Royal docks to be built.

ROYAL LONDON

FAMOUS LONDONERS

1851 The Great Exhibition is held in a Crystal Palace in Hyde Park. Profits of £186,000 from 6 million visitors go to building the Albert Hall and the Victoria and Albert Museum.

1854 Queen Victoria opens the rebuilt and enlarged Crystal Palace which had been transported to Penge Place Estate, Sydenham in South London after it closed in Hyde Park in 1851.

The Great Exhibition

LONDON'S POPULATION

1841 2.2 million.

1851 2.6 million.

1856 Fire destroys the Covent Garden Theatre again.
¤ The National Portrait Gallery is established as an historical collection rather than an art gallery at 29 Great George Street, Westminster. It opens to the public in 1859.

1857 The British Museum Reading Room is opened.

1859 On 31 May the giant bells of Big Ben, cast in the Whitechapel Foundry in East London, ring out over London for the first time.

Big Ben

1861 Fire in a warehouse at Cotton's Wharf burns for two days and destroys the dock buildings in Tooley Street.

1864 The first barrack-like block of Peabody Trust housing for the working classes is built on the Commercial Road in Spitalfields. It is one of many blocks put up with funds from a bequest by the wealthy philanthropist George Peabody.

1865 French wine merchant Daniel Nicholas, on the run from creditors in France, opens the Café Royal at 68 Regent Street.
¤ London's most up-to-date hotel, the Langham, is opened. It has hydraulic lifts.

1860 The first railway bridge crosses the Thames, taking trains from the south into the newly built Victoria Station. It is called at first the Grosvenor Bridge.

1861 Eccentric American George F. Train tries to build a horse-drawn tramway from Marble Arch along what is now Bayswater Road. He is prosecuted for digging up the roadway without permission. ¤ A new suspension bridge opens, crossing the river at the same point as the old horse ferry. Lambeth Bridge is not favoured by horse-drawn traffic and is used mainly by pedestrians.

1862 Westminster Bridge is rebuilt.

1863 The world's first underground railway opens running from Paddington to Farringdon on the western edge of the City. It is a 'cut and cover' construction just below the surface, taking a route under the New Road (Euston Road) with stations at Euston and Kings Cross. It is steam-driven with carriages lit with gas.

1864 The London, Chatham and Dover railway builds a bridge at Blackfriars for trains from the south coming in to the City.
¤ The South Eastern Railway brings its line across the Thames and builds a terminus on the site of Hungerford Market at Charing Cross.

London sewers being constructed

1865 The completion of one of the capital's greatest engineering projects: the creation of a new sewage system under the supervision of Joseph Bazalgette. From north and south of the river tunnels carry the sewage eastwards to be discharged seaward of London.

1856 The Metropolitan Works created and tasked, among other projects, to tackle the problem of pollution of the river Thames with sewage.

1857 A suspension bridge is built so that north Londoners can cross over to the newly created Battersea Park. It is called the Victoria Bridge at first, then Chelsea Bridge. Tolls are charged as on most London bridges outside the City's control.

1858 Sewage flushed into the Thames from thousands of water closet toilets produces a hideous stench which drives Members of Parliament away from the river side of the House of Commons. It is the year of the 'Great Stink' before London gets its new sewage works.

1856 An area 12-miles radius from the Post Office Headquarters in St. Martin-le-Grand is designated by Sir Rowland Hill as the London postal district. It is subdivided into ten local districts designated EC etc. ¤ The last time the Lord Mayor's show travels on the River Thames which has become horribly polluted. The Livery Companies barges are sold off.

1857 There are about 80,000 prostitutes in London.

1857 Robert Baden-Powell, founder of the Boy Scouts and Girl Guides, is born in Paddington.

1860 Competition between private gas lighting companies in London leads to wasteage and the Metropolis Gas Act divides the capital up into districts in which each supplier has a monopoly. ¤ London Trades Council founded bringing together a number of trades unions. ¤ The Temporary Home for Lost and Starving Dogs is established by Mary Tealby in Holloway, North London. It moves south of the river in 1871 to become Battersea Dogs Home.

1862 The Royal Horticultural Society Great Spring Show is held at its garden in Kensington. This becomes, much later, the Chelsea Flower Show.

1863 Middlesex County Cricket Club is founded.

1865 Evangelists William and Catherine Booth establish the East London Mission which later (1878) is named the Salvation Army.

BUILDINGS AND INSTITUTIONS

1866 The Metropolitan Fire Brigade is formed by the Metropolitan Board of Works. Renamed the London Fire Brigade in 1904.

1867 Four brass lions designed by Sir Edward Landseer are placed at the foot of Nelson's Column in Trafalgar Square.

1869 Finsbury Park is formally opened as a green retreat for north Londoners.

1866 The London terminus of the London, Chatham and Dover railway opens. Called St. Pauls, it is renamed Blackfriars in 1937. ¤ Yet another river crossing, again built by the South Eastern Railway, terminates at Canon Street station. A viaduct takes it above Upper Thames Street and over the relics of a Roman quay.

1870 One of London's engineering masterpieces, the Victoria Embankment, is completed under the direction of Sir Joseph Bazalgette. Beneath a new road running alongside the Thames is a section of the northern outflow sewage pipe and a tunnel for the Metropolitan District Railway.

1871 Official opening of the Royal Albert Hall ten years after the death of Queen Victoria's consort Prince Albert.

1872 The Albert Memorial, opposite the Albert Hall, is unveiled by Queen Victoria. However, the statue of Albert seated is not finished and put in place until 1876.

1873 Alexandra Palace is opened as a 'people's palace' on 24 May and burns down 16 days later. ¤ The Criterion Theatre is opened on the site of an old inn in Piccadilly Circus.

The Albert Memorial

THE RIVER, PORT AND TRANSPORT

1868 World's first traffic signals installed outside the Houses of Parliament. They resemble railway signals and blow up a year later injuring a policeman. ¤ The first section of what becomes the Circle Line is completed by the Metropolitan District Railway, the steam trains running from South Kensington to Westminster Bridge. ¤ St. Pancras Station, built by the Midland Railway, opens between the existing Euston and King's Cross stations.

St. Pancras Station

1869 One of the most ambitious Victorian road schemes, sometimes described as London's first 'fly-over', is opened after six years of legal wrangling and construction problems. Holborn Viaduct is designed to ease the flow of horse-drawn traffic into the City from the west crossing the steep-sided valley of the Fleet river. Whole streets are demolished and 2,000 people made homeless.

1870 The old Turnpike Trusts which raise tolls to pay for main roads lose business to the new railways and are closed down. The removal of the tolls eases traffic flow in London and other towns. ¤ An Act of Parliament permits the laying of tram lines on certain conditions. Horse tram services rapidly become popular as they are cheaper than buses. They lead to the creation of working class suburbs. The first service runs between Brixton and Kennington. ¤ Using a boring machine, the Great Shield which improves on Brunel's original design, a tunnel is cut under the Thames roughly where Tower Bridge is now to provide a rapid railway crossing. However the cramped carriage is not popular and it closes after three months, becoming a pedestrian crossing until Tower Bridge takes away its custom.

1872 Under a Public Health Act the City of London is responsible for setting up the sanitary authority for the Port of London, inspecting all ships arriving on the Thames.

SOCIETY AND CULTURE

ROYAL LONDON

1866 The last major cholera epidemic in London which hits the East End particularly hard, killing 3,000 in Stepney.

Streetscape of London in the 19th century

1868 The last public execution in London takes place at Newgate Prison.

1869 The Royal Navy shipbuilding yards at Deptford and Woolwich are out-of-date and are shut down.

1870 Thomas Barnardo opens his first home for destitute boys at Stepney Causeway in east London.

1872 Parliament grants Hyde Park the right to permit public meetings and Speakers' Corner is officially sanctioned.

FAMOUS LONDONERS

1869 Edwin Lutyens, architect and designer of the Cenotaph, is born in Onslow Square.

1870 Marie Lloyd, the music hall star, is born in Hoxton.

LONDON'S POPULATION

1871 3.8 million.

1874 The Criterion Resaurant is opened.

1875 A new Alexandra Palace is opened with a concert hall, museum, lecture hall, library and theatre.

1877 With a windfall from winnings of his racehorse Roseberry, printer James Smith opens the first purpose-built department store in London in fashionable Brixton. It has a steel frame and is named after a store in Paris, the Bon Marché (which means inexpensive).

1878 After an eventful journey in which it was nearly lost at sea, the Egyptian obelisk nicknamed Cleopatra's Needle is finally erected on the Victorian Embankment.

Cleopatra's Needle

1873 The privately financed Albert Bridge opens after years of wrangling with the owners of nearby wooden and rickety Battersea Bridge, whose owners are compensated by the Albert Bridge financiers.

1874 Built by the Great Eastern Railway, Liverpool Street station opens as a grander terminus than Bishopsgate, which becomes a goods station.

1878 640 Londoners die when a paddle steamer, the *Princess Alice*, is rammed by a collier ship. Some are trapped below decks; others fall into the horribly polluted Thames. It is the worst disaster in British inland waters in history.

1878–80 The Metropolitan Board of works spends £1,400,000 buying 11 privately owned bridges across the Thames so that the tolls can be removed and the bridges improved. There are celebrations and some old toll booths are hurled into the river.

Albert Bridge

1874 Work begins on the first stage of a new prison in west London at Wormwood Scrubs. Housed first in a temporary hut, the first block is built with convict labourers who make the bricks on site.

1875 Henry Croft, a road sweeper brought up in an orphanage, begins the Pearly King and Queen tradition in which Londoners decorate their clothes with pearl buttons sewn in patterns to attract attention to charities they support.

1877 The first Wimbledon Tennis Championship is staged for men's singles only at the All England Club's original ground in Worple Road, Wimbledon.

1878 The Telephone Company with Bell's patents is established in Coleman Street in the City with a capacity of 150 lines.

1881 Savoy Theatre built for Richard D'Oyly Carte is opened.
¤ The Natural History Museum, then a branch of the British Museum, is opened in South Kensington. Profits from the Great Exhibition are used to fund the new building designed by Alfred Waterhouse.

1882 The newly built Royal Courts of Justice are opened at the eastern end of the Strand by Queen Victoria.
¤ Operated by the company founded by the American Thomas Edison, the world's first power station is opened beneath Holborn Viaduct to provide power to light nearby streets and shops.

Royal Courts of Justice

1885 The Hotel Metropole opens in Northumberland Avenue. It is one of three built in that road by the Gordon Company founded by solicitor Frederick Gordon. The others are the Grand and the Victoria.

1886 The National Agricultural Hall opens in West Kensington, later becoming the Olympia Exhibition Centre.
¤ The Hotel Cecil, one of the largest and grandest in the world, opens on the Embankment.

1880 The Royal Albert Dock opens to the east of Victoria dock. It has three miles of quays as well as dry docks for ship repairs.

1883 To get approval for slum clearance when building stations, railway companies are obliged to offer cheap workmen's fares in the early morning. The Cheap Trains Act makes this a general requirement for all new developments.

1886 After nearly ten years of slum clearance and rebuilding Shaftsbury Avenue is opened running from Piccadilly Circus to New Oxford Street.
¤ The old wooden Putney Bridge is replaced by a stone bridge funded by the Metropolitan Board of Works. ¤ The East and West India Dock company opens a new dock at Tilbury in the Thames estuary.

Putney Bridge

1880 The first cricket Test Match staged in London is played between England and Australia at the Surrey Cricket Club ground, the Oval in Kennington. England wins by 5 wickets.

1884. Forty-one delegates from 25 nations meet in Washington DC for the International Meridian Conference. By the end of the conference, Greenwich has won the prize of Longitude 0° by a vote of 22 to 1 against (San Domingo), with 2 abstentions (France and Brazil).

Greenwich Royal Observatory, the home of Greenwich Mean Time and the Prime Meridian of the world

1886 City of London Corporation acquires the 70 acres of Highgate Woods and opens them to the public.

1883 Clement Atlee, the first post-1945 Labour prime minister, is born in Putney, the son of a solicitor.

BUILDINGS AND INSTITUTIONS

1889 The Savoy Hotel is opened on the Strand.

The Savoy Hotel

1890 The Housing of the Working Classes Act enables local authorities to build low-cost housing for the poor.

1893 The Shaftsbury Memorial fountain and statue is unveiled in Piccadilly Circus with a sculpture wrongly known the world over as Eros.

1896 The National Portrait Gallery finally has a permanent home opened at the bottom of Charing Cross Road.

1897 The National Gallery of British Art opens on Millbank on the site of the former prison. Sir Henry Tate, who made a fortune from Tate & Lyle sugar, puts up much of the money and it becomes known as the Tate Gallery.

Eros

1887 Charing Cross Road opens, built by the Metropolitan Board of Works to improve traffic flow.

THE RIVER, PORT AND TRANSPORT

1889 A five-week strike by workers in the London Docks over their demand for six pence an hour, the 'dockers' tanner', ends in victory after widespread public support.

1887 A Demonstration involving the Social Democratic League leads to clashes in Trafalgar Square between an estimated 10,000 marchers and the police. Cavalry and infantrymen stand by. Many demonstrators are badly hurt and three die.

1890 The North Metropolitan tram company experiments with electric motors powered with batteries to replace its horses. After two years it brings back horses.
¤ London's first deep-level tube is opened between Stockwell, south of the Thames, and the Bank in the City. It is made possible by the use of electric power.
¤ A new stone and iron Battersea Bridge is opened to replace the 18th-century timber crossing.

1891 London County Council (LCC), created just two years earlier, decides to exercise a legal option to take over some of the private tramways. It is the start of a policy which will see the Council running the bulk of London's trams.

1894 There is a grand opening for Tower Bridge, designed to ease the flow of horse-drawn goods traffic between the docks on the north and south of the river. However, shipping has priority, and the great bascules are raised up to fifty times a day at first meaning the bridge has to be continuously manned.

SOCIETY AND CULTURE

1888 Girls working at Bryant & May's match factory in East London stage a strike about working conditions after one of them is dismissed. With much public support and help from radical reformers the 1,400 women and girls win most of their demands.
¤ *The Financial Times* begins publication.
¤ Jack the Ripper. The brutal murder and mutilation of five prostitutes in the Spitalfields and Whitechapel area suggest a serial killer is at large. The identity of the killer has never been established.

Bryant & May girls

1897 The first, western section of the Blackwall Tunnel is opened.

1898 The term 'rush hour' is first used.
¤ The Waterloo & City Underground (tube) Line opens linking Waterloo station south of the river with the Bank in the City. It is primarily for commuters and is nicknamed The Drain. It is the second electric underground line in London.

ROYAL LONDON

1889 The first edition of the monumental social survey of London by shipping magnate and philanthropist Charles Book is published in two volumes as *Life and Labour of the People*. In this and later editions are coloured maps indicating the wealth and poverty of individual streets.

1894 The first of the Joe Lyons teashops is opened at 213 Piccadilly.

1897 The Tate Gallery on Millbank is opened showing in eight rooms 245 works by British artists dating back to 1790. This is now called the Tate Britain.

1898 London's first moving staircase, a primitive escalator, is installed in Harrods department store. Customers who dare to use it are offered a steadying glass of brandy at the top.

Tate Britain

FAMOUS LONDONERS

1888 Herbert Morrison, son of a police officer in Lambeth, is born. He becomes a leading Labour politician in London.

1889 Charlie Chaplin is born in south London.

1897 Queen Victoria celebrates her Diamond Jubilee.

1897 Enid Blyton, creator of *Noddy* and *The Famous Five* is born in East Dulwich.

LONDON'S POPULATION

1891 5.5 million.

1900

1900 London Hippodrome is opened for circus performances.

1901–10 Although Edward VII's reign is short, much of London's architecture is in a distinctive Edwardian style. This includes the tiled Underground stations of the first Piccadilly, Bakerloo and Northern lines.

1903 Nine private water companies are brought together to form a new public body, the Metropolitan Water Board charged with improving water quality in London.

1904 Newgate Prison is demolished and the Central Criminal Court, the Old Bailey, built on the site. ¤ The London Coliseum opens as the capital's most up-to-date variety theatre. It has a revolving stage on which the Derby horse-race is restaged with real horses and jockeys.

1905 Harrods Department Store in Knightsbridge is rebuilt and clad in terracotta tiles.

The Ritz Hotel

The London Coliseum

1906 The Ritz Hotel is opened in Piccadilly by Cesar Ritz who had been dismissed as manager of the Savoy Hotel.
¤ The War Office, Whitehall, is completed.

1908 The Waldorf Hotel is opened in the newly built Aldwych.

1909 The Strand Palace Hotel opens on the site of the old Exeter Hall. ¤ The American Henry Gordon Selfridge opens his department store in Oxford Street. ¤ The first game of rugby is played at the newly opened Twickenham Stadium on the site of a former market garden which grew cabbages hence the nickname the 'Cabbage Patch'. ¤ The Science Museum is officially separated from the Victoria and Albert Museum.

1900 The Central Line opens running east-west between Shepherds Bush and the Bank. It is a deep-level tube financed with private international funds and using mostly American technology. The fare is two pence and it is dubbed 'The Tuppenny Tube'.

1901 The first electric trams run by London United Tramways in west London. ¤ American tycoon Charles Tyson Yerkes takes control of the Metropolitan District Electric Traction company and, with mostly foreign capital, begins the electrification of the existing steam-driven lines.

1902 The London General Omnibus Company begins to use motor buses.

1903 The LCC inaugurates its first electric tram service. ¤ London's first petrol-driven taxi is on the road, a French-built Prunel.

1904 The first permanent motor bus service begins between Peckham and Oxford Circus run by Thomas Tilling, formerly a horse bus owner. ¤ Lots Road power station built to provide electricity for the new and existing underground lines.

1906 The Royal Commission on London Traffic finds that the average speed on the roads has fallen by 25 per cent in the previous 30 years due to congestion.
1906–7 The Bakerloo, Hampstead and Piccadilly Underground Lines open.

1907 City and South London Underground Line is extended to Kings Cross and Euston. The Northern Railway is opened.

1908 The dock companies, struggling financially, hand over to a public body, the Port of London Authority. ¤ The LCC links electric tramways north and south of the Thames with a tunnel under the newly built Kingsway.

1908 The Olympic Games, due to be staged in Italy, is switched to London when Mount Vesuvius erupts wrecking much of Naples. The length of the marathon is determined by the route from Windsor to King Edward VII's box in the newly built White City Stadium: 26 miles 385 yards. ¤ The Franco-British Exhibition is held at the White City.

1900 News that the British community beseiged in Mafeking in South Africa has been relieved and the Boers beaten back is greeted in London with wild celebrations.

1904 The London Symphony Orchestra is founded, the first independent, self-governing group of its kind in Britain.

1905 For the first time the Royal Horticultural Society Summer Show is held in the grounds of Chelsea Hospital where it settles from the 1920s.

The Chelsea Flower Show

1909 Robert Baden-Powell, founder of the boy scouts, holds a rally at the Crystal Palace which attracts 11,000 boys and a surprising number of girls. The Girl Guides are formed the following year.

Robert Baden-Powell

1901 Queen Victoria dies and is succeeded by Edward VII.

BUILDINGS AND INSTITUTIONS

1911 A new Whiteleys department store is opened in Bayswater after a huge fire destroyed its previous premises in 1887. ¤ Work begins on a new building for the Science Museum. It is not finished until 1928.

1912 The horseshoe-shaped office block Admirality Arch is officially opened. Commissioned by Edward VII in memory of his mother Queen Victoria, it forms a gateway to the Mall and the Victoria Memorial in front of Buckingham Palace.

1914 The Geffrye Museum reflecting the history of the local furniture industry is opened in Sir Robert Geffrye's Almshouses in Kingsland Road, Hackney.

1920 By popular demand the Cenotaph in Whitehall is remade in stone.

1922 County Hall, headquarters of the London County Council, is opened by King George V.

1923 The Empire Stadium, built for the British Empire Exhibition in Wembley, is finished in time to host the Football Association Cup Final.

1924 The British Empire Exhibition is opened. Most of the pavilions are temporary and will be sold off when it finishes the following year. Wembley Stadium is preserved.

THE RIVER, PORT AND TRANSPORT

1911 A trial run of an American-built escalator at Earls Court station is supervised by the Board of Trade. The novelty proves treacherous in its first week with a report of torn dresses and a passenger on crutches falling down.

1912 The United Electric Underground Railways Company of London buys up buses and trams and becomes the major provider of public transport in London. It becomes known as the Underground.

1913 The tube's circle and horizontal bar symbol, the roundel, is introduced.

1915–17 It is estimated that 300,000 Londoners seek shelter from Zeppelin and aircraft bombing raids, some taking to the Underground stations.

The London Underground roundel

1920 There are 100,000 car owners in London, with numbers rising rapidly. ¤ London's first international airport is opened at Croydon with the amalgamation of two small airfields, Beddington and Waddon.

1924 Independent or 'pirate' bus services are a problem, especially for the trams whose staff threaten to go on strike unless something is done. The London Traffic Act effectively prevents operators starting up services wherever they like and brings in some regulation.

SOCIETY AND CULTURE

1910 Dr Crippen of Holloway poisons his wife but is arrested when he flees to Canada, the first murderer caught by wireless communication.

1913 The suffragette Emily Davison is killed when she jumps in front of the king's horse at the Derby. Much suffragette action and violence. 'Cat and Mouse' Act passed allowing jailed suffragettes to be imprisoned, released, and imprisoned again.

1914–18 First World War. Unemployment falls rapidly as the London economy adjusts to the war effort. Nearly half of the men who work on the trams, buses and underground, a total of 17,669, go to the front by 1918. Women take over their jobs, the majority leaving domestic service. Woolwich Arsenal workforce increases sixfold including 28,000 women.

World War I

1915 The first of 11 Zeppelin raids on London kills seven as bombs are dropped on Hackney. Later raids by aircraft are more destructive and the final toll is 670 killed and nearly 2,000 injured. Property damage is estimated at £2 million.

1918 Wild celebrations at the news the war is over.

1921 London Fire Brigade's last horse-drawn wheeled ladder is withdrawn from service. ¤ The London County Council begins development of the Becontree Estate at Dagenham with the first of the promised 'Homes fit for heroes'.

1922 The new headquarters of the London County Council, County Hall on the south bank of the Thames by Westminster Bridge is completed. Started in 1911, building is delayed by the First World War. ¤ The first regular broadcasts, one hour a day, by the British Broadcast Company, as it was then, from the seventh floor of Marconi House in the Strand.

ROYAL LONDON

FAMOUS LONDONERS

1910–36 George V and Queen Mary are crowned in 1911. The King begins his reign as representative of the House of Saxe-Coburg and Gotha but with anti-German feeling high during the Great War and the windows of German-owned shops in London being smashed, the King changes the name to the House of Windsor. All German titles are given up. The King unveils the tomb of the unknown soldier, the Cenotaph in 1920. Huge popular celebrations in London at the King and Queen's Jubilee in 1935. Playing fields in London are named in memory of George V after his death.

1917 Vera Lynn, who entertains the troops during World War II and becomes known as 'the Forces Sweetheart' is born in East Ham.

LONDON'S POPULATION

1911 7.1 million.

1921 7.3 million.

1924 Liberty's department store which had been established on Regent Street since 1875 opens a brand new 'Tudor' store built with timbers from two battleships.

1929 Reputedly the largest office block in Europe at the time, Nobel House, headquarters of the chemical giant ICI is opened on Millbank..

1925 King George V officially opens the Great West Road, one of a number of arterial roads built around London in the 1920s with government subsidies for relieving unemployment. When new factories are built, many of them American, a section of the Great West Road becomes known as the Golden Mile.

1926 For nine days in May London Transport is reduced to a few services during the General Strike in support of the miners. ¤ Manually operated, three-colour traffic lights are installed at Piccadilly.

1929 1,362 people are killed on London's roads compared with 186 in 1901.

1926 For ten days in May London grinds to a halt during the General Strike. ¤ John Logie Baird gives the first demonstration of his primitive television, called a televisor, to members of the Royal Institution in Soho.

John Logie Baird

1927 The British Broadcasting Company becomes the British Broadcasting Corporation when it gets its Royal Charter. John Reith becomes the first Director General.

1929 Abolition of the old Poor Law Boards of Guardians, along with workhouses and the Metropolitan Asylums Board by the Local Government Act. Responsibilities transferred to the London County Council.

1928 Vidal Sassoon, celebrity hairdresser, is born in Hammersmith.

1931 Shell-Mex House, headquarters of Shell-Mex BP is built in Art Deco style on the site of the former Hotel Cecil in the Strand. ¤ The Dorchester Hotel opens on Park Lane, built on the site of the former Dorchester House. ¤ The Windmill Theatre opens in Great Windmill Street.

1932 Unilever House, headquarters of the Lever Brothers company, is completed in neo-classical Art Deco style on the site of the old Bridewell Palace at Blackfriars. ¤ The BBC moves its headquarters from Savoy Hill to a brand-new, purpose-built building, Broadcasting House, opposite the Langham Hotel.

1930 Green Line buses running to towns 30 miles from London begun by the London General Omnibus Company.

1931 The first trolley bus service to replace a tram is run by the London United Tram Company. These have bus wheels with power supplied by overhead electric cables.

1932 Cockfosters, Arnos Grove and Manor House Underground stations, designed by Holden, open. ¤ King George V opens a new Lambeth Bridge replacing the original built in 1862 which is in poor condition.

1931 Buckingham Palace and Piccadilly Circus are floodlit at night with electric lamps.

1932 The vast Becontree Housing Estate built by the London County Council is completed. With a population of 100,000 it is the largest public housing scheme anywhere in the world. ¤ Soho becomes centre of London's sex industries.

1930 Lionel Bart, writer and composer of popular music, is born in East London.

1931 Terence Conran, designer and restaurateur, is born in Kingston-upon-Thames.

1932 Actress Elizabeth Taylor is born in Hampstead Garden Suburb, north London.

1933 The open air theatre in Regent's Park has its first full season.

1934 The Geological Museum, founded in 1835, moves to new premises in South Kensington.

The Geological Museum, South Kensington

1933 The privately run Underground Group, which owns the bulk of London's public transport, agrees to the formation of a public authority, the London Passenger Transport Board, to oversee travel in the capital. ¤ The London Passenger Transport Board decides to replace all trams with trolley buses. ¤ First diagrammatic tube map, designed by Harry Beck.

1934 A beach is created on the north foreshore of the Thames by Tower Bridge with 1,500 tons of sand to give poor children from the East End the chance of a seaside holiday. In 1939, before the threat of war closes it, there are 400,000 visitors. ¤ Voluntary driving tests are introduced and a speed limit of 30 mph. ¤ Gatwick, a private aerodrome, get its first licence to be used by commercial aircraft.

1934 The Labour Party wins control of the London County Council for the first time.

1933 Michael Caine, film star, is born in St Olave's Hospital, Rotherhithe in Southwark.

1934 Mary Quant, sixties fashion designer credited with inventing the mini-skirt, is born in Blackheath, London.

1931 8.1 million.

BUILDINGS AND INSTITUTIONS

1935 The first A Station of Battersea Power Station built by the London Power Company is completed on the south bank of the Thames. There are just two chimneys: B Station with two more chimneys is completed after 1945.

1940–45 Bombing raids and rocket attacks on London destroy about 50,000 houses in inner London and 66,000 in outer London, with more than 290,000 houses badly damaged. In the City of London about a third of all floor space is lost.

1935 Driving tests made compulsory.

1936 The world's first circular terminal, nicknamed 'The Beehive', opens at Gatwick Airport. Passengers board the first scheduled flight from there to Paris.

1946 The Air Ministry takes over a former Royal Air Force base and begins the creation of a civil airport, named Heathrow after a local village.

THE RIVER, PORT AND TRANSPORT

1935 In between the world wars London is a boom town, and semi-detached suburbia grows at a tremendous rate.

1936 Oswald Moseley and the British Union of Fascists march through the East End of London with its large Jewish population. Pitched battles with communists, anarchists and anti-fascists follow. A Public Order Act is passed requiring police permission to hold marches. ¤ After walking 300 miles from their home on the Tyne in the north-east of England the Jarrow marchers present a petition to Parliament protesting at the closure of the shipyards which provided them with their livelihood. There is great sympathy for them along the route and in London.

1937 About 20,000 German Jews arrive in Britain, most settling in London, as the Nazis' anti-semitism becomes violent.

1940 Germans, Italians and other potential enemy 'aliens' in London are rounded up and interned. Of 1,560 Italians sent to Canada on the *SS Arandora Star*, 600 die when it is torpedoed in the Atlantic. ¤ At 5PM on Saturday 7 September, a warm late summer evening, the roar of hundreds of German bombers is heard over the East End of London and

bombs began to fall on factories and houses. The Blitz has begun. Londoners take to the tube station as the nightly raids continue, defying an official ban which is later lifted. ¤ In October a new evacuation scheme has 89,000 children and some mothers sent out to the countryside, where they are not always welcome.

The Blitz

1941 In May, Hitler abandons plans to invade Britain and the German Luftwaffe is sent to support the assault on Russia. The Blitz is over. ¤ The United States declares war on Japan after the attack on Pearl Harbour. Hitler declares war on the United States.

1942 American GIs begin to arrive in London. They bring with them racial attitudes which make life more difficult for black people in London.

SOCIETY AND CULTURE

1939 Preparations for war are made with the digging of trench shelters, the removal to safekeeping of national treasures, the stockpiling of sandbags and the distribution of gas masks. ¤ Within a few weeks of the declaration of war with Germany on 3 September around 750,000 children are sent away to the country. The evacuation is followed by the anti-climax of the 'Phoney War' when the expected assault by German bombers does not happen. By Christmas about half of the children evacuated from London have returned home.

1944 On 13 June the first of the V1 flying bombs nicknamed Doodlebugs hits London as the D-Day Landings get under way. On 8 September the first of the V2 rockets hit Chiswick.

1945 On 8 May the war in Europe is over. Londoners celebrate in Trafalgar Square into the night. Many street parties are held in the following days. The Labour Party wins a surprise victory in the July election. VJ Day when Japan surrenders on 15 August after atomic bombs are dropped on Hiroshima and Nagasaki.

Jamiacans arriving in London

ROYAL LONDON

1936 On the death of his father, Edward VIII becomes king but abdicates after less than a year so that he can marry the American divorcee Wallis Simpson. He is not crowned.

1936–52 Edward's brother Albert becomes king using his second name George and is crowned George VI with his wife Elizabeth Bowes-Lyons as queen in 1937. During the war they win the hearts of Londoners by staying at Buckingham Palace, despite the bombing.

1948 The ship the *Empire Windrush* arrives at Tilbury with 493 Jamaicans seeking a new life in London. ¤ The National Health Service comes into being. ¤ The Olympic Games are staged in London with an opening ceremony at Wembley Stadium.

FAMOUS LONDONERS

1945 Ken Livingston, former leader of the Greater London Council and the first elected London Mayor, is born in Lambeth.

1937 Actress Barbara Windsor is born in Shoreditch.

1947 Singer David Bowie born in south London.

LONDON'S POPULATION

No census in World War II

MODERN LONDON

1951 The Festival of Britain, 100 years on from the Great Exhibition, is staged on the south bank of the Thames.

The Festival of Britain

1958 The London Planetarium opens on the Marylebone Road.

1952 On a misty morning on 8 October express trains crash into a local train at Harrow in north London killing 112 and seriously injuring 157.

1957 London smog causes the Lewisham railway disaster in which 87 people die.

1958 The Queen officially opens the new Gatwick Airport on 9 June. In the first seven months 186,172 passengers pass through the airport which is 'state of the art.'

1952 Londoners still rely on coal fires for heating and a bad winter 'smog' takes many lives.

1956 A Clean Air Act is passed enabling local authorities to ban coal fires and to create smoke-free zones.

1958 Teddy Boys attack West Indian immigrants in Notting Hill and there are nights of rioting with police arresting 140 mostly white youths. ¤ First boutique, His Clothes, opens in Carnaby Street which becomes a symbol of Swinging London.

1959 The original Notting Hill Carnival, staged in response to the riots the year before, takes place indoors at St. Pancras Town Hall and is a great success.

1952 Queen Elizabeth is crowned in 1953 amid huge celebrations in London with crowds queuing overnight to get a view of the Royal Procession. Royal pageantry focused on Buckingham Palace becomes an important London tourist attraction.

The Coronation

1960 The BBC Television Centre at White City is officially opened.

1963 The Hilton Hotel opens on Park Lane.

1965 The Post Office Tower is officially opened by prime minister Harold Wilson. At 620 feet from the ground to its tip, it is the tallest building in London for some years.

1966 Centre Point, 32 stories high, is completed at a major road junction at Tottenham Court Road, Oxford Street and Charing Cross Road. Controversially, it remains empty for years.

1967 The Queen Elizabeth Hall is opened on the South Bank.

1968 The Hayward Gallery opens on the South Bank.
¤ The collapse of a tower block, Ronan Point, in Newham after a gas explosion blows out a prefabricated wall so that one side falls like a pack of cards.

1963 A tunnel under the Thames is opened at Dartford charging a toll for the crossing.

1968 The London Bridge, erected in 1831 which has been put up for sale by the City of London, is bought by the American oil tycoon Robert P. McCulloch and shipped to a theme park at Lake Havasu City in Arizona to be re-assembled as a tourist attraction. ¤ The first section of a new tube line – the Victoria Line – opens between Walthamstow Central and Highbury and Islington. ¤ A brand-new Euston Station, built to reflect the age of electrification of mainline trains, opens amid controversy over the loss of the Euston Arch, a valued feature of the old station.

1969 The Victoria Line is officially opened between Brixton and Walthamstow by the Queen who buys a 5-pence ticket and travels from Victoria Station to Green Park, handy for Buckingham Palace.

1962 The Commonwealth Immigrants Act puts Asians living in Uganda, Kenya and Tanganyika in a difficult position. They have to chose between retaining British citizenship or taking citizenship of countries which are becoming independent and pursuing a policy of 'Africanisation'. Large numbers decide to head for Britain between 1965 and 1968 when the law is changed. Many settle in London.

1965 The Greater London Council (GLC) replaces the London County Council providing an authority which takes into account the great growth of the capital. Old boroughs are amalgamated to form new larger authorities.
¤ The Notting Hill Carnival is staged for the first time in the open air in Notting Hill.

The World Cup

1966 Jubilation when England, hosting the football World Cup, beats Germany in the final at Wembley.

1968 The Kray twins Ronnie and Reggie are imprisoned for their gangland crimes. One of their victims is rumoured to be buried in the concrete of the Hammersmith flyover.

1962 Mick Jagger and his rhythm and blues group appear for the first time as the Rolling Stones at the Marquee Jazz Club in Oxford Street.

The Lloyd's building

BUILDINGS AND INSTITUTIONS

1972 Trellick Tower, a block of flats 32 stories high, is built in North Kensington.

1973 Covent Garden Market moves to new buildings at Nine Elms, Vauxhall, south of the river. ¤ The British Library is formed by the amalgamation of collections of the British Museum, several other libraries and the Patent Office.

1976 The Museum of London, comprising several existing collections, opens in a new building as part of the Barbican redevelopment.

1978 The Central London Mosque is opened in Regent's Park.

1980 The London Transport Museum re-opens in Covent Garden.

1981 The 600 ft (182.9m) NatWest Tower, designed by Seifert, is built.

1986 The new modernist building designed by Richard Rogers for Lloyd's insurance is opened in the City.

1989 The Design Museum on Butler's Wharf opens.

THE RIVER, PORT AND TRANSPORT

1973 On 17 March the Queen officially opens a new London Bridge, the one that is there today.

1975 Moorgate tube crash kills 41 and injures 74.

1979 The first phase of a new tube, the Jubilee Line, is opened between Stanmore and Charing Cross stations. The name is inspired by the Queen's 1977 Jubilee two years earlier.

1980 A second tunnel under the Thames is opened at Dartford.

1982 The Thames Flood Barrier at Woolwich is completed.

1984 Smoking is banned on London Underground trains.

1985 The smoking ban on the Underground is extended to all underground stations.

1986 Terminal Four is completed at Heathrow Airport. ¤ The M25 is completed.

1980 Iranian separatists hold staff and journalists hostage in the Iranian embassy, killing one man. SAS troops storm the building, killing five terrorists. A hostage also dies.

1987 An automated, driverless elevated railway is opened in the redeveloping docklands area and is known as the Docklands Light Railway. ¤ A new airport is opened on the site of the disused Royal Victoria Dock and becomes known as the London City Airport. ¤ A fire at King's Cross Underground station started beneath an escalator suddenly shoots up to the booking hall killing 31 people, including a fireman, in seconds.

1989 A pleasure boat, the *Marchioness*, carrying 131 passengers, staff and crew on a birthday trip on the Thames is struck by a dredger, the *Bowbelle*, and sinks in a few seconds. 51 are drowned in one of the worst disasters on the river.

SOCIETY AND CULTURE

1973 The start of a sustained IRA bombing campaign with the 'Provisionals' planting four car bombs in London in March and bombs in Swiss Cottage on Christmas Eve.

1974 Three more IRA bomb attacks in London including one at the House of Commons that injures 11 people.

1975 Two more IRA bombings, one at the Hilton Hotel which kills two and injures 63.

1978 A Bulgarian exile, Georgi Markov, is killed on Waterloo Bridge when an assassin pricks him with a poisoned hypodermic needle disguised in an umbrella.

1981 Riots break out in Brixton, south London, as tensions between the police and young black people rise. Shops are burned and some looted and 56 police vehicles are set on fire. ¤ Two more IRA bombings, one at Chelsea Barracks and another in a Wimpy Bar in Oxford Street which kills the police officer trying to defuse it. ¤ The first London Marathon.

1983 Workmen cleaning drains in Muswell Hill, north London, discover human body parts. Dennis Nilsen confesses to multiple murders.

1984 Police officer Yvonne Fletcher is shot from within the besieged Libyan embassy while policing a protest outside the building.

1985 Riots follow tensions between predominantly black young people and police. Police officer Kenneth Blakelock is killed at Broadwater Farm estate, Tottenham.

1986 News International moves its main titles, the *Times, Sunday Times, Sun* and *News of the World* from Fleet Street to a fortified site in Wapping. ¤ Margaret Thatcher's Conservative government abolishes the Greater London Council led by Ken Livingstone.

1987 The worst storm to hit England since 1703 causes millions of pounds worth of damage in London.

ROYAL LONDON

A London street party in 1977

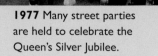

1977 Many street parties are held to celebrate the Queen's Silver Jubilee.

1981 The wedding of Prince Charles and Lady Diana Spencer.

The Royal Wedding

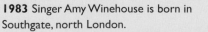

FAMOUS LONDONERS

1975 Footballer David Beckham born in Leytonstone, east London.

1983 Singer Amy Winehouse is born in Southgate, north London.

1988 Singer Adele is born in Tottenham.

LONDON'S POPULATION

1971 7.4 million.

1981 6.7 million.

MODERN LONDON

1991 The first phase of the Canary Wharf development in the regeneration of docklands is complete, including the building One Canada Square which for a time is the tallest builing in London.

Canary Wharf

1993 Buckingham Palace opens to the public.

1995 County Hall is converted into flats and a hotel.

1997 The new Globe theatre opens, a replica of Shakespeare's original.

1999 The London Eye is erected on the south bank of the Thames and is for a while the tallest Ferris wheel in the world.

2000 The Millennium Dome opens in Greenwich.

2003 Wembley Stadium's twin towers demolished.

2004 An office block nicknamed the Gherkin is completed on the site of the old Baltic Exchange in the City of London.

2007 The New Wembley Stadium is opened.

2008–12 Construction of huge Olympic Park in Statford, east London.

2012 At a height of more than 1,000 ft (304.8m) a new office block, the Shard London Bridge, is topped out.

The Shard

1991 Smoking banned on London buses. ¤ The Queen Elizabeth II Bridge opens to carry southbound road traffic across the Thames at Dartford. The existing tunnels take the northbound traffic.

1994 The terminus for the Eurostar service between London and Paris is opened at Waterloo Station.

2000 The Millennium Bridge opens by St. Pauls.

2003 Congestion charging introduced in central London.

The Millennium Bridge

2007 The terminus for Eurostar trains between London and Paris opens at St. Pancras International. The Waterloo terminus closes.

2010 A bicycle sharing scheme is introduced with 5,000 bikes in 315 docking stations. It is officially called Barclays Bicycle Hire after Barclays Bank which sponsors it. ¤ Researchers record 125 different species of fish living in the tidal Thames as it runs through London.

2012 The Emirates Air Line cable car Thames crossing opens.

1991 The Provisional IRA attempt to kill the prime minister, John Major, and members of the Cabinet meeting at 10 Downing Street by firing rockets at the building. They fail when two do not explode and a third goes off in the garden.

1992 A huge one-ton bomb in a lorry blows off the front of the Baltic Exchange in the City killing three and injuring 91 people. The Provisional IRA take responsibility and set off four other bombs in London during the year.

1996 The IRA bombs Canary Wharf tower.

1999 A neo-Nazi, David Copeland, called the London 'nail bomber', plants home-made bombs in Brick Lane, Brixton and Soho targeting Asians, West Indians and gay men. He kills three people, including a pregnant woman, and injures more than 100 others. He is convicted of murder.

1997 Widespread public mourning at the funeral of Lady Diana with a service in Westminster Abbey after her death in a car crash in Paris.

2000 The first elections for a new-style London Mayor as a Greater London Authority replaces the former GLC. Ken Livingstone wins. ¤ London celebrates the New Millenium with street parties and a massive firework display.

2003 A daytime congestion charging scheme is set up in central London in an effort to ease the flow of traffic.

2005 A terrorist attack by four Islamic suicide bombers kills 52 and injures hundreds, many losing limbs. Three bombers board Underground trains, a fourth, unable to get to his intended target, boards a bus and blows himself up. A follow-up attack two weeks later fails. ¤ The International Olympic Committee choses London to host the 2012 Olympics.

2002 Celebrations of the Queen's Golden Jubilee.

The Opening Ceremony at the London Olympics

2011 Riots break out in several parts of London and other cities.

2012 The London Olympics take place.

2012 Queen's Diamond Jubilee celebrations include a Royal Flotilla and procession. Buckingham Palace displays many of the diamonds worn by the Queen and other monarchs over the past 200 years.

The River Pageant

1993 Bobby Moore, born in Leyton, east London and captain of England's World Cup-winning team in 1966, dies of cancer at the age of 51.

2011 Amy Winehouse dies of alcohol poisoning.

1991 6.9 million.

2001 7.2 million.

THE THAMES
The ebb and flow of history

- **The slender Millennium Footbridge, which spans the river**
- **between St. Paul's Cathedral on the north bank and the Tate**
- **Modern art gallery directly across the water to the south, is a fine**
- **place to begin a historical study of the Thames.**

Look down through the silver suspension wires of the Bridge and on the swirling brown surface of the river you will notice flotsam and jetsam is racing westwards, towards Parliament, away from the sea. The Thames, it seems, is running backwards, flowing strongly 'up stream'. Later the river will turn, and the water level along the Embankment walls will begin to fall rapidly, revealing gravel beaches. At the turn of the tide, roughly every six hours, there are a few minutes of calm water, then the Thames is on the move again, rushing into London from the sea.

This observation of the flow of the tides in the midst of a great city reveals one overwhelming historical fact about the River Thames: it is tidal, all the way from the wide estuary to Teddington, Middlesex, on the western fringes of the capital. This flow of water, running at a treacherous six or seven knots, packs enormous power and was used for centuries to supply London with everything from food to building materials, right up to the age of electricity.

On the north bank, St. Paul's stands testimony to the power of the Thames tides. Most of the stone and timber used to build it between 1675 and 1710 came up the river, in the days when the roads in England were pot-holed tracks, there were no canals to speak of and steam railways were a futuristic dream. On the South Bank, the building materials for Bankside Power Station, now the Tate Modern art gallery, also came up the Thames.

In his poem *The Wasteland* the American T.S. Eliot called the river 'a strong brown God'. If that was true of the Mississippi of his childhood in St. Louis, it was even more so of the Thames which Eliot knew well from the many years he spent in London. The tides which made the building of London possible sometimes threaten to destroy it. A North Sea surge of water could overwhelm the Embankment walls and the capital has had to protect itself

**Top: Statue of Father Thames;
Above: Old London Bridge.**

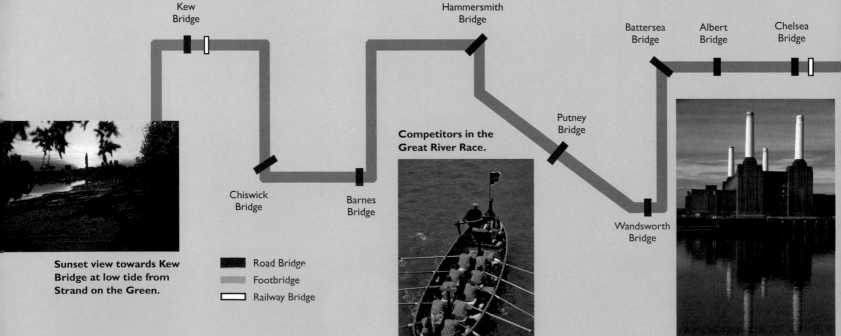

Sunset view towards Kew Bridge at low tide from Strand on the Green.

Kew Bridge

Hammersmith Bridge

Battersea Bridge

Albert Bridge

Chelsea Bridge

Putney Bridge

Competitors in the Great River Race.

Chiswick Bridge

Barnes Bridge

Wandsworth Bridge

■ Road Bridge
■ Footbridge
□ Railway Bridge

Battersea Power Station.

against disastrous flooding by building a barrier between the city and the sea.

Now that the Thames has lost most of its commercial traffic it has become one of London's great natural resources, once again full of fish and clean enough for tourists to enjoy a pleasure trip down to Greenwich or up to Windsor.

OLD LONDON BRIDGE

The London Bridge of today bears no resemblance at all to the historic Old London Bridge which stood, just to the east of the present bridge, from its completion in 1209 until 1831. This first stone bridge spanned the river on 19 arches, each of which was supported by two 'starlings', boat-shaped break-waters which cut through the force of the tides and river flow. For five centuries the narrow roadway of Old London Bridge was like a tunnel between the shops, houses and chapel built along its length.

A modern pleasure boat could not pass under any of the arches of Old London Bridge. There was, for a long time, a small drawbridge near the centre and tall ships could pass through it if they paid a toll. But, in effect, the Bridge held back the flow of flood tides and was a barrier dividing the tidal Thames, where ocean-going vessels moored, from the upper reaches of the river.

Most historians now believe that the Old Bridge was not built primarily as a river crossing. Whereas for the Romans the bridge at Londinium provided a short-cut from the Kent coast to East Anglia and northern England, for the Anglo-Saxons, and later the Normans, the purpose of a bridge was different. The wooden bridges the Saxons built were intended as a defensive barrier to repel invaders who sailed up the Thames from the east coast. They were defending not the old Roman London but Lundenwic further west.

In AD 994 the Vikings burned and ransacked London and they tore this bridge down in 1014. According to the Olaf sagas they rowed up to it, tied ropes

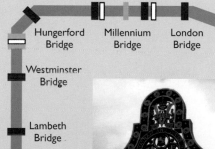

The London Eye.

Tower Bridge.

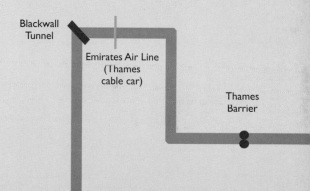

Since 1982 the Thames Barrier has protected London from floods.

Waterloo Bridge · Blackfriars Bridge · Southwark Bridge · Tower Bridge · Rotherhithe Tunnel · Hungerford Bridge · Millennium Bridge · London Bridge · Westminster Bridge · Lambeth Bridge · Vauxhall Bridge · Blackwall Tunnel · Emirates Air Line (Thames cable car) · Thames Barrier

The sign for the old Blackfriars Railway Bridge dated 1864.

The river police force, based in Wapping, was founded in 1798.

Headquarters of the secret service, MI6, completed in 1993.

Built in 1869, the tea clipper, the *Cutty Sark*, (now at Greenwich) beat the world record by sailing from London to China in 107 days.

to the piers and then set off down stream, carried no doubt by the ebb tide, taking the wooden bridge with them. Many people believe this is the ancient origin of the children's nursery rhyme 'London Bridge is falling down'. However, that was not the only disaster to befall the wooden Saxon bridges – one was washed away by high tides, others simply collapsed. Until the arrival of the Normans and the construction of a much sturdier structure, London Bridge kept on falling down.

The Normans ruled London by the time the last wooden bridge had to be replaced. Their decision to rebuild in stone presented a formidable technological challenge: there was no question of spanning the Thames with two or three elegant arches. But as the bridge was almost certainly regarded as part of London's defences, like a long arm thrown across the river from the City to hold back river-borne attack, the obstacle it presented to shipping was not an issue.

It took 30 years to build Old London Bridge and it cost a fortune. Peter of Colechurch, who was the mastermind behind it, died before it was completed. Money was raised with a special tax on wool exports and many people made bequests to 'God and the Bridge'. To

pay for the cost of up-keep, houses and shops were built on it, the rents going to a bridge fund – except on occasions when the income was purloined by kings in search of a ready form of cash. The roadway between the buildings was only 20 feet wide, another indication that the first purpose of the bridge was not to make it easier to cross the Thames.

When the tide was running, water raced through the arches of Old London Bridge as if tumbling over a weir. It could bank up several feet higher on one side than the other. The arches were not of even dimensions and the watermen who learned to 'shoot the bridge' gave names to each of the treacherous openings: Long Entry, Chapel Lock, Gut Lock, Rock Lock and, the largest where there was a drawbridge, Draw Lock. When the tide was high, head clearance for a boat shooting the lowest lock could be down to eight feet. The rush of water through the Bridge was always treacherous: at one time one of the shops on the bridge specialised in selling cork life jackets.

One of the wonders of medieval Europe, Old London Bridge ensured over the centuries that the bulk of the nation's wealth accumulated in the City. Ships carrying goods brought from around the

world moored just below the bridge, creating a busy and ever more congested sea-port. Coal, wheat, quarry stone, and timber brought from around the coast were also routed to London Bridge, and much of it was taxed, swelling the coffers of the City and its merchants. The up-keep of the Bridge was paid for out of a trust and the City staunchly opposed the building of any new bridges up-river which might threaten its age-old monopoly.

The opening of Westminster Bridge in 1750 sealed the fate of Old London Bridge as it lost its monopoly as the only permanent river crossing. The shops and houses came down and in the autumn of 1757 a temporary wooden bridge was built alongside the old bridge so that traffic could still cross while the buildings were being taken down. But this bridge was severely damaged by fire and the demolition work had to be speeded up. Compensation was paid to those who lost their properties and toll charges were brought in to defray the cost – even the watermen had to pay for risking their lives shooting the bridge. The tolls were very unpopular and were lifted when Parliament helped to bail the City out of its plight.

When Old London Bridge was finally demolished entirely and replaced in August 1831 by a new bridge just a little upstream, the old barrier was gone and the tides raced even further inland. The City, now immensely wealthy, could afford to allow the river traffic to flow. Great docklands had already been built to the east to ease the pressure on the Pool of London, and there had been a spate of bridge building, some of it funded by the City itself.

The bridge of 1831, designed by the father and son team of architects John Rennie, lasted until 1968 when it was taken down, stone by stone, and shipped across the Atlantic. It was bought by the McCulloch Oil Corporation and re-assembled at Lake Havasu City in western Arizona.

THE BRIDGE OF FOOLS

In May 1736 an Act of Parliament giving the go-ahead for the first bridge in central London to challenge Old London Bridge was passed on the grounds that it would 'be advantageous not only to the City of Westminster but to many other of His Majesty's subjects and to the Publick in general'. To turn the proposed Westminster Bridge into reality, 175 commissioners were appointed, among them many members of the aristocracy and the Archbishop of Canterbury, who was to be compensated for loss of income from the Lambeth horse ferry.

Parliament decided it could raise £625,000 by running state lotteries. Imagining there would be great public enthusiasm for a flutter on London's new bridge, 125,000 lottery tickets were put on sale at £5 each. The satirical novelist Henry Fielding, with some foresight, dubbed the enterprise 'The Bridge of Fools'. He thought all lotteries were corrupt and accused the government of trying to fund public works by diverting the public interest away from the popular pastime of throwing dice. After a year only £40,000 had been raised.

Another lottery failed to raise the money needed and, with work beginning on the bridge, there were five lotteries between 1737 and 1741, at which point the government, still short of the necessary funds, gave up and provided an annual grant to keep the works going. Over the next decade all kinds of troubles attended the painfully slow progress of the bridge across the river: barges coming from up-river hit the arches and caused damage and in 1748 a pier sank, suggesting that the structure was fundamentally unsound. By February 1750 it was nearing completion, however, and some Londoners had already taken a hazardous trip across it when an earthquake rattled the Palace of Westminster. Another followed in March and though there was widespread panic, the bridge stood up. Work was completed by mid November and Westminster Bridge was finally opened officially. It was lit at night by 32 oil lamps.

FREEING THE BRIDGES

You can stroll or drive over any of London's bridges today without putting your hand in your purse or pocket and paying a toll. In the past, however, although the City of London kept London and Blackfriars (opened in 1769) free, private promoters of new crossings did not have reserve funds and had to raise income somehow.

They all, initially, made a charge for both pedestrians and horse-drawn vehicles.

An early private venture was up-river between Battersea on the south side of the river and Chelsea to the north. There was a ferry but it was considered to be unreliable and hazardous, so a local landowner, Earl Spencer (ancestor of the late Lady Diana Spencer), pushed through an Act of Parliament to replace it with a bridge. He tried to raise money for a stone bridge but the scheme failed so he settled instead for a timber bridge which was opened in 1776 as Chelsea Bridge. A charge of a half-penny was made for foot passengers and there was a scale of tolls for horse-drawn vehicles rising to a shilling for the largest.

There followed a spate of privately funded bridge building in the early 1800s. The first iron bridge across the Thames was opened in June 1816 with tolls of a penny for pedestrians and up to one shilling and sixpence for carriages. It was originally called the Regent's Bridge but was later renamed Vauxhall Bridge and, like all London bridges, it was rebuilt at a later period. While work on this was going on another enterprise called the Strand Bridge Company was planning a crossing from Somerset House on the north bank to Watermen's Stairs on the Lambeth side. Faced in granite from Wales and designed by John Rennie, it opened in 1817 just a year after Vauxhall Bridge. It was to have been called the Strand Bridge but was renamed Waterloo in honour of the Duke of Wellington's victory over Napoleon Bonaparte two years earlier. Again the toll revenues did not give the investors in the bridge any return.

Less than two years after the completion of Waterloo Bridge a private company sought to profit by building a

Waterloo Bridge, built between 1811 and 1817.

new crossing between Blackfriars Bridge and London Bridge. There were fierce objections from the City and from watermen as the river was now becoming crowded with bridges making navigation much more difficult. But a design by the engineer John Rennie which would leap the river and provide the minimum obstruction for shipping won the day and Parliament approved the plan. Rennie, a Scotsman, looked north of the border for the stone for the abutments and shipped granite blocks down from Peterhead on the east coast, as well as from Dundee and Edinburgh. Huge iron castings were made in Rotherham, Lancashire and the girders winched into place and bolted together. This new crossing, Southwark Bridge, was opened officially when St. Paul's struck midnight on 24 March 1819. This bridge never paid its way and was notable for its lack of traffic.

As more bridges were built south London began to develop, attracting more traffic and putting more pressure on the road system and increasing demand for yet more river crossings. After 1830 the

railways arriving from north, south, east and west brought in more passenger and goods traffic, all of which was hauled ponderously in horse-drawn vehicles so, by the 1860s, congestion had become a serious problem. Private companies continued to believe that they could profit from new river crossings. Lambeth Bridge opened in 1862 but with a steep approach, goods vehicles tried to avoid it. Like Southwark Bridge, it took most of its paltry income from commuters walking from the southern suburbs to work.

The Albert Bridge Company began work on yet another crossing in 1864 but it ran into trouble as a new Embankment was being built and Parliament dithered over its exact positioning. Work was delayed for nearly a decade and it did not open until 1873, by which time the company promoting it was more or less insolvent and could not recoup its cost with toll charges.

Though they never returned much in profits, toll charges did limit the use of bridges: toll gates narrowed the entrances, payments slowed everything up, and the

cost discouraged movement across the river. The first to recognise this was the City. In 1849 they leased Southwark Bridge from the company that had built it and made it toll-free, buying it outright in 1866. The Metropolitan Board of Works, the only London-wide authority, decided to buy the other toll bridges and remove all charges. Starting in 1878 it spent £1,400,000 to 'free' 11 bridges. In celebration, the Prince and Princess of Wales criss-crossed the river on Queen Victoria's birthday, 24 May 1879, in a carriage which took them over Lambeth, Vauxhall, Chelsea, Albert and Battersea bridges.

In the end private enterprise, as so often in London's history, was bailed out by the public purse. However those who lived downriver of London Bridge and had contributed their rates (or local taxes) to freeing the river crossings in town argued that they had been hard done by. The solution was to provide a free ferry at Woolwich for both vehicles and pedestrians who were taken across the river in paddlesteamers. Opened in 1889 the ferry still runs – on diesel – and remains a quaint and amusing way of crossing the Thames.

Every one of the bridges the Metropolitan Board of Works bought was later replaced: the lifespan of river crossings on the tidal Thames has mostly been short, with the notable exception of Old London Bridge.

THE 'WOBBLY' BRIDGE

In central London no new river crossings had been built for a century when, in May 2000, Queen Elizabeth II inaugurated officially the opening of the strikingly original Millennium Footbridge which links St. Paul's Cathedral with the Tate Modern art gallery across the Thames. An unanticipated structural problem which made the bridge vibrate alarmingly under the footfalls of hundreds of people led to the closure of the bridge for more than a year. It was re-opened to the public in February 2002 and offers fine, traffic-free views of the Thames.

Hard on the heels of the Millennium Bridge, two new footbridges were built alongside Brunel's original Hungerford Market crossing. Work on these was delayed by the fear that there might be unexploded bombs from the Second World War in the river-bed, as the Luftwaffe made the Victorian railway bridge that the new Hungerford bridges follow on either side a target in the Blitz. Also, the Thames had been so burrowed under here with underground railway tunnels there was concern that these might be breached when the pilings were sunk. Happily there were no explosions and no terrifying punctures of the tube tunnels and the latest walkways across the river are now open.

FROST FAIRS

For a very long time the Thames tides have been too strong, and the climate too clement, for a 'frost fair' to be held on the river. The last was staged in the winter of 1813–14 a few years before Old London Bridge was pulled down. And it was the Old Bridge, just as much as the colder climate, which had made the fairs possible, for the flow of the river above the bridge was held back by the arches so the Thames froze more readily. But, spectacular though they were when they were held, frost fairs were rare events. The first was in the winter of 1564–5, the second more than a century later in 1683–84, then 1715–16, 1739–40 and finally 1813–14. In 1789 there was a huge fair upriver from London Bridge at Putney.

Two days before Christmas 1683 the Thames was frozen across and, on New Year's Day, 1684 streets of tent-like booths appeared on the ice forming an avenue which was instantly named Temple Street since it ran from the Temple Stairs. Horse-drawn carriages were able to cross the ice and a bull ring was set up close to London Bridge. Watermen, desperate for trade, hitched their boats to horses and sleighed up and down the river. A printing press was set up on the river and the diarist John Evelyn noted: 'The people and ladies took a fancy to have their names printed, and the day and year set down when printed on the Thames: this humour took so universally, that it is estimated the print gained £5 a day, for printing a line only, at sixpence a name, besides that he got by ballads etc'.

King Charles II, his brother James, the Duke of York and Queen Catherine, Infanta of Portugal, all had their names printed on the frozen Thames. Oxen were roasted without a hole appearing in the solid ice, which remained frozen for about a month so that the booths and festivities extended further and further from London Bridge and sightseers rode in coaches from one end to the other.

One of the longest spells of freezing weather began in December 1789 and lasted through until February. But there was a sudden thaw in between. A Frost Fair had begun on Christmas Day and by 21 January many stalls were set out above London Bridge. Overnight the weather warmed and an extraordinary scene greeted the people who lived on the west side of the bridge when they awoke the following morning. All the stalls had drifted into each other in the thaw, and then froze again in a jumble. However, the Frost Fair continued until 14 February when the Thames suddenly dissolved and smashed ice into the bridge, badly damaging it.

Ice on the Thames was not all jollity. During the winter of 1763–64 the water between all but one of the piers froze solid so that the entire force of the river was concentrated on the remaining arch. The rush of water so scoured the river bed that it undermined the foundations of the bridge. Again in 1814–15 the last great Frost Fair ended in sudden thaw which drowned many people and smashed ice and roaring water into the piers. Repairing the damage was extremely costly and the City finally took the decision to build a new bridge. Although the Thames did freeze again on

A Frost Fair, 1814.

occasions there were no more Frost Fairs. The last significant amount of ice formed in the bitter winter of 1962–3.

THAMES FISHERIES

The Thames was a salmon river. The season ran from March to September when the adult fish, after spending four years in the North Sea, returned to their spawning grounds in the shallows upriver. There were fisheries at Wandsworth, Battersea, Putney, and Fulham, while the Lord of the Manor at Chelsea had the fishing rights from Battersea to Lambeth. In the eighteenth century these fishing villages were still sending salmon to the London market and there is a record of Fulham catching 130 in a single day in 1776. There were some astonishing catches that century. In 1784 the *London Chronicle* carried this story on 13 April: 'A salmon which weighed near 30lb was taken off one of the starlings of London Bridge by two watermen, who saw it leap out of the water at low-water mark, and immediately put off in their boat'.

The Thames salmon fisheries survived until the early 1800s though the spawning grounds were being rapidly destroyed by the building of locks upriver and the dredging of shingle banks to improve

Billingsgate Market in the 1880s.

navigation. In 1812 a weir was built across the river at Teddington, Middlesex, which proved to be an almost impenetrable barrier for the salmon and today marks the official tidal limit of the Thames. There were still annual salmon runs but the pollution of the river with sewage began to kill off the fish in the 1820s. By the time a Salmon Fisheries Commission took evidence in 1861 there were no signs of salmon at all.

The classic Thames fish was not salmon but much smaller smelt, delicate little fish which, when fresh from the water, smell of cucumber. Like salmon they were seasonal, caught between March and May when the adults came up through London to breed. The City of London had most of the fishing rights on the river.

Most of the Thames fisheries had been destroyed by pollution before London got an effective sewage system in the 1860s. In his *A History of British Fishes*, published in 1859, William Yarrell wrote: 'Formerly, the Thames from Wandsworth to Putney Bridge, and from thence upwards … to the bridge at Hammersmith produced an abundance of smelts, and from thirty to forty boats might then be seen working together, but very few are now to be taken, the state of the water it is believed, preventing them from advancing so high up'.

After World War II, the Thames as it ran through London was biologically dead. There then unfolded one of the least well known, and yet most spectacularly successful, ecological triumphs of the twentieth century. Fish populations recovered with remarkable speed. Cucumber smelt returned, flounder, another fish which comes upriver to spawn, and a range of freshwater fish were found in the very heart of London. By 1990 more than 100 species had been recorded, and by 2012 the total topped 120 with the return of lampreys, the rather unappetising-looking, eel-like fish which – as many know – put an end to an English king. Henry I, third surviving son of William the Conqueror, is reputed to have

died of food poisoning caused by 'a surfeit of lampreys' in 1135.

The Thames Water Authority was sufficiently encouraged to re-stock the upper reaches of the river with salmon in the hope that they would migrate to the sea and return as adults to spawn. Salmon ladders were built to help them past the weirs and locks. By 1988 the salmon were running again, and in one year 300 were recorded at Molesey in the freshwater river. In that murky brown water below you as you peer over the bridges there are plenty of fish, unlikely as this may seem.

FLOODS

London is built in the wide, shallow valley of the Thames and a very large part of it lies within the natural floodplain of the river. Tens of thousands of commuters go to work each day in offices below the river's high-water mark. Though most Londoners never give the danger a thought, the threat of flooding is ever present. The biggest hazard is the weather in the North Sea, which can drive a wall of water down the east coast of Britain into the Thames estuary and all the way up the river into the centre of the capital. At the same time, heavy rainfall within the Thames valley can fill the tributaries of the river and send a surge of freshwater downstream to meet the oncoming tide. These are not new threats to London brought about by climate change, but age-old.

There is a record in the *Anglo-Saxon Chronicle* in 1099 that 'on the festival of St Martin the sea flood sprang up to such a height and did so much harm as no man remembered that it did before'. An account of a thirteenth-century flood says that in the great Palace of Westminster 'men did row with wherries in the midst of the Hall'. Samuel Pepys described in his diaries a great flood on 7 December 1663 when all Whitehall was 'drowned'.

When the Victorian embankments were being built between 1869 and 1874

Flooding at Westminster, 1928.

an estimate was made of the highest possible tides. The Metropolitan Board of Works ordered the owners of riverside properties to have defensive walls 17 feet, 6 inches high (5.33m). That was enough to hold back tidal surges in 1874 and 1875. But not everyone complied and in 1881 the Thames rose to the Board's height limit and overflowed its banks.

The embankment walls had to be raised and though there were scares towards the end of the nineteenth century the 1881 level was not reached again for nearly half a century. When it happened it was not anticipated. On the night of 6 January 1928 the predicted high water at London Bridge was a safe 12 feet, 5 inches (3.8m) and the tide was expected to turn at 1.37 AM. But a North Sea surge, pushed by strong winds, drove the tide inland where it met a strong flow of freshwater from upriver. The Thames rose alarmingly and at 1 PM it was 18 feet, 3 inches (5.5m). At Millbank a wall collapsed under the pressure of water and 14 people were drowned.

After this calamity the flood defences were raised again, and a programme begun to attempt to predict dangerous tides. But nothing was done until the aftermath of the great floods which inundated large parts of Eastern England and the Thames estuary on the night of 31 January 1953. On Canvey Island 57 people died when the

sea defences were breached, unleashing a wall of water which smashed into houses and flooded them instantly.

To guard against another exceptional tide the embankment walls would have to be raised again, but it was obvious that in time this would mean the river Thames would be hidden from view and it would become impossible to seal the docks in an emergency. The only long-term solution was some kind of barrier or barrage across the Thames to the east of London which could be shut to hold back a predicted tidal surge.

It took 20 years to resolve the technical and administrative problems. The barrier scheme that exists now was begun in 1974 and went into operation in October 1982. It was first closed against a dangerous tide in February 1983 and officially opened by the Queen in 1984. Downstream, all the flood defences had to be raised as a closure would naturally raise the river levels there. But the Thames Barrier is only a temporary measure and will gradually become less and less a guarantee against disaster as the water level of the Thames continues to rise at nearly half an inch per year. (1.27cms) The barrier will only provide protection until 2030, and already the government's Environmental Agency is working on new solutions for London.

THE WEST END
From the 'Season' to a shopping centre

If the City of London is where a great deal of wealth accumulates, the West End is where a great deal of it is spent and that has been true from the very beginnings of the creation of this most fashionable part of town. Before the Great Fire of 1666 drove many of London's wealthiest merchants out of the City, the development of upper class housing to the west had already begun with the building of Covent Garden Piazza by the Duke of Bedford. At the same time as the City's richest residents were leaving the old Square Mile, the establishment of the Royal Court and Parliament at Westminster drew the aristocracy into London and it was their presence here from the early seventeenth century that gave the West End the opulent character it still has today.

The statue of Eros (actually the Angel of Christian Charity) in Piccadilly Circus.

THE LONDON SEASON

The wealthiest families in England had their homes on their estates in the countryside. However in the seventeenth century a ritual arose in which they stayed in London for three months of the year when Parliament was sitting. As a rule, titled gentlemen were also Members of Parliament and would be required to be in Westminster. This was the origin of what became known as the Season, the annual round of balls, dinner parties and sporting events which took place in and around Parliament. Those in town for the Season needed somewhere to stay so fine squares were developed as the town houses of those whose main home was a mansion in the country. Landowners developed them in exactly the same way as other parts of London: the land was leased to builders who put up the fine terraces. Because the tenants were to be from the very pinnacle of society, the building leases stipulated the standard of housing should be appropriately grand.

Because there were only a few landowners in the area it was possible to plan the road system. An aerial view of the famous squares such as Bedford, Russell and Tavistock reveals a neat grid pattern which illustrates the way this upper-class district was carefully planned. A great many have been redeveloped since the eighteenth century, but Bedford Square in Bloomsbury remains a fine example.

When the upper crust were in town they required a great many servants and there were hundreds of tradesmen, such as furniture- and coach-makers, to support the lavish lifestyle of the wealthy. Some idea of the teeming life of these districts when they were newly fashionable can be gathered from a detailed survey carried out by historians of the Grosvenor Estate in Mayfair in 1790.

In Grosvenor Square itself no less than 31 of the 47 householders were titled; and on the estate as a whole there were 37 peers, 18 baronets, 15 'Honourables' and 39 'Ladies'. But this was only a small proportion – less than ten per cent – of the inhabitants. Among the other residents were foreign diplomats and professional people such as civil servants or Court officials, including the king's organist. There

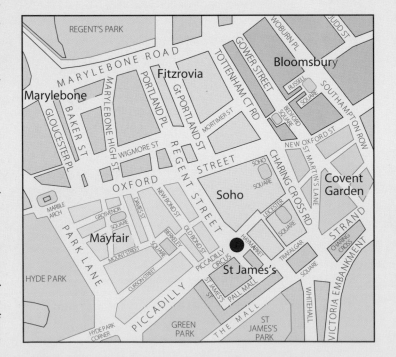

A pre-Raphaelite statue in Berkeley Square, surrounded by 30 tall plane trees planted in 1789.

were army officers, doctors, architects and lawyers. But by far the largest group of estate residents were tradesmen, who lived above their shops. The main shopping streets were Davies Street, Duke Street, Mount Street, North and South Audley Street, Oxford Street and Park Street.

Among the tradesmen there were 55 butchers who at that time would still drive livestock, bought at market, to their shops in Mayfair, where they would be slaughtered. As well as butchers, there were other suppliers of food and wine, dairymen (including a cow-keeper), carpenters, bricklayers, masons, plumbers, upholsterers, cabinet-makers, dressmakers, tailors, milliners and so on.

Every member of a rich family would have a wardrobe of expensive, handmade clothes for every different type of social occasion, changed and supplemented every 'Season' according to the dictates of fashion. The most famous members of this industry were the bespoke tailors who populated the streets either side of Regent Street and on the Burlington estate. Later they congregated in Savile Row.

REGENT STREET

During the nineteenth century this West End society and economy expanded enormously as new estates were developed to the West. The single most important development marking out the West End from the rest of London in the nineteenth century was the building in the 1820s of Regent Street and the laying out of Regent's Park. This was a scheme devised by John Nash, the architect favoured by the Prince Regent, carved out of Crown land, though built, like everything else, as a speculation. It is about the only example to be found in London of grand planning on a scale common in European cities, and typically it was never completed and was altered not long after what had been built was finished.

Nash's plan was to create a kind of aristocratic garden city on open fields in Marylebone, just north of the New Road (now Euston Road/Marylebone Road) – then virtually the northern boundary of built-up London. He envisaged individual villas set in landscaped parkland from where there would be a broad street running down to Carlton House, providing an exclusive thoroughfare between the Park and the Prince Regent's residence.

To avoid the impression that the new Regent Street simply crossed the New Road and Oxford Street, circuses were to be built, providing elegant junctions which continued the style of the dominant thoroughfare. Regent Street, moreover, was to turn its back on London to the east – less salubrious areas such as Soho, where common mechanics lived – and to look to the west. Few roads were allowed in from the east, and the whole project was deliberately designed as a social barrier marking off the West End.

Not all of the scheme was finished: the fine terraces around Regent's Park certainly did become very fashionable residences, as they are today, but the circus on the New Road was only half-completed, and Marylebone Park never

Regent Street at Christmas.

61

Princes Arcade, a boutique shopping centre in Piccadilly.

did get off the ground as an aristocratic suburb. But Regent Street itself, after a faltering start, became one of *the* most fashionable haunts of 'London Society'. As Nash had intended, it was to rival the attractions of Bond Street, with shops all the way along, and exclusive lodgings above for bachelors, beaux, and visitors to town. Butchers, greengrocers and the like were not allowed to trade there. Regent Street was not, in the way it is now, a main road in London: rather, it was a genuine shopping centre in which the rich could park their carriages and parade up and down, the ladies popping into shops between the fashionable hours of two and four in the afternoon, while their footmen waited outside. 'Only here,' wrote Francis Wey, a visitor in the first half of the nineteenth century, 'could you find the fashionable world so perfectly at home in the middle of the street'.

Though the Season is not what it once was now that the presentation of debutantes to Her Majesty the Queen no longer takes place, and the aristocracy no longer gather on Rotten Row in Hyde Park in their carriages and on horseback, some of it lingers on. The well-to-do like to be in town for the Ascot races and a

Test Match at Lord's Cricket Ground, but far fewer will now own or lease a property in town. A middle-class West End, stretching all the way out to Notting Hill Gate with row upon row of gigantic 'wedding cake' terraces covered in white stucco – a kind of mock stone cladding – arose with a new kind of shopping in the large department stores such as Harrods and Selfridges. In fact, when the American Gordon H. Selfridge opened his store in Oxford Street in 1909 many thought he had built it in the wrong place, beyond the social world of the then West End. The new stores aimed to provide a complete day out for their customers, more and more of whom were visitors to the West End rather than local residents. Restaurants were provided, as well as 'retiring rooms' – that is, lavatories – for ladies, who could spend the day not only buying things, but reading magazines, drinking and chatting, just as men had been able to do in their West End clubs in Pall Mall and St James's.

WEST END ENTERTAINMENT

It was in the last decades of the nineteenth century that entertainment became more refined. New theatres were built with stalls rather than the raucous pit and

Soho still contains stripclubs, but is also home to bars, clubs and theatres.

audiences which had once hurled abuse at the villain took to sitting in silence. The rougher music halls, which had developed from inns or drinking clubs, were superseded by plush variety theatres, the most glamorous of which was the Coliseum, opened in 1902, which had a revolving stage on which the Derby was re-run with real horses and jockeys.

In the inter-war years, by which time variety was on its way out and the cinema was hugely popular, there was an invasion of the West End by Americans and American culture. The most conspicuous transformation that took place was the rebuilding of much of Park Lane, where two of the grandest aristocratic mansions, Grosvenor House, home of the Dukes of Westminster, and Dorchester House, were demolished in the 1920s to make way for hotels and flats. The new Grosvenor House Hotel was designed specifically to cater for the American market, and though the building may not look very transatlantic to us today, it was the first hotel in London to have a separate entrance lobby to each bedroom, and separate bathrooms with running iced water: a peculiarly American taste. Two years after Grosvenor House Hotel was completed in 1929, the Dorchester was built, and it was said that Park Lane was beginning to resemble Fifth Avenue in

Chinatown in the West End.

New York. Regent Street, too, was largely rebuilt in the 1920s between Oxford Circus and Piccadilly Circus in a variety of architectural styles which reflected American influences. It was officially re-opened in 1927.

Although some districts of the West End retain something of the old aristocratic quarter, in the post-war years it has become a tourist magnet for people from other parts of the country as well visitors from abroad. For Londoners themselves it might be expensive, but it is no longer exclusive. After World War II many of the older houses became offices.

BELGRAVIA

This was an entirely new estate of grand, stucco-clad houses built on what had been marshy wasteland on the north bank of the Thames. It was owned by the Grosvenor family who named the new district after Belgrave, a small village in the Midlands where they had a country estate. The main contractor was Thomas Cubitt, one of the finest and most successful London builders who put the first houses up in the 1820s. Early leases banned the shooting of duck on Sundays: it was still marshy at the edges then. Earth

from the excavations of St. Katharine's Dock was used as infill.

Belgravia was instantly fashionable as it was close to Buckingham Palace and Westminster and the housing was of the highest quality.

FORTNUM AND MASON

Like nearly all of London's most famous stores, Fortnum and Mason had modest beginnings. In 1705 Hugh Mason had a shop in St. James's Market and a spare room in which he put up William Fortnum, who had come to London as a builder after the Great Fire. When Fortnum got a job in Queen Anne's household as a footman he discovered that the many wax candles burned every day left a residue which he could sell. This brought him into business with Mason. They imported goods from the East India Company and gained a reputation for stocking exotic foods. The store has never lost its early cachet and is popular today, although the present shop only dates from the 1920s.

CARNABY STREET

Once a fashionable address, Soho lost its aristocratic residents when the West End was developed. Regent Street turned its back on the little streets to the East, and the district was, literally 'beyond the pale' for the well-to-do.

Soho became London's principle red-light district as well as an enclave for foreign residents. However, the reputation of this district was transformed in the 1960s when a new kind of streetwise fashion caught the attention of the world. The shorthand term for the daring new clothing was Carnaby Street, the modest road in which the leading designers set up shop. According to the American magazine *Time* in 1966:

'In this century every decade has its city ... Today it is London, a city steeped in tradition, seized by change, liberated by affluence ... In a decade dominated by youth, London has burst into bloom. It swings, it is the scene'.

In a way this was a new, more democratic, post-war West End re-inhabiting its oldest quarters. Carnaby Street has adapted with the times and Soho gets smarter every year, now with a lively Chinatown to the south of Shaftesbury Avenue.

Carnaby Street, one of the centres of Swinging London in the Sixties, is still fashionable today.

THE CITY
From the first Lord Mayor in 1189, the pivot of finance, ceremony, exchange and trade

The City of London, often referred to as the Square Mile, is one of the world's great financial centres. It has arisen on the site of the very first London built by the Romans and resettled later by the Anglo-Saxons and Normans, and has survived several great fires, plague and the Blitz.

A bustling river port town in the Middle Ages, London began to grow well beyond the boundaries of its old walls as suburbs arose and the built-up area spread to Westminster. Although the City became engulfed in the tide of building to all directions of the compass in the nineteenth century, it steadfastly held on to its ancient system of government and refused to either take responsibility for the London that grew around it or to be absorbed by it. So in the Corporation of the City of London it retains its unique form of self-governance, which it guards jealously, and has its own Lord Mayor who, for centuries, was one of the most important political figures in the capital.

It has been a peculiar feature of the City that it has retained many ancient traditions and organisations while transforming itself into an international financial powerhouse which occupies mountainous, towering office blocks. In this outwardly very modern district ancient Livery Companies survive though the trades they once oversaw have long disappeared. Each year they engage in pageantry at the Lord Mayor's Show which attracts sightseers from all over the world.

The refusal of the City authorities to have any responsibility for the districts that grew up around the Square Mile created a crisis in the capital. When the rapidly expanding northern industrial towns were given a modernised form of local government by an Act of 1835, London missed out. It was not until 1889, when county councils were created, that London beyond the City got an authority with overall responsibility, the London County Council (LCC). Within the area of the LCC, boroughs were created and have been reformed many times since. The LCC was replaced by the Greater London Council in 1965, and when this was abolished by Margaret Thatcher in 1986 a government department took on the GLC's responsibilities, though local borough councils remained. In 2000 the Greater London Authority was created with a new Mayor of London in charge. All the while, the City of London remained aloof, retaining its structure and ancient traditions while Greater London was reformed several times over.

To avoid confusion, the Lord Mayor of London is now referred to as the Lord Mayor of the City of London, an office that is rather different from that of the Mayor of London. Whereas Greater London has a population of more than 7 million, the City has only 9,000 residents. However, each day more than 300,000 arrive in the Square Mile to work, and a special system of voting at local elections reflects this with firms of all kinds allocated votes according to the number of their employees.

Although the City has retained its independence and held aloof from Greater London, it does have responsibility for looking after two important open spaces, Hampstead Heath and Epping Forest.

A view of the majority of the City from the top of the Monument.

It also looks after four London bridges: Southwark, Blackfriars, Tower and London. A Bridge House Trust, which has funds donated over the centuries, dispenses around £15 million in charitable donations each year.

THE FREEDOM OF THE CITY

Each year around 1,700 people, both women and men, become Freemen of the City of London, an ancient right which is retained despite the fact that, in practical terms, it means little or nothing. The ceremonial and ritual is everything. In the past, it was not possible to trade or work in the City unless you were a Freeman, and qualification was dependent on membership of one of the Worshipful or Livery Companies. This was changed in 1835 and there have been many revisions since in the qualifications required.

According to the City Corporation's own account of the history of this office, ancient privileges associated with the Freedom of the City included the right to herd sheep over London Bridge, to go about the City with a drawn sword, and if convicted of a capital offence, to be hanged with a silken rope. Other, less dubious, advantages are said to have included the right to avoid being press-ganged, to be married in St. Paul's Cathedral, buried in the City and be drunk and disorderly without fear of arrest. Freemen used to

The Royal Exhange.

be given a casket in which to keep their Freedom certificate: it was a document that was carried around as we would carry a driving licence today.

Today, when they are sworn in, Freeman make the following Declaration: 'I do solemnly swear that I will be good and true to our Sovereign Lady Queen Elizabeth the Second; that I will be obedient to the Mayor of this City; that I will maintain the Franchises and Customs thereof, and will keep this City harmless, in that which in me is; that I will also keep the Queen's Peace in my own person; that I will know no Gatherings nor Conspiracies made against the Queen's Peace, but I will warn the Mayor thereof, or hinder it to my power; and that all these points and articles I will well and truly keep, according to the Laws and Customs of this City, to my power'. Non-British and British Commonwealth Citizens have the option to substitute 'our Sovereign Lady' with 'Her Majesty'.

THE BANK OF ENGLAND

This venerable institution, housed now on a three-acre site in the heart of the City, has a history going back to 1694 when it was created as a way of raising money for the Government. From small beginnings in a Livery Company's hall it has been

The Monument.

housed as it grew in ever-larger buildings. Its grandest home, designed by Sir John Soane, was mostly demolished in the 1920s when the Bank was rebuilt, to the horror of many architectural bodies. Soanes' great wall remains. Today the Governor of the Bank of England is an important figure in the regulation of the British economy. The Bank fixes the base rate at which money is lent by other banks and building societies. There is a museum in the Bank with an account of its history.

THE LONDON STOCK EXCHANGE

The London Stock Exchange can trace its history back more than 300 years. Starting life in the coffee houses of seventeenth-century London, the Exchange quickly grew to become the City's most important financial institution.

THE BARBICAN

This huge development built between 1965 and 1976 covers a 35-acre bombsite at Cripplegate. After the devastation of the Blitz only 48 people lived in the area, and the resident population of the City as a whole was only 5,324. The Barbican almost doubled that by the time it was finished, and although the grey concrete facades have been described as examples of the 'new brutalism' in architecture, it is very popular and the apartments very expensive. Within the huge complex there are concert halls, a cinema, restaurants and, adjoining it, the Museum of London. It is one of the most vibrant arts centres in London, rivalling the South Bank. Despite the criticism of the architecture it was given a Grade II listing.

LLOYD'S

From a modest beginning in 1688 in Edward Lloyd's coffee house in the City, this association of wealthy men who gambled on insuring ships, where there were high risks and great rewards, created one of London's most dynamic and successful companies. Lloyd's has an unusual history and structure because its members had to devise a unique form of association when the creation of joint stock companies was strictly controlled after the disaster of the South Sea Bubble in 1720. Such were the national losses on the investments on worthless ventures that speculations by groups acting together were outlawed. Lloyd's got round this by operating as individuals or "Names" who risked their money on their own.

When, in the 1820s, the law was changed so that any company could go into the business, the Lloyd's system was badly rattled. It survived, and still survives, because it had developed an information system on shipping, with agents around the world, which gave it an advance on others in terms of intelligence on insurance risks – and it always paid up. By the mid-century, it was insuring not only ships but also property and all kinds of other risks worldwide.

Today Lloyd's is still not a company as such but a marketplace for insurance and insurers who club together in syndicates to take risks. In 1986 it moved into its distinctive modernist building designed by the architect Richard Rogers.

The Lloyd's building in Leadenhall Street. The stainless steel reflects light and constantly changes colour.

Some of Lloyd's covers:

The showmen For many years, Ringling Brothers: Barnum and Bailey, promoters of circuses and ice shows, have been covered at Lloyd's. Underwriters have been asked to write insurance for King Tusk, an elephant, and for a 'unicorn' – in both cases against non-performance due to ill health or death.

Satellites Insurance against death or injury caused by a piece of disintegrating satellite falling from the sky.

Spiders A company in Australia that clears houses of poisonous spiders whose bite can be serious or fatal. This spider is often found under lavatory seats. The fumigation company gives a written promise to pay a cash sum to any clients subsequently bitten.

Crocodiles A Lloyd's syndicate covers against crocodile attack.

Aircraft Insurance has been provided for the smallest twin-engine aircraft, which takes off from the top of a Mitsubishi Shogun at air shows.

Cosmonauts The Russian cosmonauts who went to the MIR space station on the American space shuttle had personal accident cover underwritten at Lloyd's.

Lottery winners Employers can buy insurance against two or more of their staff winning the UK national lottery and not returning to work.

Polar cover A team of 21 British women who walked more than 600 miles from northern Canada to the North Pole was covered at Lloyd's for personal accident, search and rescue, equipment, supplies and recovery.

Bomber aircraft Lloyd's underwriters insured a World War Two German Heinkel bomber. This was airlifted from Spain to Cambridgeshire, slung beneath a German Army Sikorsky helicopter. The bomber belonged to The Old Flying Machine Company, which provides vintage aircraft for air shows and films.

Chinese wine For a French exhibition, the underwriters insured a 2,000-year-old wine jar complete with contents that were blue with age.

Monster risk Cutty Sark Whisky offered a £1 million prize to anyone who could capture the Loch Ness monster alive. The company guarded against loss by taking out a Lloyd's policy.

Extra-terrestrial Cutty Sark Whisky again insured against loss at Lloyd's before offering £1 million for an authentic extra-terrestrial device.

Sport Many major sporting events are covered in the London insurance market, including the Olympic Games and the World Cup Football Championships. Sports personalities covered include footballers, boxers, tennis stars, racing drivers, plus entire American teams for basketball, baseball, ice hockey and football.

Up in smoke For a premium of 50 pence, what was then the world's largest cigar (length 12.5 feet/3.8m weight 242lbs/110kg) – rolled to celebrate the launch of a new brand – was insured during a London exhibition for its retail value of £17,933.35. The cigar would have needed 339 days and nights of uninterrupted smoking to be consumed!

Snowed under A car dealership in the town of Omaha in Nebraska, USA, took out insurance at Lloyd's after offering $10,000 to anyone who bought a car from the company during December – if it snowed on Christmas Day in Omaha. More than 65 customers qualified.

Making sense Food critic and gourmet, Egon Ronay, insured his taste buds for £250,000. A whisky distiller once insured his nose.

Star cover Lloyd's has insured many film and stage personalities. These include Gene Kelly, Mae West, Elizabeth Taylor, Frank Sinatra, Bob Hope, Bing Crosby, Richard Burton, Sir Laurence Olivier and Betty Grable, with her 'million dollar legs'. Actress Kerry Wallace, whose head had to be shaved for a *Star Trek* film, insured against the possibility of her hair failing to grow back again properly.

Lloyd's also insure rock stars. These have included Eric Clapton, Dire Straits, Bob Dylan, Michael Jackson, The Beatles, Genesis, Elton John, Led Zeppelin, Status Quo, The Rolling Stones, Rod Stewart, Stevie Wonder, The Who, Jason Donovan and Kylie Minogue. Bruce Springsteen insured his voice for £3.5 million.

Bath-tub A merchant navy officer, who sailed from Dover to France in a sea-going bathtub, insured his vessel for £100,000 in third party liabilities. The underwriters accepted the risk, provided that the plug stayed in place at all times!

FACTS ABOUT THE CITY

- Sir Francis Child, Lord Mayor in 1698, is credited with having founded the banking profession when he left his goldsmith business to work entirely in finance.
- King Ethelred levied the earliest customs duty in 979 and the first Custom House was built in 1382, close to the present building.
- Lombard Street has traditionally been a street of banks. Many had their own special emblems on display – an eagle for Barclays, a grasshopper for Martins, a cat and fiddle for the Commercial Bank of Scotland and an artichoke for Alexanders.
- Carved mice on a building in Philpot Lane commemorate the fact that, during its construction, one workman was pushed to his death on suspicion of stealing sandwiches. But the real culprits were, in fact, the hungry local mice.
- One Lord Mayor built a small bridge over Seething Lane to connect his two houses but had failed to seek official permission. The fine imposed was a freshly plucked rose and his descendents still give one fresh rose each year to the current Lord Mayor.
- A man working on sewers in 1836 discovered a tunnel leading into the bullion vaults of the Bank of England. He sent a note arranging to meet the directors there at midnight and duly emerged from below a flagstone. He was rewarded for his honesty and the tunnel was blocked in!
- The Monument, which marks the start of the Great Fire, is the world's tallest freestanding stone column.

CITY SIGHTS

Financial institutions such as the museum of the Bank of England and the Royal Exchange, London's first financial trading marketplace, are not the only places to visit in the City. Other museums include the Museum of London and the Geffrye Museum; St. Paul's Cathedral and John Wesley's House and Chapel represent the range of religious institutions; and historic sites vary from parts of the Roman London Wall to Dr. Johnson's House, the Guildhall (built in 1411 for the medieval trade guilds), and Mansion House, the official residence of the Lord Mayor of London. The City also manages to squeeze in more modern sights such as the Cartoon Art Trust!

GENTLEMEN'S CLUBS AND TRADING COMPANIES
Steeped in tradition

- **London has for centuries been a city where men and women**
- **have grouped together in trade associations and clubs to meet**
- **with like-minded associates not only to be sociable, but also to**
- **further their economic and political interests. The oldest of these**
- **associations originally brought together men (and some women)**
- **from particular trades and devised their own special ceremonial**
- **dress or livery. Not only have many of these survived from the**
- **Middle Ages until the twenty-first century, but also new guilds are**
- **forming today. Gentlemen's clubs have a very different history.**
- **The earliest can trace their origins back to the opening of the**
- **first coffee houses in the seventeenth century while some of the**
- **grandest, such as the Atheneum in Pall Mall, were founded in the**
- **nineteenth century.**

CLUBS

The very oldest, and today the most exclusive, gentlemen's club is White's in St. James's Street which has among its members Prince Charles. Its beginnings, like that of some other venerable clubs, was modest enough. It was called Mrs White's Chocolate House, located in Chesterfield Street in the West End, and was opened by an Italian called Francesco Bianco (Francis White). Chocolate was an expensive novelty when White's first began to serve it in 1693 and those enjoying it would have been wealthy young men. They were also fond of gambling, a financially disastrous addiction for many after they moved to their present premises in 1778.

Among the other surviving West End clubs with a history going back to the eighteenth century is Brooks's, favoured by Whigs (roughly equivalent to today's constitutional monarchists), and Boodle's, favoured by Tories (traditionalist monarchists), both in St. James's Street. Founded by aristocrats,

The Athenium Club.

they were generally named after their head waiter.

Though these old West End clubs are the most exclusive, the heydey of the gentlemen's clubs was the nineteenth century. Typical of these is the Atheneum in Pall Mall which was founded in 1824 by a group of distinguished scientists, authors and artists including Humphry Davy, Michael Faraday and Walter Scott. It

was rather like a communal palace where, for a subscription, members could enjoy a grand building, designed especially for them by a leading architect. Jules Verne, the French science fiction author, was never a member, but he had his quintessential English hero Phileas Fogg make the wager here that he could go round the world in 80 days.

Other major London clubs include the Reform, the Carlton, the Oxford and Cambridge, the Army and Navy, the East India and Sporting, and the Naval and Military, founded in 1862 because the existing clubs for servicemen were full.

One exclusive club is the Garrick in Covent Garden, founded in 1831 and named after the famous eighteenth-century actor David Garrick. This club brought together aristocrats – among the first members were 24 peers –and actors and writers. Charles Dickens was a member as was W.S. Gilbert of Gilbert and Sullivan fame.

CITY LIVERY COMPANIES

London's Livery Companies are the direct descendants of the medieval guilds, religious fraternities which grew up round the City's churches in late Anglo-Saxon times. After the Norman Conquest many of these began to develop into associations of workers, in particular crafts or trades. The word 'guild' derives from the Saxon word for payment, since membership of these fraternities has always been paid for. The word 'livery' refers to the uniform worn by guild members on ceremonial occasions. There are no records for the very early formation of the Livery Companies but some almost certainly existed before 1066. Guilds, sometimes called mysteries, from the Latin 'misterium', meaning professional skill, are not unique to the City of London but were common in other parts of the country and, in fact, throughout Europe.

During the medieval period, the Livery companies checked the quality of goods and sought to ensure weights and measures were accurate and honest. They also controlled imports, set wages and working conditions and trained apprentices. From their earliest days, the guilds also looked after the welfare of their members, and they built almshouses all over the country. The celebrated City Guild member and former Lord Mayor, Richard Whittington, left a fortune for almshouses when he died in 1423 and the Trust he founded still exists.

The earliest known record of a guild is that of the Weavers, which is mentioned in a document dated 1130. In 1155 there is a record of a Royal Charter given to the Weavers by Henry II in return for payment into the Exchequer. These Royal Charters awarded to Livery Companies were a way of buying privileges acknowledged by the Crown. The leading City Livery Company, the Mercers, have a record in

The Mercers' Maiden, the symbol and coat of arms of the Mercers' Company. She first appeared on a seal in 1425.

their archives indicating that they were formed with elected members as early as 1348. In the following year the Worshipful Company received its Royal Charter from Richard II.

At one time most Livery companies had their own halls, but the Great Fire of 1666 took its toll of the earliest halls and the Blitz took away many of those which were rebuilt. Today, only 40 Companies have halls in London, the oldest of which is of the Worshipful Society of Apothecaries, dating from 1672.

THE GUILDHALL

The City of London's Guildhall, much of which dates back to the fifteenth century and survived both the Great Fire of 1666 and bombing in the Second World War, is used now more for ceremonial occasions and corporate hospitality than day-to-day business of the City. The original withstood fire because much of it was of stone and the timbers solid oak. It is the only secular, stone building in the City dating before 1966. It was both the council chamber for the City and, for a long time, the scene of trials which required a large hall. These included the trial of Lady Jane Grey and her husband, Lord Guildford Dudley, in 1553.

Order of precedence of Worshipful Companies, with date of first records of existence or grant of Royal Charter:

1. Mercers (general merchants) 1394
2. Grocers 1428
3. Drapers 1364 (wool and cloth merchants)
4. Fishmongers 1272
5. Goldsmiths 1327
6. Merchant Taylors (tailors) *1327
7. Skinners (fur trade) *1327
8. Haberdashers (thread and sewing articles) 1371
9. Salters (salt and chemical merchants) 1394
10. Ironmongers 1463
11. Vintners (wine merchants)1364
12. Clothworkers 1528
13. Dyers 1471
14. Brewers 1437
15. Leather sellers 1444
16. Pewterers 1384
17. Barbers (also surgeons and dentists) 1308
18. Cutlers (knife, sword and cutlery makers) 1344
19. ** Bakers 1486
20. Wax chandlers (now supports beekeeping and honey production) 1484

*The original order was settled by the Lord Mayor in 1515 but, to take into account an earlier dispute, the Merchant Taylors and the Skinners alternate the 6th and 7th position. There are now 108 Livery Companies, with the last, formed in 2004, for Security Professionals.

**To ensure they were never accused of giving short weight, members of the Bakers' Company gave a small, extra piece of bread with each loaf – and 13 loaves for every 12 bought, hence the term 'a baker's dozen'.

THE EAST END
The haunt of cockneys, costermongers and Jack the Ripper

- In 1800 the East End of London, which was to become a byword for poverty, sweated labour and crime, was no more than a few villages downriver of the City of London. Even in the mid-nineteenth century, when Charles Dickens was writing about the London underworld, he did not find it here, for he rarely wrote about anything east of Aldgate Pump. His world of thieving and murder was in the central London slums or the terrible rookeries south of the river in places like Bermondsey. The East End was then chiefly a town of sailors and shipbuilders.

On the north bank of the Thames there was a string of hamlets from the Tower to Limehouse. These housed stevedores and lumpers who loaded and unloaded cargoes, rat-catchers, ship repairers, ship's bakers, marine-store dealers and watermen. The servicing of sailors provided much work for the women of Wapping and Shadwell, who would launder their washing.

In Limehouse there were shipbuilding yards – as distinct from cargo docks – and these, along with a thriving shipbuilding industry in Deptford, south of the Thames, supported communities of skilled sailmakers and other craftsmen. The villages of Poplar and Blackwall were built around the East India Company's main shipyards, and the Company shaped the life of the whole community. Time was told by the Company's shipyard bell, most local people worked in the yards making and repairing East Indiamen, they worshipped at the Company chapel, their children went to the Company school, and they often ended their days at the Company almshouses.

THE NEW DOCKS

All this was changed radically by the building of new enclosed docks to the East of the City from the early 1800s onwards. When all merchant ships had to moor in the Pool of London, the area of the Thames just below London Bridge, pilfering of cargoes was rife. However, the new West India Docks, built far to the east of the City on the Isle of Dogs, were surrounded by high walls and had their own police force. One by one the spread of the new docklands changed the character of this part of London, and the image arose of the East End as a vast area of poverty and hardship. Work in the docks was always uncertain and when ships came in men would fight for work.

At the same time as the docks arose, a distinctive form of London industry developed: the 'sweated' trades in which men and women laboured long hours in attic workshops turning out clothing and all kinds of fancy goods, many destined for parties in the wealthy West End. And some of the more unpleasant industries were evicted from the City and re-established to the East. The once fashionable housing around Spitalfields lost its appeal and in time was mostly demolished, though some fine eighteenth-century terraces can still be seen.

The East End was also the district to which immigrants congregated, in particular

Church bells have been cast at Whitechapel Bell Foundry for over 500 years.

Jews who were fleeing persecution in Russia and Europe. For a long time they gave this part of London a distinctive character, though, today, the synagogues they built are often now superseded by the mosques of the Muslim Bangladeshi community.

Many of the Irish immigrants who came to London in the second half of the nineteenth century congregated around the docks and worked as stevedores, the elite men who were responsible for loading ships and making sure cargoes were securely packed so that they would not shift dangerously in stormy seas.

This tough, but vibrant world has changed beyond all recognition in the past half century. Every single enclosed cargo dock has closed down. St Katharine's, the closest to the City, is now a popular tourist attraction. The Museum of Docklands has been housed in some of the original West India Dock warehouses. A great tower block has arisen at Canary Wharf where bananas were once unloaded. Redevelopment of Docklands has turned much of it into an extension of the City.

The area of Whitechapel, centre of the Bangladeshi community, is really the only part that retains some of the old East End feel. But it is no longer the home of the celebrated London cockney.

SPITALFIELDS
Now a newly fashionable part of London full of restaurants and design firms, this was a Roman burial ground and later the site of the twelfth-century New Hospital of St. Mary without Bishopsgate. The land by the hospital became known as Spitalfields, the 'Spital' probably a shortened version of Hospital. When Henry VIII dissolved the monasteries most of this building was destroyed. Later this area, just outside the walls of the City and therefore free of the control of the Guilds, was settled by French Huguenot silk weavers who had fled France after the religious intolerance

of Protestants. There were around 14,000 of these weavers, the most successful of whom built fine town houses with lofts at the top for the looms. Some of these survive today in, for example, Fournier Street. The popularity of cotton cloth from the late eighteenth century and the development of new machinery to create it cheaply destroyed their livelihood by the early nineteenth century.

WHITECHAPEL
Like Spitalfields, Whitechapel is considered by many to be the heart of the East End. A notoriously rough area in the late nineteenth and early twentieth centuries, prostitution was rife there and murder was a common occurence. Britain's most infamous serial killer, Jack the Ripper, committed his crimes in the Whitechapel and Spitalfields areas.

The Whitechapel Road is the East End's main street. Here is the Whitechapel Bell Foundry where the bells for Westminister Abbey were made. Big Ben was also recast here when the original bell cracked.

THE ISLE OF DOGS
This once marshy wasteland formed by a great loop in the River Thames was reclaimed by Dutch engineers who drained it in the seventeenth century. There are many suggestions as to how this

great expanse of London got its name but none is convincing. It was once called Stepney Marsh, and is sometimes referred to as The Island. It was still remote grazing land when the first of the great enclosed docks was carved out in 1802. A system of docks led to its development for warehousing and the servicing of ships. When this nineteenth-century infrastructure was abandoned in the 1970s it became an area of widespread dereliction until its resurrection by the London Docklands Development Corporation. The Docklands Light Railway now provides a public transport link with the City and the rest of London.

The changes in the East End have been dramatic – this example of grand, modern Docklands architecture replaced a dark and grimy alley in Whitechapel.

FACTS AND FIGURES ABOUT THE EAST END

- Bells have been made at Whitechapel for more than 500 years.
- Charles I's executioner, who lived in Rosemary Lane (Royal Mint Street) in Whitechapel, obtained an orange stuffed with cloves from the king's pocket and sold this for a princely ten shillings.
- We know Shakespeare lived at Bishop's Gate, Shoreditch because he was noted in records as a tax defaulter! ... The new Globe Theatre is set just 200 yards from Shakespeare's original playhouse.
- More than 300 people were put to death on Tower Hill and for several hundred years, pirates were regularly hanged at Execution Dock, Wapping: these included Captain Kydd. Ever a place of seafaring men, Wapping was home to explorer Captain Cook, Zachariah Hicks (who first sighted Australia) and Captain Bligh of 'Mutiny on the *Bounty*' fame.
- Brick Lane is so-called because it was the route the carts took from the brick kilns in nearby fields.
- Jack the Ripper killed at least six victims in Whitechapel in 1888.
- From 1788 until 1960, London was the biggest port in the world. During the 1930s some 100,000 men handled 35 million tons of cargo.
- During excavations prior to building the Royal Mint Court, by Tower Bridge, some 760 skeletons were uncovered. This was the site of plague pits where corpses of Black Death victims were slung in 1348 and 1350.
- As well as the redeveloped docklands areas, East London contains some of the city's great visitor attractions, such as the Tower of London and Tower Bridge. The warship HMS *Belfast* is moored near Tower Bridge, while the Design Museum and London Dungeon offering contrasting exhibits. There is even a working city farm to visit, the Mudchute Park and Farm on the Isle of Dogs.

THE COCKNEY

There is an old saying that to be a true cockney, that is to say a real Londoner, you had to be born 'within the sound of Bow Bells'. To the east of the City of London is a district called Bow and it is often assumed that the peeling of the bells of a church out there defined the true East Ender. In fact, the naming of the cockney goes back to the time when a curfew was still rung in the City of London to warn that the city gates would be closed at night. The bells which chimed the end of the day were those of St. Mary-le-Bow in Cheapside, so a cockney was someone born within the boundaries of the City of London, long before the East End developed. In time the term cockney was used to describe the distinctive accent of Londoners, particularly the street sellers of the Victorian period, but the origin of the term remains obscure.

A traditional East End occupation was that of costermonger, selling fruit and vegetables from a barrow in the street.

Converted dock buildings.

HMS *Belfast.*

COCKNEY RHYMING SLANG

Cockney Rhyming Slang has now become a part of London's heritage, and has spread beyond the confines of those Londoners born within hearing distance of Bow Bells. It has percolated right through the East End – and beyond.

Adam and Eve	believe
apples and pears	stairs
April showers	flowers
Aristotle	bottle
Artful Dodger	lodger
Bath bun	son/sun
Beecham's Pill	bill
bees and honey	money
Bristol Cities	titties (Bristols)
butcher's hook	look
'take a butcher's'	

The dramatic architecture of One Canada Square (often called just 'Canary Wharf').

china plate	mate
'my old china'	
cobbler's awls	balls (testicles)
'a load of cobblers'	
cocoa	say so
'I should cocoa'	
dog and bone	phone
Donald Duck	luck
Duchess of Fife	wife
'me ole Dutch'	
dustbin lids	kids
Hampton Wick	prick (penis)
'on me wick'	
jam jar	car
Jimmy Riddle	piddle
rabbit and pork	talk
'she don't 'arf rabbit on'	
Rosy Lee	tea
rub-a-dub-dub	pub

Scapa Flow	go
'we'd better Scapa'	
Sexton Blake	cake
skin and blister	sister
tea leaf	thief
tiddle wink	drink
'a bit tiddly'	
tin tank	bank
tit for tat (titfer)	hat
Tod Sloan	alone
'on his tod'	
trouble and strife	wife
Uncle Ned	bed/head

WESTMINSTER, PARLIAMENT AND THE GOVERNMENT

For centuries, the centre of the British political scene

- Though today Westminster City Council is just one borough within the Greater London Authority area, its origins go back to a time when it was a place quite distinct from the city that had grown up two miles east along the Thames. The development of Westminster as the home of royalty and the seat of government began in 1042 when Edward the Confessor decided to build a palace close to the Abbey that he had built on Thorney Island. Nothing remains from this time except the tradition that this was where kings and queens would be crowned. The earliest part of the Parliament building that survives today is a remnant of Westminster Hall, built by the Conqueror's son, William II.

Around the Palace and the Abbey founded by King Edward a town grew in time, and by the thirteenth century it was thought to have a population of around 3,000. Efforts were made by royalty to turn it into a commercial centre to rival the City. But, instead it developed as a town which provided services and entertainment for those who gathered around the Royal Palace and the Abbey. It was not by any means a pious place for it teemed with prostitutes and there were around sixty alehouses in the area around the Abbey in the fifteenth century.

Rebuilding of the Abbey started in the thirteenth century and was not completed until 500 years later with the final additions designed by Nicholas Hawksmoor in 1745. A kind of bureaucracy grew up around the Palace in Westminster as it became both a Court and the place where the first parliaments met. It was this concentration of political power

Detail of the front of the Houses of Parliament. The statue is of King Richard I (the Lionheart).

and wealth which created the modern Westminster: dominated by the Houses of Parliament overlooking the Thames and the magnificent Abbey in which monarchs are still crowned and funeral services for the elite are held.

THE HOUSES OF PARLIAMENT

The name parliament is derived from the French *parler* meaning 'to talk'. British Parliament is made up of three parts: the Crown, the House of Lords, and the House of Commons.

In the years when the House of Commons and the House of Lords were becoming established they had no purpose-built home but found rooms in the old Palace of Westminster. Between 1824 and 1827 something like a modern Parliament building began to take shape with rebuilding works designed by John Soane. But most of this was destroyed by fire in

1834. The Exchequer still used wooden tally-sticks which were regularly burned, and it is believe an oven consuming them overheated.

The Houses of Parliament which survive today were built in the Victorian Gothic style while Members of both Houses 'camped out' as best they could. The Lords Chamber was completed in 1847 and the Commons in 1852. The chief architect was Charles Barry. During the Blitz Parliament was hit many times and an incendiary bomb burned out the House of Commons chamber, which had to be rebuilt in a simpler style.

The term 'Westminster' is used often as shorthand for Parliament and the Government.

After a general election, a Parliament will last for a maximum of five years if

The Speaker's Chair in the House of Commons. The Speaker is an MP who has been elected to act as Chairman during debates in the House of Commons. He or she must ensure that the rules laid down by the House for the carrying out of its proceedings are observed.

there is no reason to dissolve it earlier. Within that time there are annual Parliamentary 'sessions' and at the start of each of these there is a State Opening. For this the Queen goes in procession from Buckingham Palace to Westminster escorted by the Household Cavalry to give a speech which, by convention today, sets out some key aims of the party in power. State openings were formerly in November but have recently been moved to the Spring. It is a ritual that can be dated back to the sixteenth century and acquired its modern form in 1852 at the first opening of Parliament after the fire of 1834.

THE YEOMEN OF THE GUARD

These are a military corps founded by Henry VII in 1485. Since then, they have been the bodyguard of the sovereign, although their duties today are purely ceremonial. They wear a distinctive red uniform dating back to Tudor times and are commonly known as Beefeaters.

Before the State Opening of Parliament, the Yeomen Warders search the cellars of the Houses of Parliament to ensure there is no repeat of the Gunpowder Plot, when Guy Fawkes was arrested in the cellars while attempting to blow up the building.

BIG BEN

If there is an unmistakable landmark which says to anyone from anywhere in the world 'London' it is the Clock Tower of the Houses of Parliament which contains the Great Bell that booms over Westminster when its hammer strikes the hour. Strictly speaking, the nickname 'Big Ben' refers only to the giant bell cast

especially for the Tower, but it has come to mean the whole structure as if it were one huge grandfather clock.

The history of the clock is fascinating. Architect Charles Barry handed over the work on the Clock Tower to Augustus Pugin, whose design was one of the last he ever produced. After some controversy, the design of the Great Clock itself was awarded to a lawyer and amateur clockmaker Edmund Beckett Denison, who worked in tandem with a professional clockmaker Edward Dent. Their brief was set by George Airy, Astronomer Royal,

who decreed: 'The Great Clock should be so accurate that the first strike for each hour shall be accurate to within ONE second of time'. It was thought by many to be an impossible task, but they achieved it. They designed the clockwork mechanism or 'escapement' which keeps the ticking regular. The Great Bell was cast in Whitechapel Bell Foundry and hauled to the Clock Tower by a enormous team of 16 brightly beribboned horses. It chimed for the first time on 31 May 1859.

Two months after it first chimed the time, the Great Bell cracked. It turned out that Denison, self-styled giant clock expert, had had the hammer made twice as large as intended by the bell founder. The time was rung by one of the smaller bells for three years after that while a smaller, more suitable hammer was made. The bell was turned so the crack was away from the hammer point and it rings to this day with a slightly imperfect tone.

The origin of the name Big Ben remains a matter of contention. Some say that at the time the bell was cast there was a heavyweight boxer known as Big Ben and anything huge was named after him. Others say the name came from Sir Benjamin Hall, in charge of government works, who was known as Big Ben. The name was certainly used in newspapers before the bell first rang out.

WHITEHALL

Just as 'Westminster' can be short for Parliament so 'Whitehall' is used as shorthand for government offices. Once the site of the Palace of Whitehall, occupied first by Henry VIII, most of the palace was destroyed by fire except for the Banqueting House designed by Inigo Jones in 1622. The wide thoroughfare called Whitehall, running from Trafalgar Square through to Parliament Square via

A Yeoman of the Guard, also known as a Beefeaters.

built by the profiteering contractor whose name they bear'. By the time he was resident there the building had been substantially enlarged and improved, first of all by Sir Robert Walpole, who was the first prime minister to take up residence in 1735. After Walpole left it was another 20 years before a prime minister moved into No. 10. In 1770 Lord North moved in and made more improvements to the house, which by then had become the recognised home of prime ministers. As crowds tended to gather outside it, for security reasons gates were put up at the entrance from Whitehall.

PRIME MINISTERS

- Britain's first Prime Minister was Robert Walpole (Whig Party, in office 1721–42).
- Britain's youngest Prime Minister was William Pitt the Younger, who came to power in 1783 at the age of just 24.
- William Gladstone was Prime Minister four times: 1868–74, 1880–85, 1886 and 1892-94.
- Winston Churchill was one of most famous twentieth-century Prime Ministers. He held office from 1940–45 and 1951–55.
- Margaret Thatcher was Britain's (and Europe's) first woman Prime Minister and the first British Prime

Minister of the twentieth century to win three consecutive elections.

THE MAYOR OF WESTMINSTER
In addition to the Lord Mayor of the City of London and the Mayor of London who heads the Greater London Authority, all the boroughs in the capital have a mayor too, with just one exception (Richmond). Again with a few exceptions, these mayors are appointed rather than elected and carry out essentially ceremonial functions wearing official regalia. Westminster City Council accordingly has its own mayor who serves for one year and is stationed in what is known as the Mayor's Parlour in the local council offices, Westminster City Hall.

M16
M16, the British Government's secret intelligence service, occupies a surprisingly conspicuous building on the south bank of the Thames at Vauxhall. Rumour has it that there is a tunnel running from the M16 building under the Thames to the Houses of Parliament.

- Westminster Hall is the largest Norman hall in Europe. It has hosted the trials of Charles I, Guy Fawkes and Sir Thomas More.
- James Boswell claimed to have made love on Westminster Bridge.

Parliament Street, houses some of the most important government offices and departments: the Ministry of Defence, HM Revenue and Customs, and the Cabinet Office. Just off Whitehall is the traditional home of prime ministers, No. 10 Downing Street.

10 DOWNING STREET
This row of terraced houses was designed by the great Christopher Wren for a seventeenth-century diplomat and property developer, George Downing. Between 1682–1684 up to 20 houses were built on the north of the street named after the speculator: the exact number of original houses is not known as some were later demolished. Despite the elevated reputation of their architect, the houses were shoddily built on weak foundations. As Winston Churchill put it, the houses were 'shaky and lightly

ROYAL LONDON
Traditions, palaces and processions

- Britain has a constitutional monarchy, so the Queen does not
- create or pass legislation. However, the monarch carries out an
- important constitutional role and undertakes a wide range of
- duties as the head of the nation. Royal ceremonies and pageantry
- form some of London's most exciting events.

Queen Elizabeth II in procession.

TRADITIONS AND PALACES

An estimated 300 million people around the world watched on television the Royal Wedding of 2011, when Prince William married Catherine (Kate) Middleton at Westminster Abbey. A further one million people stood on the streets of London to watch the processions to and from the Abbey, and to cheer when the Royal Family made their now traditional appearance on the balcony of Buckingham Palace before the wedding reception there.

The crowds, the street parties, the interest from all round the world shows that fascination with Britain's Royal Family is as strong as ever, and nowhere has as many associations with royalty as London. Even before it became England's capital, it was the country's largest city, so kings, queens, princes and princesses all had residences there. Many of those are no longer royal homes, but several magnificent buildings around London have associations with the monarchy, such as Queen's House in Greenwich or Somerset House.

THE QUEEN AND HOUSEHOLD

Queen Elizabeth II is the UK's Head of State and is also Head of the Commonwealth.

The Queen's staff are referred to as the Royal Household which currently numbers around 1,200 employees working in five departments: the Private Secretary's Office; the Master of the Household's Department; the Privy Purse and Treasurer's Office; the Lord Chamberlain's Office; and the Royal Collection Department. The Lord Chamberlain, as the most senior member of the Household, has overall authority.

THE CROWN JEWELS

The Crown Jewels have been stored in the Tower of London since 1303. Over the centuries, they have been kept in various places within the Tower, and today, they can be viewed in the Jewel House, which was opened by Queen Elizabeth II in 1994.

The first king to assemble a collection of regalia was Edward the Confessor (reign 1042–66). Many pieces in the current collection of Crown Jewels were made for Charles II's coronation in 1661. They are believed to be copies of the jewels that were lost when the Protectorate took over from the monarchy in 1649. The current collection includes regalia for coronations, other crowns and pieces donated by various monarchs, insignia, robes, medals and royal christening fonts. Among the many priceless pieces are the famous diamonds the Cullinan I and the Koh-i-Noor, while the Imperial State Crown alone contains 2,868 diamonds, 273 pearls, 17 sapphires, 11 emeralds and 5 rubies.

Several sets of crown jewels have been lost, stolen and even pawned! The most famous attempt at stealing the Crown Jewels was made in 1671 by Colonel Thomas Blood, who was caught at the East Gate of the Tower of London with the crown, one sceptre and the orb.

ROYAL RESIDENCES

St. James's Palace

St. James's is the senior palace of the Queen and is also the 'court' to which foreign ambassadors and high commissioners are accredited. It was built between 1532

The gatehouse of St. James's Palace.

and 1540 by Henry VIII on the site of the Hospital of St. James, Westminster, then for more than 300 years it was the primary London residence of the kings and queens of England.

Today, St. James's Palace contains the London residences of Princess Anne (the Princess Royal) and Princess Alexandra. It also houses the offices of the Prince of Wales, the Royal Collection, the Marshal of the Diplomatic Corps, the Central Chancery of the Order of Knighthood and the Chapel Royal: the coffin of the late Diana, Princess of Wales, lay there prior to her funeral.

Clarence House and Lancaster House

Clarence House, the London home of the late Queen Mother, is located within the grounds of St. James's Palace, as is Lancaster House, which is used for government conferences and receptions. The Duke and Duchess of Cornwall (Prince Charles and his wife Camilla) currently live at Clarence House, as does Prince Harry in a separate apartment which he used to share with his brother Prince William before William married Kate Middleton and moved to Kensington Palace.

Buckingham Palace

Until 1689, British sovereigns used the Palace of Whitehall as their London residence. They then moved to St. James's Palace until 1837 when Queen Victoria moved to Buckingham Palace.

Originally called Buckingham House (and still commonly known as Buck House), Buckingham Palace had gained its royal links in 1761 when George III purchased it for his wife, Queen Charlotte. George IV inherited the house in 1820 and six years later set about remodelling it into a palace. The house was refurbished and doubled in size. In the courtyard, a triumphal arch, known as the Marble Arch, was erected

Buckingham Palace and the Victoria Monument from St. James's Park.

to commemorate the British victories at Trafalgar and Waterloo.

When the Houses of Parliament burnt down in 1834, William IV offered Buckingham Palace as a new home for Parliament. His offer was declined, however.

Queen Victoria removed the Marble Arch from the courtyard in the 1840s to create a new wing to the Palace (Marble Arch now stands on the northeast corner of Hyde Park), and today's forecourt of Buckingham Palace was formed in 1911 as part of the Victoria Memorial Scheme.

In addition to being the official London residence of the Queen, Buckingham Palace is the administrative headquarters of the monarchy. As with her other homes, when the Queen is in residence, the Royal Standard – a flag showing the symbols of England, Scotland and Wales – is raised above the palace. When she is not at home, the Union flag is flown.

Queen Victoria's ballroom was once the biggest room in London, measuring 37 metres (122 feet) long, 18 metres (60 feet) wide and 13.7 metres (45 feet) high.

More than 50,000 people visit

Buckingham Palace each year, as guests at banquets, lunches, dinners, receptions and Royal garden parties. In addition, the staterooms of Buckingham Palace are open to the public at certain times of the year, and another attraction to visitors is the Changing of the Guard outside the Palace. The Army's Household troops have guarded the Royal Family since 1660, and today the ceremony of the changing of the watch takes place every day in the summer and every second day during the rest of the year.

In a ceremony lasting around 45 minutes, the New Guard marches to the Palace from Wellington Barracks in nearby Birdcage Walk, and the Old Guard hands over; new sentries take their positions outside the Palace and the Old Guard returns to barracks. The New Guard then marches to St. James's Palace.

Kensington Palace

This palace first fell into Royal ownership when William III bought the Jacobean mansion (then called Nottingham House) from the Earl of Nottingham. Queen Victoria was born and raised in

Kensington Palace Gardens.

Kensington Palace, and it was widely believed that she would continue to live there after her accession to the throne in 1837. However, she surprised everyone by moving to Buckingham Palace almost immediately.

Today, Kensington Palace contains the offices and residences of the Duke and Duchess of Cambridge (Prince William and his wife Kate), the Duke and Duchess of Gloucester, the Duke and Duchess of Kent and Prince and Princess Michael of Kent. It was also home to Diana, Princess of Wales. In July 2000, the Diana Memorial Playground in Kensington Gardens was opened in the memory of Diana, Princess of Wales, on the site of an earlier playground funded by *Peter Pan* author, J.M. Barrie. It features a fully rigged pirate ship and a stone crocodile. Later, in July 2004, Queen Elizabeth II opened another unique memorial to Diana, in the form of the Diana, Princess of Wales Memorial Fountain in Hyde Park.

Hampton Court Palace
Situated on the north bank of the river in the Royal Borough of Richmond upon Thames, this palace first came into royal possession in the 1520s when Cardinal Wolsey gave it to Henry VIII.

George II (reigned 1727–60) was the last reigning monarch to occupy the palace and in 1851 Queen Victoria conferred it on the British Government. Today, the staterooms are open to the public along with the gardens and the famous maze, which was commissioned around 1700 by William III. The famous gardener 'Capability' Brown planted the current 'Great Vine' in about 1770. This is the oldest and largest known grapevine in the world.

The Banqueting House
This is the only surviving part of Whitehall Palace, the sovereign's London residence from 1530–1689, until destroyed by fire. Built by Inigo Jones (completed 1622), the Banqueting House was first used for plays, state banquets and masques, and is still used for state occasions.

The Banqueting House is most famous for being the venue for the execution of Charles I, after he was found guilty of treason. On 30 January 1649, a scaffold was set up against the walls and the monarch was beheaded. Although the event drew massive crowds, it was a controversial execution. The head executioner refused to behead his former king, and his assistant could not be found. Eventually a hooded individual, whose identity was never revealed, executed the king. According to legend, the king asked for an extra shirt because the weather was cold, and if he shivered from the cold, he did not want the watching crowd to think that he was afraid.

Kew Palace
Kew Palace is an unassuming, redbrick mansion set in the grounds of the Royal Botanic Gardens at Kew. It was originally one of three palaces at Kew and was bought by George II. The only monarch to live there was George III, who was confined there from 1802 as doctors tried to cure his 'madness'.

ROYAL PARKS
London has eight royal parks, some of which date back to the reign of Henry VIII. These are St. James's, Greenwich Park, Kensington Gardens, Hyde Park, Regent's Park, Bushy Park, Richmond Park and Green Park. They cover 8,000 acres of land and are all open to the public.

ROYAL TRAVEL
Today's Royal Family has a number of beautifully crafted, horse-drawn coaches for state processions and other special

The Banqueting House.

occasions. The oldest coach in use is the Gold State Coach first used by George III when he opened Parliament in 1821, and since then used for every coronation. The coach currently used for the State Opening of Parliament is the Irish State Coach, so-called because the Mayor of Dublin built it in 1851. In addition to the collection of horse-drawn coaches, the Royal Family also maintains a fleet of motor vehicles.

Housed in the Royal Mews are eight specially built state limousines, three Rolls-Royces, three Daimlers and two Bentleys, while the Royal fleet also includes several Volkswagen 'people carriers'. As state vehicles, the Rolls-Royces and Bentleys do not have number plates.

The first royal to travel in a motor car was Queen Victoria's son Edward, Prince of Wales (later to become Edward VII). He developed a great interest in motoring and by the time of his coronation in 1902, he owned four cars, all Daimlers, though there is no proof that he himself could drive a car. The first monarchs that were known to drive were Edward VIII and George VI.

HOUSES OF PARLIAMENT

The two Houses of Parliament (House of Commons and House of Lords) are based in the Palace of Westminster, a medieval royal residence until a major fire in 1512. Since Parliament had already been meeting at the palace, the rebuilt structure continued as the centre of government while the monarchs moved to other palaces.

Every year, parliament is opened by the reigning monarch in a ritual steeped in tradition. Since Guy Fawkes' attempt to blow up parliament in 1605, the day has begun with a search of the building's cellars. At 11 AM, the monarch's procession travels to the Houses of Parliament for the king or queen's speech. On the sovereign's arrival, the vice chamberlain is

The Irish State Coach.

'kidnapped' and held by Palace officials to guarantee the safe return of the monarch! After the speech, the procession returns to Buckingham Palace, and the vice chamberlain is freed.

THE TROOPING OF THE COLOUR

This military parade by the Queen's personal troops (the Household Division) celebrates her official birthday in June. The custom of 'trooping the colour' dates back to Charles II's reign when the colours of a regiment were used as a rallying point in battle. To ensure that every soldier could recognise the colours of his own regiment at a glance, they were trooped in front of the men every day.

THE QUEEN'S DIAMOND JUBILEE

2012 saw the latest Royal event with celebrations marking 60 years of the reign of Elizabeth II.

From pageants, concerts, a thanksgiving ceremony and the lighting of a line of beacons across the country, the celebrations confirmed the enduring popularity of Britain's Royal Family.

A drum horse.

THE QUEEN'S DIAMOND JUBILEE
Celebrating sixty years on the throne

- **Only the second British monarch – after Queen Victoria – to reign**
- **for sixty years, Queen Elizabeth II celebrated her Diamond Jubilee**
- **in 2012 with a year of public engagements around the country.**
- **But it was in London, Her Majesty's capital, where the festivities**
- **mainly took place.**

Queen Elizabeth II celebrated 60 on the throne of the United Kingdom with a year full of special events in 2012. The highlight of the ceremonies was the Diamond Jubilee Weekend, four days in June that allowed the whole country to celebrate with Her Majesty the Queen and the Royal Family.

A keen follower of horseracing, the Queen began the Diamond Jubilee Weekend with a visit to the Epsom racecourse on Saturday June 2nd, the start of the official celebrations. There the Red Devils aerobatics team parachuted on to the course with a large Union Jack, before the Queen watched the Epsom Derby festival including the Diamond Jubilee Stakes race.

THE RIVER PAGEANT

Sunday June 3rd saw an estimated 1.2 million people lined up in rain along seven miles of the River Thames in central London to watch the Queen in the golden Royal Barge near the head of a 1,000-boat flotilla. In addition, about 90,000 people packed the special viewing areas of large screens in Battersea Park.

It was the grandest event on the river for 350 years, and one of the largest flotillas ever, making its way at a stately four miles an hour from upstream of Battersea Bridge to downriver of Tower Bridge. The Royal Barge, the *Spirit of Chartwell,* was a converted Thames pleasure cruiser, adapted with half-a-million gold buttons to form the

Top: The flotilla nears Tower Bridge. Below: Queen Elizabeth II on her gilded Royal Barge during the River Pageant.

royal coat of arms, with gilded carvings and with special ceremonial scarlet dress for the Royal Watermen.

The Queen was accompanied on the Royal Barge by Prince Philip, the Prince of Wales and the Duchess of Cornwall (Prince Charles and Camilla), the Duke and Duchess of Cambridge (Prince William and Kate), and Prince Harry. The family members symbolised the Queen's selfless desire for the celebrations to emphasise royal succession, rather than concentrating solely upon herself.

A massive floating belfry was the actual spearhead of the flotilla, ringing out the Jubilee as it triumphantly led the procession. Weighing 12 tons and 180 feet (54.9m) long, it carried eight specially cast bells. Also in the flotilla was a Jubilee gift to the Queen, the 94-foot (28.6m), gilded royal rowbarge, *Gloriana.* The 18 oarsmen were led by Sir Steve Redgrave, multiple Olympic gold medal winner.

A Maori war canoe, kayaks, narrowboats, small rowboats and powerful launches were all part of the noisy, colourful river procession. Lifeboats and fireboats symbolised duty and service, while pleasure boats represented the celebratory aspect of the day. There were also ten barges carrying orchestras. The very last boat in the formal procession carried the London Philharmonic Orchestra, entertaining the crowds with the tune 'Singing in the Rain'. The Thames Barrier was closed in the morning of the procession to slow the river from its usual five miles an hour current to about half that. This not only made sailing smoother for the boats, but also kept the river at its high tide level to make it easier to see the flotilla from the banks.

The Queen's new royal rowboat, *Gloriana*.

GLORIANA

Gloriana was the title given to the first Queen Elizabeth (1533–1603), whose defeat of the Spanish Armada led to her becoming a cult figure, an image of invincible majesty. In the 'Ditchley Portrait' Elizabeth I is depicted with celestial symbolism wearing a cream dress with gold embroidery. For the River Pageant, Queen Elizabeth II wore a dress and jacket of ivory bouclé embroidered with gold and silver spots and Swarovski crystals, an outfit that emphasised the overall continuity of Britain's royal families.

STREET PARTIES

Street parties took place throughout the country on all days of the Jubilee Weekend, with one of the largest a 500-seat picnic table set up along Piccadilly for the 'Big Jubilee Lunch'. The street is home to Fortnum and Mason's and the

The Prince of Wales and the Duchess of Cornwall at a street party in Piccadilly.

Ritz hotel among other outlets, offering party-goers slightly different street-party fare than usual.

DIAMOND JUBILEE CONCERT

Held on Monday June 4th outside Buckingham Palace on a stage specially built at the end of the Mall, the concert featured music from the six decades of the Queen's rule. She attended part of the concert, which was organised by the BBC and Take That singer Gary Barlow.

Gary Barlow and Andrew Lloyd Webber co-wrote a special Jubilee song, 'Sing', which saw its first performance at the concert by a choir drawn from several Commonwealth countries.

Comedians performed during the interludes, and for the Grand Finale the Queen lit a beacon fire, the last in a chain of National Beacons that crossed the country to mark the Jubilee.

SERVICE OF THANKSGIVING AND STREET PROCESSION

On Tuesday June 5th the official Queen's Diamond Jubilee celebrations finished with a morning Service of Thanksgiving at St. Paul's Cathedral, attended by the Queen and members of the royal family. A Diamond Choir of about 40 children from all over the country performed an anthem 'The Call of Wisdom', commissioned especially for the occasion. The Queen then attended

a reception at Mansion House, followed by lunch with 700 people including family and dignitaries at Westminster Hall, before a spectacular carriage procession back to Buckingham Palace began.

Accompanied by Prince Charles and the Duchess of Cornwall, the Queen travelled in her 1902 State Landau. In another open-top landau the Duke and Duchess of Cambridge followed behind.

At Buckingham Palace the Queen and members of her family made a balcony appearance, watching the RAF's Battle of Britain Memorial Flight perform a fly-past in a Dakota, two King Airs, four Spitfires, a Hurricane, and the last flying Lancaster. The Red Arrows next paid their own tribute, trailing smoke in red, white and blue lines from their fly-past, then members of the Buckingham Palace Guard of Honour completed the official Diamond Jubilee Weekend with a feu de joie, a celebratory cascade of rifle fire.

With Queen Elizabeth only the second British monarch after Queen Victoria to celebrate a Diamond Jubilee, the year saw the whole country, but London in particular, offer all the pomp and pageantry that the city and its visitors love.

Fireworks celebrate the Jubilee.

UNDER LONDON
Life under the streets

- Apart from the London Underground, this is the city that few
- people ever see – the many layers of tunnels, hiden rivers
- and vaults below the city streets.

THE CAMDEN CATACOMBS

This complex of tunnels and vaults is used by British Rail for storage, but was once stabling for horses and pit ponies used for shunting railway wagons. Cast-iron grilles set into the road provided a source of light for the horses below.

HARRODS

The Knightsbridge store has its own system of tunnels leading to its warehouse in Trevor Square. Frosty Way leads to the deep-freeze rooms and Wine Cellar Close to wine stocks. The Lock Up is used to hold shoplifters. Green electric trolleys run under Brompton Road.

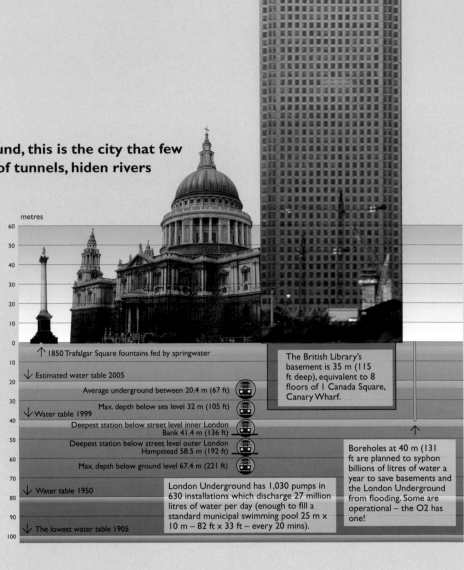

metres

↑ 1850 Trafalgar Square fountains fed by springwater

↓ Estimated water table 2005

Average underground between 20.4 m (67 ft)

Max. depth below sea level 32 m (105 ft)
↓ Water table 1999

Deepest station below street level inner London Bank 41.4 m (136 ft)

Deepest station below street level outer London Hampstead 58.5 m (192 ft)

Max. depth below ground level 67.4 m (221 ft)

↓ Water table 1950

↓ The lowest water table 1905

The British Library's basement is 35 m (115 ft deep), equivalent to 8 floors of 1 Canada Square, Canary Wharf.

Boreholes at 40 m (131 ft are planned to syphon billions of litres of water a year to save basements and the London Underground from flooding. Some are operational – the O2 has one!

London Underground has 1,030 pumps in 630 installations which discharge 27 million litres of water per day (enough to fill a standard municipal swimming pool 25 m x 10 m – 82 ft x 33 ft – every 20 mins).

CRYPTS

In the 1960s, the crypt at St. Stephen's Walbrook was rediscovered by the founder of the Samaritans and equipped as their telephone operations room. St. John's, Smith Square, is now a concert hall – the crypt serves as a restaurant and bar. Below the old *News of the World* building in Carmelite Street is a fourteenth-century vaulted crypt. In Fleet Street, the Cheshire Cheese Inn retains the vault from an ancient monastery. The Adelphi Arches, once wine cellars and coal vaults, run 12 metres (40 feet) down from Charing Cross Station to the Savoy Hotel. Under the Ministry of Defence is a wine cellar that was part of Cardinal Wolsey's Whitehall Palace. The Café in the Crypt, St. Martin-in-the-Fields, Trafalgar Square, is an award-winning eating place.

CHANCERY LANE SAFE DEPOSIT

When this was bombed and flooded during World War II, some safes were opened. Inside one was a pair of Edwardian frilly lace knickers, with a label inscribed, 'My life's undoing'.

HIDDEN WATERWAYS AND RIVERS

Many rivers still flow below the city streets. The Walbrook (between St. Paul's and Mansion House) was covered over from 1463. The River Fleet (hence Fleet Street) was once called the 'river of wells' due to the numerous healing wells along its banks. Navigable as far as Holborn, it was wide enough for pirates who, in 1310, attacked a vessel carrying King Edward II. The Fleet joins the Thames under Blackfriars railway bridge, and from 1732 work began on covering it over. In 1846, a build up of foetid gases made the Fleet explode; a tide of sewage swept away three houses in Clerkenwell, inspiring Alexander Pope to write:

...where Fleet-ditch with
disemboguing streams
Rolls the large tribute of
dead dogs to Thames.

In a rainstorm, Jonathan Swift noted that:
Sweepings from Butchers' Stalls,
Dung, Guts and Blood,
Drown'd Puppies, stinking Sprats,
all drench'd in Mud,
Dead Cats and Turnip-Tops come
tumbling down the Flood.

North of the Thames
- Stamford Brook
  Wormwood Scrubs to Chiswick
- Counters Creek
  Wormwood Scrubs to Chelsea
- Westbourne
  Hampstead to Chelsea via Hyde
  Park and Serpentine
- Tyburn
  Hampstead to Westminster
- Fleet
  Highgate and Hampstead to the City
- Walbrook
  Islington to Cannon St.
- Black Ditch

Stepney to Poplar
- Hackney Brook
  Hornsea to River Lea

South of the Thames
- Beverley Brook
  Wimbledon to Barnes
- Wandle
  Merton to Wandsworth
- Falconbrook
  Tooting to Battersea
- Effra
  Norwood to Vauxhall
- Peck / Earls / Sluice / Neckringer
  East Dulwich to Bermondsey and

Rotherhythe
- Ravensbourne
  Bromley to Deptford

TUNNELLING UNDER THE THAMES

As early as 1798 a company had been formed to dig a tunnel downriver between Gravesend and Tilbury, but the technical problems defeated them. Cornish mining engineers tried at the same time to use their specialist skills to create between Rotherhithe on the south and Limehouse in the north a tunnel for 'Horses and Cattle, without carriages, and

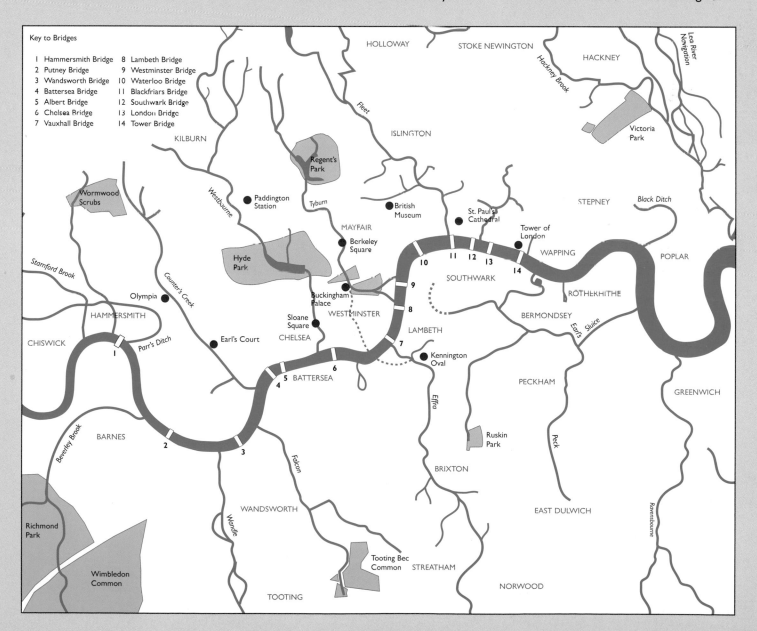

Foot Passengers'. The engineer Robert Vaize, known as 'The Mole', was joined by the Cornish giant, wrestler and engineer Robert Trevithick and together they dug some way under the river. But the tunnel caved in, very nearly drowning Trevithick.

The next attempt was begun in 1824 by Marc Isambard Brunel, father of the more famous Isambard Kingdom. Brunel senior, who had invented a new way of making pulley blocks for Navy ships, spent a good deal of time down at the Naval Dockyard in Deptford. At the time, a little mollusc called *teredo navalis*, or the shipworm, was playing havoc as it could sink a ship by boring into the timbers of the hull with its sharp shells. As it burrowed it secreted a substance which left a miniature tunnel in the timber. Brunel senior, according to legend, always carried a magnifying glass, and he took a close look at the burrowing techniques of this pest. This inspired Brunel to invent a giant version of *teredo navalis* for boring through the soft, clay sub-soil of the Thames Valley. He called it his 'Great Shield' – a large rectangular iron cylinder which was forced bit by bit through the ground with workmen bricking up the sides of the tunnel as it inched forward.

In 1824 a Thames Tunnel Company was formed and raised £150,000 on the promise of 'Great Publick Advantage if a Tunnel for the Passage of Carriages, Cattle and Passengers were made from some part of the Parish of St John Wapping to some part of the Parish of St Mary Rotherhithe'. Parliament, approving the scheme, allowed seven years for it to be bored out and permitted tolls of two pence for pedestrians and a scale up to two shillings and sixpence for carriages drawn by six or more horses. Work began on the south side of the river in 1825 with an iron hoop 50 feet (15.24m) in diameter and weighing 25 tons. Church bells were rung and the Thames Tunnel project was underway.

The 'Great Shield' worked, but the sub-soil was not consistently the malleable clay that Brunel had wished for, and they hit sand and gravel which washed into the machine parts and held up the work. A huge labour force of 450 men forcing the shield forward, bricking in the back of the tunnel and pumping out water drained the company's resources. In 1827 a flood tide rushed into the tunnel through a breach and washed 120 men back to shore, all of them miraculously surviving. Fortunately, when the tide ran out the river was low enough to seal the breach. But the trouble was not over: Brunel senior became ill from overwork, and although in time his son Isambard continued the scheme, it took more than 18 years to complete the tunnel, by which time the newspapers were dubbing it 'The Great Bore'. It opened with a fanfare on Saturday, 25 March 1843 when 10,000 Londoners paid to inspect it. Later Queen Victoria and Prince Albert were rowed downriver in her State barge to inspect this wonder and in the first year more than two million people handed over their toll money to experience the delights of the Brunels' tunnel.

Although wide enough for horse-drawn vehicles, the company could not afford the cost of building approach roads and it remained a pedestrian crossing. It became a popular tourist attraction and 'grand fancy fairs' were held in it. But none of this gave the directors a return on their money and the tunnel went into social decline, a favourite haunt of prostitutes. It was sold in 1862 to the East London Railway and trains began to run through it in 1870. The only way to go

The Underground post office system at Mount Pleasant ran from 3 December 1927 to 31 May 2003. Covering 23 miles of track in 25 minutes, the system handled about 7 million bags of mail a year on tracks 70 feet (21 metres) below the streets of London.

through it today is on the Underground's East London Line between Wapping and Rotherhithe.

Twenty years before Tower Bridge was opened, a second Thames tunnel had been bored between Tower Hill in the north and Tooley Street on the South Bank. An adaptation of Brunel's 'Great Shield' was developed by the bridge engineer Peter William Barlow using a cylindrical cutter and cast iron rather than brick linings. With this more efficient burrowing device a Tower Subway Company planned to create a kind of prototype tube train, a

14-seater carriage hauled through the tunnel on a pulley system. The cutter worked well, burrowing under the river at the rate of ten feet a day so that in just five months the tunnel was complete. Passengers were promised rapid transit under the river in just two minutes. But the machinery frequently broke down and was eventually removed leaving the tunnel as a walkway. It was little used and closed in 1897. It now carries cables of various kinds.

BURROWING MANIA

There was a kind of burrowing mania in the last two decades of the nineteenth century as engineers and private promoters sought to find a way of linking the dockland regions north and south of the river below London Bridge. As with bridge building, most private enterprise schemes ran into financial trouble. It was the Metropolitan Board of Works which, in its last days, finally got a successful tunnelling scheme going. It was the brainchild of their celebrated engineer Joseph Bazalgette, designer of the sewage system and several bridges, and was planned out on a route between Blackwall on the north bank and Greenwich to the south. Bazalgette did not see it through, however, for a new authority, the London County Council, took over from the Metropolitan Board of Works in 1889 and a new engineer, Alexander Binnie, took over. He brought in an American specialist firm S. Pearson & Son whose engineer E.W. Moir had just finished a tunnel under the Hudson in New York.

The art of tunnelling was becoming more sophisticated. The Blackwall tunnel was designed with a carriageway for horse-drawn vehicles and two footpaths for pedestrians. It was opened on 22 May 1897 and within a year more than four million people had walked through it while road traffic was counted at over 300,000 horse-drawn carts and carriages.

This proved to be, as it still is, the main road route across the Thames between Tower Bridge and the Dartford Tunnel and the Queen Elizabeth II Bridge.

Several years before the Blackwall Tunnel was opened the new London County Council (LCC) had wanted to start a ferry service between Rotherhithe and Radcliffe to ease the flow of traffic between the southern and northern docks. This scheme was abandoned on the grounds that the ferries would be a hazard to shipping, so a tunnel scheme was pushed through instead once Blackwall had opened successfully. The Rotherhithe Tunnel was opened by King George V and Queen Mary on 12 June 1908 with a narrow roadway and two footpaths.

There was still opposition to these river crossings even in the late nineteenth century and when the LCC proposed in 1896 that a tunnel for pedestrians should be built between Poplar and Greenwich, there were protests from watermen, the London and Blackwall Railway and even the trustees of Greenwich Hospital, which owned Greenwich Pier. To push the scheme through the LCC had to pay £30,000 in compensation for lost business. But, the Greenwich foot tunnel opened in 1902 and was well used. There is now a quicker way under the river since the

Sewer inspection.

extension of the Docklands Light Railway to Greenwich in November 1999, but the foot tunnel, now a listed building, is still popular and is especially useful for cyclists who cannot use the railway.

Yet another foot tunnel was opened in 1912 between the terminals of the Woolwich Free Ferry because of complaints that the boats were constantly being held up in London fogs which descended every year before the Clean Air Act of 1956 took effect. The Woolwich Subway, was also built by the LCC and is still open. With the redevelopment of docklands since the 1980s these easterly river crossings are likely to become much more popular than in the days when the area languished in dereliction after the closure of one dock after another.

A TIMELINE OF THAMES TUNNELS

- 1843 Thames Tunnel
- 1870 Tower Subway
- 1890 Borough (Southwark) to King William Street (City)
- 1897 North Greenwich to Poplar: Blackwall Tunnel
- 1898 Waterloo & City Line
- 1902 Greenwich Foot Tunnel
- 1906 Bakerloo railway (Baker Street to Waterloo)
- 1908 Rotherhithe Tunnel
- 1912 Woolwich Foot Tunnel
- 1926 Northern Line (Charing Cross Branch)
- 1963 Dartford Tunnel
- 1967 Second Blackwall Tunnel
- 1971 Victoria Line Tunnel
- 1999 Jubilee Line (North Greenwich to Canning Town and Westminster to Waterloo)
- Docklands Light Railway (Island Gardens to Cutty Sark)
- 2009 Docklands Light Railway (Woolwich Arsenal to George V Dock)

Bazalgette's low-level sewer has remained in use since the 1860s.

SEWERS

The construction of the London sewers was one of the most important engineering feats of the Victorian age. The earliest open-ditch sewers in London sloped toward the Thames, which ultimately took this waste into the sea. In fact, the term 'sewer' derives from 'seaward' in Old English. The ditches often overflowed, depositing garbage and human waste into streets, houses and marketplaces. Epidemics of cholera, typhus and other illnesses would plague London for more than four centuries.

1550s

By the late 1500s, the city housed more than 2 million people in crowded conditions and the situation was deteriorating. King Henry VIII wrote an edict making householders responsible for clearing the sewer passing their homes.

Eighteenth century

By the early eighteenth century nearly every residence had a cesspit beneath the floors. Nauseating stenches permeated homes, often even worse than in the manure filled streets. After

industrialisation, the 'night air' was laden with coal smoke and sulphurous industrial outpourings, so doors and windows of homes and factories were sealed shut at sunset to protect the occupants. As a result, entire families and crews of workers died during the night, perhaps due to asphyxiation by hydrogen sulphide, oxygen deficiency or methane explosions – conditions common in sewers, septic tanks and confined spaces even today.

Cesspits overflowed via culverts to a partially open sewer trench in the middle of the street. This waste soaked into foundations, walls and floors, and since culverts were frequently blocked, sewage spread to contaminate cisterns, wells and waterways. The Thames and its tributaries became the only major disposal routes, and by the mid-1800s. the river became so foul that it was described as a 'Stygian Lake'. Some homeowners stored huge quantities of 'night soil' to sell as a fertiliser for crops; to harvest this, they crawled on hands and knees through the wastes and dragged it to the surface.

Nineteenth century

A report on sewer working conditions stated:

12 January, 1849

The smell was of the most horrible

description, the air being so foul that explosions and choke damp were frequent. We were very nearly losing a whole party by choke damp, the last man being dragged out on his back through two feet of black fetid deposit in a state of insensibility.

February 21, 1849

Explosions occurred in two separate locations where the men had the skin peeled off their faces and their hair singed ... The deposit deepens to 2 feet 9 inches, leaving only 1 foot 11 inches of space in the sewer. At about 400 feet from the entrance, the first lamp went out and, 100 feet further on, the second lamp created an explosion and burnt the hair and face of the person holding it.

In 1850, the sewage generated by 2.5 million Londoners was simply dumped in the streets, most of it finding its way into the river. In the mid-1800s, 60,000 died in a nationwide cholera epidemic and London had four outbreaks – but the link between dirty water and disease was still not understood. The theory of airborne infection still prevailed; many – including Florence Nightingale – believed that diseases came from the atmosphere. However, sanitary reformer Edwin Chadwick questioned slum dwellers, explored sewers, and promoted obtaining water from pure lakes and reservoirs, rather than from the fetid Thames. His Public Health Act ultimately reduced the death toll. He also attacked the greed of homeowners who objected to cleansing propositions because they received money for manure.

The construction of large, central, covered sewers had begun by 1844. Meanwhile, Commissioners investigated the 'soil-pan or watercloset principle' and 'tubular drainage' ideas to carry away solid or semi-solid matter. Hundreds of designs for potential water closets arrived. In fact, the earliest flushing lavatories added to the Thames' pollution and smell – and some people still drank the water! However, when Sir Thomas Crapper's efficient flush toilet arrived, at last London's sanitation problems were addressed successfully.

The Great Stink

In 1858 'The Great Stink' from the backed-up Thames caused thousands to flee the City, although Parliament remained in session. The windows of the parliament building were draped with curtains soaked in chloride of lime, to allow the government to continue. Upper class residents fled the city or drenched sheets with perfumes to mask the odours.

Sir Joseph Bazalgette

London's ingenious system of sewers was the work of the great engineer Bazalgette. During the hot summer of 1858 when the 'Great Stink' struck, his scheme was finally approved by the Government. His grand system of intercepting sewers (82 miles/132 km long) carried foul water to new pumping stations and holding tanks. Embankments (such as Victoria Embankment) were created to accommodate low-level sewers and helped keep the river clean. Waterborne diseases like cholera and typhoid were all but eradicated. Bazalgette's sewer system made a huge contribution to the health and economy of London and the nation.

THE UNDERGROUND WAR ROOMS

The underground Cabinet War Rooms, under Storey's Gate in Westminster, are a system of 120 rooms, many of which are now open to the public. Here Winston Churchill and his War Cabinet directed operations during World War II. Churchill insisted on having immediate access to the Map Room and his office/bedroom was sited next door, with a communicating door. He slept there occasionally but, generally, used a suite of rooms just above the underground complex. In case of bombing, the room above here was filled with solid concrete. To enable visitors today to walk through to the Map Rooms, a passage has been drilled through this tunnel.

Far right: Churchill's underground bedroom in the Cabinet War Rooms.
Right: Transatlantic Telephone Room: in 1943 a direct telephone link in the underground war rooms was installed between the prime minister and the American president.
Below: The Map Room, once a hub of activity, still houses maps, charts, and pin boards. Black, red, green, and white telephones are lined up on the long desk.

TRANSPORT

From Roman roads to light railways ...

- **The first London built by the Romans was small enough for people**
- **to be able to walk from one side to another. As is well known,**
- **the Romans were excellent road builders and established a long-**
- **lasting network of routes which linked London with other towns.**
- **When the Romans left, the Anglo-Saxon town, Lundenwic, to the**
- **west of the Roman ruins, was compact too. For both towns, the**
- **river was an important highway, especially for trade. As London**
- **was re-established inside the old Roman walls and developed**
- **by the Normans, the Thames became even more important for**
- **London transport.**

When Old London Bridge crossed the river on 19 arches with just a central drawbridge, the waterman had to learn to 'shoot' the bridge, flying through on the run of the tide like white-water rafters. Even when the first carriages appeared in the sixteenth century, London's watermen provided the bulk of the transport and on old maps of London you can see marked all along the banks 'Stairs'. These were steps down to the river where the watermen would wait shouting 'Oars!' As road traffic increased in the eighteenth century and more bridges were built across the river, the watermen's job became more difficult: competition for passengers increased and they had to learn the run of the tides as they rowed through the arches. But what really made their lives impossible was the arrival of the steamboats in the early nineteenth century. These large paddle steamers created a wash which tossed the rowing boats about in an alarming way.

Watermen had complained about the rise of the horse-drawn hackney coaches and tried to get them banned in the seventeenth century. But by then London was expanding away from the river and some new form of road transport was needed. In the eighteenth century, stage coaches began to bring in commuters from the newly built suburbs, but it was not until the hackney cab monopoly of picking up and setting down passengers in the City was broken that the first horse-drawn buses could become profitable. These were running everywhere in the central area of London by the time of the Great Exhibition in Hyde Park in 1851. But they were pricey, and most Londoners got about on their own two feet. A cheaper form of transport arrived in the 1870s with the horse tram, called 'street cars' in America. Running on rails, trams could carry more passengers than buses and were cheaper. For a while they were the most widely used form of London transport. At the very end of the nineteenth century these tramlines were rapidly electrified and, for a time, it seemed the electric tram, brilliantly lit at night, would be the transport of the future.

London's first mainline railway stations were kept out of the central area by Parliamentary decree and by the 1860s the amount of traffic, both goods and passenger, they brought to the capital was becoming a problem. The solution was to build a linking railway, resulting in the world's first underground line opened in 1863 from Paddington to Farringdon. It followed the line of the New Road built in the mid-eighteenth century (now Euston/Marylebone Road) and the tunnel was just below the surface: a cut was excavated large enough for two lines and then covered over. The carriages were hauled by steam trains. Railways were run commercially, and more lines followed as

Excavating in 1901 with the help of a shield originally patented by Sir Marc Brunel.

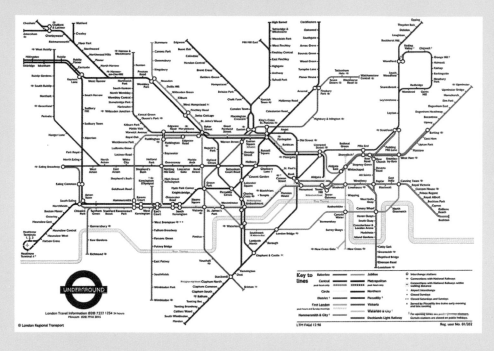

The Tube Map, originally designed by Harry Beck in 1931, was first seen by the public in January 1933.

1933 one large company, the Underground Group which owned buses as well as tube lines, dominated transport in London. In that year they handed over to the London Passenger Transport Board which went under the assumed name of London Transport. The Board also took over the London County Council trams and the supervision of buses by the police.

Between 1933 and the mid 1980s, London Transport was a publicly owned and run service. Then privatisation began with the underground hived off to a public-private partnership and the bus routes put out to tender. A new authority, Transport For London, oversees the tube lines, the buses, the Docklands Light Railway and the Overground. Although the farming out of the Underground proved to be a failure and it was taken back into public ownership, London Transport as a whole today carries a huge number of passengers. The buses and trains have had to cope with a steadily rising population. In the years since 2000 car journeys have fallen while trips on public transport have risen. Cycling has become popular, and in 2011 25,000 journeys were made

investors were persuaded that they could make a killing by offering new commuter services to London's steadily growing population.

DEEP LEVEL TUNNELS

When a method of tunneling through London clay was made possible by Marc Brunel and his son Isambard with the opening of the Thames Tunnel in 1843, the technology was there to drive deep level tubes under London. Intended for horse-drawn traffic, the Thames Tunnel was used first only by pedestrians and then to carry a steam railway line in 1869. It could be said to be the first deep level tube. However, that record is normally given to the line built between Stockwell, just south of the river, and King William Street in the City. It was to have been cable-hauled, but the technology to make it electric arrived in time for its opening in 1890. The Central Line followed in 1900, built with mostly American technology and funds from international investors. As more underground lines were proposed, two American financiers fought for the right to fund and build them. The winner was a convicted fraudster by the name of Charles Tyson Yerkes. He arranged

funding for the first sections of what are now called the Northern, Piccadilly and Bakerloo Lines. The stations, all opened around 1906–7, had distinctive 'ox liver' coloured tiles and many of these survive.

In the years just before the outbreak of war in 1914, London transport took on a dazzlingly new appearance with its electric trams (those of the London County Council were publicly owned), underground stations and the replacement of the old horse buses with motor buses. Motor cars appeared as well, but were not to become common until the 1930s. Between 1918 and 1939 London Underground was extended and new stations built, which were regarded as wonders of the world. In particular, the warren of Piccadilly Circus escalators and tunnels with its Art Deco design was visited by dignitaries from all over the world after it was opened in 1928. The 'Tube' was extended out into the countryside. Until

Christmas decorations in a London Underground shelter in 1940.

per day with bikes hired under a scheme sponsored by Barclays Bank.

LONDON TRANSPORT ROUNDEL

In order to give a sense of coherence to an underground system run by different companies, a symbol, which became known as the Roundel, was agreed on and began to appear in 1908. In 1916, Frank Pick of the Underground Group commissioned the typographer Edward Johnston to design a company typeface. The Roundel was redesigned to incorporate this now familiar and elegant lettering. From 1919

The famous roundel logo first appeared in 1908 but was redesigned by calligrapher Edward Johnston in 1919.

it was used on publicity posters – often witty and created by leading artists of the day – as well as for other advertising. A similar design was developed for the General buses. In the 1930s the new tube stations designed by the modernist architect Charles Holden had the symbol built into their entrance. A Holden station is instantly recognisable, Arnos Grove on the Piccadilly Line being one of the best known. He also designed the former head office of London Transport at 55 Broadway.

UNDERGROUND LANDMARKS

- In 2007 the Tube carried four million passengers on one day for the first time.
- During the 2010–11 financial year passenger numbers exceeded 1.1 billion for the first time.

UNDERGROUND GHOST STATIONS

Over the years around forty Underground stations in London have fallen into disuse for one reason or another. Most date from the early days of the tube and are easily recognisable from the street if their ox-liver coloured tiles have been preserved. One or two can be glimpsed from the tube as you hurtle through the tunnels. These ghost stations include:

Brompton Road

During the Second World War part of the disused station at Brompton Road was converted into offices and a four-storey, anti-aircraft control centre, since used by the Territorial Army and Ministry of Defence.

During the War, between Knightsbridge and South Kensington on the Piccadilly Line, a small cinema screen was painted on the wall at the end of one of the bricked-up platforms – for the screening of information. This screen is still there today complete with a 'no smoking' sign painted beneath! Some of the maps used are still in place on the walls of the lift-shaft operation rooms. There remains a section of the façade on a side street just off Brompton Road.

British Museum

When the Underground was amalgamated, it was decided that Holborn and British Museum stations were so close to each other that there was need only for a single station at Holborn, so in September 1933 the British Museum station was closed. At one time the deserted station was used by the Ministry of Defence as offices and was considered a potential London District Military Command centre in time of crisis.

Charing Cross and Trafalgar Square

Old Underground maps show an extra station named Trafalgar Square on the Bakerloo Line. When the Jubilee Line was built in the late 1970s, a passenger walkway and an escalator link were provided between Trafalgar Square and Charing Cross so the two stations became jointly known as Charing Cross. Name changes can be confusing: Aldwych was originally named Strand; Embankment was first called Charing Cross, and Charing Cross was originally known as Strand.

Jubilee Line

When the Jubilee Line (originally named the Fleet Line) was first constructed, the aim was to extend it further east via Charing Cross towards the City. This is why there were two platforms at Charing Cross with tunnels continuing on from both. With the closure of the platforms, access to the redundant escalators down to the Jubilee platforms was walled off but they can still be seen through a little window at the Northern Line end of the station. Transport for London often hires the Jubilee Line platforms here to film-makers wanting Underground scenes.

King William Street

The first deep-level tunnel built on the London Underground ran from Stockwell to King William Street, just a few metres away from the surface entrance to Monument station. Opened in 1890, it suffered technical problems including steep inclines and sharp corners. Often the trains had insufficient power to complete the final sharp incline into King William Street, and would have to pull back and make another attempt! Sometimes a second engine had to be enlisted to help. When a new tunnel was built just north of Borough, King William Street closed in 1900, only to be opened briefly as an air raid shelter during World War II. Today, the only access to the station is via the basement of an office block where several IT companies use some of the tunneling to convey fibre optic cables. The old tunnels run directly above the existing Bank Northern Line platforms – if you look up you can see directly into them through ventilation grilles in the roof.

South Acton

South Acton station was located at the end of a short branch line that closed in 1959 due to low usage. It is said that some of the staff called this line the Tea Run, since it was so short that a kettle could be placed on the fire and would be coming to the boil just as the train arrived back at Acton Town on its return journey.

Down Street Station

Down Street Station, between Hyde Park Corner and Green Park, was closed in 1932. During the war, Prime Minister Winston Churchill and the War Cabinet used the sub-surface rooms at the station.

Down Street 'ghost' station was used as safe accommodation by Churchill and the War Cabinet during World War II.

LONDON BUSES

More than 90 per cent of Londoners live within 400 metres of one of the 19,500 bus stops in the capital. The network requires constant management and development to meet the changing needs of travellers.

Approximately 7,500 London buses carry more than six million passengers each weekday on a network serving all parts of Greater London.

In 2001 a new kind of long, single-decker, articulated or 'bendy' bus was introduced on 12 routes in London. They were not popular (some caught fire), and the last one was withdrawn from service in May 2012. An updated version of the old favourite the Routemaster bus was introduced instead.

TRAMS AND TROLLEY BUSES

The electric trams that first ran in the early years of the twentieth century were intended to be the future of London Transport above ground, but by the 1930s they were regarded as noisy and troublesome on roads increasingly crammed with cars and buses. They were phased out and replaced by a hybrid vehicle, the trolley-bus, which looked like a conventional double-decker but was powered by electricity from overhead wires. It took a while to rid the streets of trams and tram lines which had provided such good service since the arrival of horse trams in the 1870s. The last one ran in 1952 and the tunnel under Kingsway which connected lines north and south of river was closed down.

The trolley bus was not favoured for long, and very soon old tram routes were taken over by diesel driven buses. Many of the trolley buses were sold off in 1948 and they disappeared from London streets in 1962.

Trams returned to the satellite town of Croydon in 1997 and have been in full operation since 2000.

The popular Routemaster bus.

DOCKLANDS LIGHT RAILWAY

When the huge area of London's abandoned docklands was being redeveloped on the Isle of Dogs it was recognised that a new form of transport would be needed for those commuting to work there or moving into the new housing that was being built. But there was not much money available. Unmanned rolling stock of a new Docklands Light Railway (DLR) was the answer, running along existing railway lines, and using one section of an old line by the West India docks. When the first lines were opened by the Queen in 1987 there were just 11 trains and 15 stations. The line has been extended several times with two lines which now go under the Thames to Lewisham and Woolwich Arsenal. A new station, Stratford International, was opened next to the 2012 Olympics site. There are now 100 trains and 40 stations and the DLR carries more than 70 million passengers a year.

A London County Council class E/1 electric tram which ran from 1908 until the closure of the system in 1952. This was the supreme example of Edwardian public transport.

LONDON ROADS

There is nothing new about traffic congestion in London, and it long pre-dates the arrival of motor vehicles. Before the City was burned down in 1666 the roads were very narrow and it was difficult to get a single cart down many of them. In his seventeenth-century diaries, Samuel Pepys writes about going to Whitehall with his liveried watermen 'for speed'. After the fire, roads were widened which made it easier for carriages and carts to move around the City. Much of London's food arrived either by river from farmland on the upper Thames or the rural banks on the south side or, in the case of cattle and sheep, on the hoof. Drovers brought their livestock into the abattoirs in town. Milk was supplied by cows kept in urban dairies. As London grew in the eighteenth century, new roads were built for bringing livestock and other goods into town. These, like the New Road from the West into the City (now Euston Road) were created by Turnpike Trusts which raised money by charging anyone using the road a fee or toll. Tolls varied according to the damage the animals or vehicles were likely to inflict on the surface (which was often pitted with potholes).

Traffic remained predominantly horse-drawn until the end of the nineteenth century. While the railways took away the trade of the long-distance stagecoaches they increased the demand for carriages and carts in London by bringing more people in to town. Horse traffic created tremendous problems. For fuel they needed a huge quantity of hay and oats and they deposited on the streets thousands of tons of dung. Horse-drawn vehicles, if they were heavy, were very slow and had great difficulty both going up and coming down hills. London saw many horse troughs put up by associations of people who hated to see horses suffer.

At that time, roads were not surfaced with tarmac. Some were cobbled, producing a deafening traffic noise, while many had a soft surface. In wet weather they would cover pedestrians in mud. The arrival of motor vehicles greatly improved the flow of traffic in the early days of the twentieth century and roads became cleaner with a smoother surface. Local councils began to take over from the Turnpike Trusts and later government took a hand in major road building. From the mid-eighteenth century, paving and lighting laws began to produce roads that we still see today in the older surviving districts of the capital. Gas lighting of streets made a huge difference to the night-time atmosphere of the central areas from early in the nineteenth century.

Between the two World Wars new roads were built to ease traffic congestion in the main streets of satellite villages around London. These 'arterial' roads, such as the Great West Road, took on an American appearance in places as they were lined with factories put up by US companies. They were quickly lined too with semi-detached houses, many with garages, for the new car-owning Londoners who liked to go for a 'spin' out in the countryside over the weekend.

The great increase in car ownership from the 1960s began to create serious traffic problems. A solution often suggested, and eventually, after much controversy given the go-ahead, was to create circular routes around the outer core of London so that cross-town traffic did not have to go through the centre of town. These roads, such as the North and South Circular routes, were put together bit by bit as was the later M25 motorway which almost defines the outer limit of built-up London.

In 2003 a congestion charging scheme was introduced for the central area of London. Black cabs and cars which use electric power are some of the few exemptions, but other vehicles pay a daily fee to enter the restricted zone. Special cameras which record licence plate numbers 'police' the congestion zone.

LONDON BUSES

- In 1829, George Shillibeer ran the first horse-drawn omnibus service along Marylebone Road.
- By 1835, 600 omnibuses were operating in London.
- The first London bus with stairs appeared in 1864.
- The first bus stops appeared in the 1930s. Prior to this, passengers hailed buses in the same way as cabs.

'BLACK CABS' AND MINICABS

London's black cabs, which have a golden 'Taxi' sign lit up when they are available, are the only taxis which can legally be hailed on the street. For the privilege of the right to 'ply for hire' in the street, the black cab driver has to pass a demanding test of his or her experience of London streets. This is known as the *Knowledge*,

All London taxis were plain black until the 1980s, when first advertising, and then coloured taxis, arrived.

first introduced in 1865, and it can take a would-be cabby several years to pass it. They study 320 routes in central London not so much with maps, but first hand, exploring the streets on motor scooters. They have a written test on 80 routes and are interviewed on the other 240. Everything must be memorised so that they have their own internal 'sat nav'. Finally they have to take a driving test.

For many years black cab drivers were licensed by the Carriage Office run by the Metropolitan Police. Today Transport for London is in charge and there around 250,000 licences current. Not all black cabs look alike: some are covered in advertisements, some are cream coloured or red, and they are not a uniform model. All modern taxis have to be able to take passengers in wheelchairs.

Private hire or minicab firms are strictly regulated: they have to display an official Transport for London disk in their window., and they can only take bookings over the phone or at their offices.

LONDON OVERGROUND TRAINS

For a long time, overground trains running across London were out of fashion with transport planners and the lines were allowed to deteriorate to the point where it appeared they would all be closed down. However, a new initiative in 2007 modernised and extended the system. New carriages with a corridor running from the front to the back, the electrification of lines and new routes make this one of the most exciting ways of travelling around London. By the end of 2012 there were 83 stations on the network which runs both north and

south of the river. The original Brunel Thames Tunnel, which carried the old East London Railway, is now, confusingly, part of the Overground network.

CANALS

Before the railways there was the canal age in which industrial parts of the country were linked by newly excavated waterways that cut across country on aqueducts and through tunnels, with locks to take boats up and down hills. With the development of railways and then modern road transport the canals fell into disuse and became for a long period blighted, slum waterways. However, many have been revived for pleasure trips

and tourism and London has a number of attractive canal walks. Camden Lock market has grown up around an old canal lock and centre, and the Regent's Canal which runs along the northern edge of Regent's Park is especially picturesque. Little Venice is a fashionable area in Maida Vale built on a canal junction.

London's transport system never sits still. The city's public transport has one of the longest histories in the world, but London is always looking to modernise. It has a heliport in Battersea and the London City Airport in Docklands; Crossrail, the new east-west link, is set to revolutionise journey times across the city; and a cable car river crossing is in place.

The canal at Little Venice.

MUSEUMS AND ART GALLERIES
From Egyptian mummies to modern art

- **London is regarded as a museum capital of the world with about 240 museums and many more art galleries. The museums cover a vast range of subjects and interests, from the macabre to the esoteric, from the British Museum to the London Dungeon; there is even a museum devoted to pipes and tobacco. Sports bodies such as Arsenal Football Club offer specialized collections, while the Science Museum has on display material that is literally out of this world in the form of a replica moon lander. The city's art galleries offer famous classic paintings through to the modern and postmodern.**

In size London's museums vary from small personal collections up to vast national institutions. From royalty — Buckingham Palace's state rooms, Queen's Gallery and Royal Mews — to criminals in the Clink Prison Museum, the city's collections cater for every taste and age group.

Meanwhile art enthusiasts can discover great and famous paintings or revel in small, specialist galleries. Permanent displays in both museums and galleries are constantly augmented by special exhibitions and points of focus.

SOME OF LONDON'S MUSEUMS

Apsley House (Wellington Museum)
While the current duke continues to live in the upper floors of Apsley House, W1, the lower floors are now known as the Wellington Museum. It is dedicated to the memory of Arthur Wellesley, the 'Iron Duke' of Wellington, one of Britain's military heroes after his victory over Napoleon Bonaparte at Waterloo. The building is often (wrongly) called Number One, London.

Bank of England Museum
Detailed history of the Old Lady of Threadneedle Street from 1694 when it received its royal charter. Items include a £1 million note, genuine gold blocks, relics of a Roman mosaic pavement discovered when the bank was rebuilt in the 1930s and muskets and pikes used by the bank guards in former times.

British Museum
Situated in the heart of Bloomsbury, the

The British Museum. The new roof over the courtyard was designed by Foster and Partners.

British Museum holds in trust a huge collection of art and antiquities from ancient and living cultures including the Elgin Marbles and Egyptian mummies. The museum was founded in 1753 in a bid to promote greater public understanding of the world through the arts, natural history and science. The museum is one of London's most popular attractions, and its Great Court is London's largest covered public square.

Clink Prison Museum
This occupies a site on which a real prison stood from the fifteenth century until its destruction in 1780. Today, the museum

The Clink Museum on the site of the old prison. The term 'in the clink' derived from the original gaol.

shows visitors how grim prison life was at a time when convicts had to give up their human rights as well as their freedom. Highlights include various reconstructions of cell interiors and a hands-on display of both original and reproduction devices for restraining and torturing prisoners.

Design Museum
Housed in an old warehouse, this exhibits an unpretentious collection of mass-produced industrial design classics from cars to Tupperware.

Freud Museum
In Sigmund Freud's old house, the ground floor study and library look exactly the same today as they did when Freud lived there.

Horniman Museum
Frederick Horniman was a tea trader in the late 1800s. He amassed an impressive and eclectic collection on his travels. Some of the weirdest exhibits include a tiny, mummified kitten, an orangutan's foot and Arabian shoes complete with flaps to scare away scorpions!

Imperial War Museum
Dedicated to twentieth-century warfare, exhibits range from tanks and aircraft to personal effects such as ration books and letters. All aspects of life in wartime are

The Imperial War Museum is housed in the old lunatic asylum of Bedlam.

covered. Branches are: the Cabinet War Rooms, a fortified basement in Whitehall where the Government lived, worked and slept during World War II; HMS *Belfast* – a cruiser used extensively in World War II and now moored in the Thames; and the Duxford Imperial War Museum, which specialises in military aircraft.

Jewish Museum
Founded in 1932, the museum has one of the world's finest collections of Jewish ceremonial art at its Camden centre. The Finchley Centre houses the museum's social history collections, including an oral archive featuring some 400 taped memories.

London Aquarium
Part of what use to be County Hall and set on the banks of the Thames close to the London Eye, this has a collection of hundreds of varieties of fish and sea life from around the world – including sharks, stingrays, piranha, sea scorpions and cuttlefish. Many of the exhibits have never been seen in Britain before.

London Dungeon
Arguably London's scariest museum – visitors travel through underground catacombs and relive events from London's gory past including the famous Jack the Ripper serial killings in the Victorian period.

London Transport Museum
This uncovers the story of 200 years of London and its public transport, the oldest in the world. Old buses, trains and trams make up the bulk of the exhibits, alongside a good deal of interactive entertainment geared towards children. Also on display are London Transport's stylish posters

and maps, many commissioned from well-known artists.

Madame Tussaud's
This famous waxworks museum is a favourite with young visitors to London, with life-like figures of the famous, whether royalty, sports and pop personalities or characters from history. The Chamber of Horrors is always a great attraction.

MCC Museum
Situated next to the hallowed turf of Lord's Cricket Ground, this repository of

SEA LIFE London Aquarium: part of what used to be County Hall.

cricket memorabilia and history includes a stuffed sparrow that was accidentally bowled to death by Jehengir Khan in 1936.

Museum of Childhood
Housing the Victoria and Albert Museum's child-related objects, this Bethnal Green site has a fantastic display of dolls' houses, some of which date back to the 1600s. It features toys, books, games and costumes from times past.

Museum of Garden History
The first museum of its type in the world, this is situated in the Church of St. Mary-at-Lambeth, next to Lambeth Palace. Outside, a section of the church graveyard has been transformed into a seventeenth-

century-style garden, reflecting the work of John Tradescant, gardener to Charles I and James I.

Museum of London
Diverse exhibits that use artefacts and images to display London's rich history. In addition to permanent exhibits, the museum also features temporary exhibitions that deal with all manner of people and events connected with London.

National Maritime Museum
First opened to the public in 1937, this Greenwich museum includes the seventeenth-century Queens House and the Royal Observatory that are set within its grounds, as well as the sailing ship the *Cutty Sark*. The museum has the most important holdings in the world on the history of Great Britain at sea, including maritime art and cartography, ship models, many navigational instruments, costume, ecology and astronomy. Exploration, trade, migrants and naval power are explained. At the Royal Observatory it is possible to be in both eastern and western hemispheres by standing astride the Prime Meridian which marks 0^0 longitude.

Natural History Museum
This has a vast amount of exhibits, including the famous plaster cast of a *Diplodocus* dinosaur skeleton and the model of the Blue Whale.

Red House (William Morris's home)
The museum houses a permanent display of fabrics, rugs, wallpaper and furniture designed by both Morris and his contemporaries such as Edward Burne-Jones and Dante Gabriel Rossetti.

Royal Armouries, Tower of London
A fine collection of weapons and armoury including suits of armour, cannon and artillery, plus the famous Tower execution block and axe.

The fine façade of the Natural History Museum.

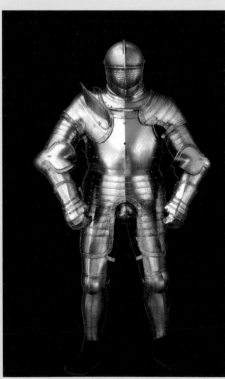

Exhibits in the Royal Armouries Museum include Henry VIII's armour (made at Greenwich in 1540).

Royal Artillery Museum
Opened in the historic Royal Arsenal in southeast London, this museum brings together the significant collections of the Royal Regiment of Artillery.

Royal Botanical Gardens
The world-famous Botanical Gardens at Kew began life as pleasure gardens, created in 1731 by Prince Frederick, son of King George II. After Frederick's death, his widow Princess Augusta established Kew's first botanical gardens. Some of the earliest specimens were brought to the gardens by the great explorer, Captain Cook. Since then, the Gardens have grown from their original 8 acres to 300 acres and now contain over 50,000 species.

The Royal Mint Sovereign Gallery
Relates the 500-year-old history of the famous gold coin.

Science Museum
Seven floors of exhibits drawn from every conceivable area of science including: computing, time, telecommunications industry, photography, medicine and space travel. The museum also holds special temporary exhibitions that deal with specific disciplines.

Sherlock Holmes Museum
Housed in a building claiming to be 221B Baker Street, the museum is dedicated to the life and times of the famous detective. The interior has been faithfully recreated to match the descriptions in Sir Arthur Conan Doyle's stories.

Sir John Soane's Museum
Housed in the architect's former residence, which Soane designed to display his collection of antiques and art.

Tower of London
One of London's oldest buildings; its earliest structural foundations can be

Imperial State Crown, Jewel House, Tower of London.

traced back to the time of William the Conqueror. The Tower has a bloody history but today is primarily a museum. Its most famous attractions are the Crown Jewels and the Yeoman Warders in their distinctive uniforms. Visitors may also see some more unusual exhibits such as the headless figure of Anne Boleyn as the Tower is renowned for its ghosts!

Westminster Abbey Museum

Housed in the eleventh-century vaulted undercroft of St. Peter, one of the few surviving Norman sections of the Abbey. Exhibits include royal death masks of Edward III and Henry VII plus wax funeral effigies of Charles II, William III and Lady Frances Stuart, who was the model for Britannia on the old penny coins.

Victoria and Albert Museum

The largest and most influential museum of decorative arts in the world. The building contains 145 galleries with exhibits ranging from sculpture, ceramics and jewellery to textiles and dresses. Its collection spans 2,000 years. The museum

The Victoria and Albert Museum, completed in May 1899.

was founded in 1852 as a Museum of Manufactures to inspire British designers and industry by building on the success of the Great Exhibition, which had been held the previous year. It was renamed the V & A in 1899.

Wesley Museum

This tells the story of the founder of Methodism, John Wesley. It is housed in the basement of the chapel next to Wesley's house.

Wimbledon Lawn Tennis Museum

Set in the world-famous All England Tennis Club, the museum traces the origins of the modern game from its medieval roots. Exhibits include the social history of tennis, the development of equipment and films of great players.

Winston Churchill's Britain at War Experience

Recreates life in the capital during the Second World War. Inside, visitors can view a number of contemporary re-creations including a bombed department store, a London Underground air-raid shelter, a wartime theatre dressing room and a GI nightclub.

The Royal Collection

One of the finest art collections in the world, this comprises paintings and drawings, furniture, porcelain, silver, sculpture, jewellery, books, arms and armour, and textiles – all gathered by sovereigns and other members of the Royal Family over the last 300 years. Some items belonging to earlier monarchs, such as Henry VIII, also survive. All this is held in trust by the Queen, not as a private individual but on behalf of her successors and the nation. This is the only collection of major national importance that does not receive any government or outside funding. It is administered by the Royal Collection Trust, a registered charity.

Most of the Collection is on display or in use at the principal royal residences which are open to the public: Buckingham Palace, Windsor Castle, the Tower of London, Hampton Court Palace, Kensington Palace, the Banqueting House and Osborne House (and the Palace of Holyroodhouse in Scotland). The official royal residences, which are administered by the Royal Collection Trust, have a programme of special exhibitions to show more of the Collection to the public.

ART GALLERIES

There are about 300 art galleries to explore in London, covering classical to modern art. They include:

Barbican Centre

This includes an art gallery that has a range of thematic exhibitions throughout the year, covering a diverse range of subjects and themes.

Dulwich Picture Gallery

Called 'the most beautiful small art gallery in the world' by the *Sunday Telegraph* newspaper, it houses a magnificent collection of old masters including works by Rembrandt, Poussin, Rubens and Gainsborough.

Hayward Gallery

Situated in a purpose-built 1960s building, this is one of the largest and most versatile temporary art exhibition spaces in Britain. Exhibits tend to focus on twentieth-century work.

Kenwood House

Houses the Iveagh Bequest, plus important works by Vermeer, Rembrandt and Reynolds.

The National Gallery had just 38 pictures when it was founded in 1824. Now it has thousands of exhibits.

Leighton House

This was originally the home and studio of Frederic, Lord Leighton (1830–96), the classical painter and president of the Royal Academy. The house was built in the mid-nineteenth century to designs by George Aitchison as an expression of Leighton's vision of a private place devoted to art.

National Gallery

This houses one of the country's premier art collections. The works span from about 1260 to 1900 and nearly every well-known Western artist from this period is represented. In World War II, National Gallery works were stored in a North Wales slate mine.

National Portrait Gallery

Founded in 1856 to collect the likenesses of famous British men and women, this is today the most comprehensive of its kind in the world.

Royal Academy

Founded in 1768, the Royal Academy is the oldest fine arts institution in Britain. It is famous for its one-off exhibitions, including the world-famous Summer Exhibition, where the public can submit work to be displayed (and sold) alongside the work of recognised artists.

Serpentine Gallery

Housed in a former tea pavilion, this was opened in 1970 by the Arts Council of Great Britain. It displays work by new and established modern artists.

Tate Britain

Tate Britain houses the national collection of British painting from 1500 to the present day and the Turner Collection. It includes works by Blake, Constable, Hockney, Rossetti, and Sickert.

Tate Modern is an inspiring transformation from a disused power station to a new national art gallery.

Tate Modern

Housed in the former Bankside Power Station, Tate Modern displays the Tate collection of a wide range of international modern art from 1900 to the present day. Exhibits include works by Dali, Picasso, Matisse, Moore, Rothko and Warhol.

Wallace Collection

This is both a museum and the finest private collection of art ever assembled by one family. It was bequeathed to the nation by Lady Wallace in 1897 and opened to the public in 1900. Among its exhibits is a remarkable collection of seventeenth-century paintings.

THEATRES

'All the world's a stage and all the men and women merely players' W. Shakespeare

- **London has enjoyed a longstanding reputation as one of the world's major theatrical centres. For hundreds of years, the city has acted as a magnet for writers and actors keen to seek fame and fortune. Throughout the centuries, London theatre has evolved from the bawdy Southwark playhouses of Shakespeare's time to the palatial Victorian theatres that now occupy prime sites in the West End and its surrounds – with more than 100 venues showing up to 200 shows at any one time and several new openings each week. The Theatre Museum in Covent Garden explores many facets of theatre, past and present.**

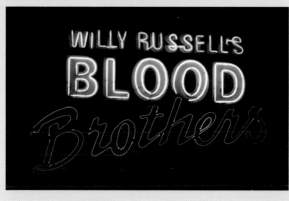

Theatre façades change dramatically with each new production.

Today, London theatre can be divided into three categories:

WEST END
West End theatres are mainly commercial enterprises, staging productions by well-known writers that are likely to attract large audiences. Productions such as *Les Miserables* and *The Mousetrap* are all performed in West End theatres.

SUBSIDISED THEATRE
Unlike their West End counterparts, the Royal Shakespeare Company (RSC) and the Royal National Theatre (RNT) are subsidised and they can afford to take risks with less commercial productions that may not appeal to a large audience.

However, some of the most popular productions have transferred to the West End. The RSC's London home was for many years at the Barbican Centre, but since 2002 the company has not had a permanent London base, and instead stages performances at various venues around the city. The RNT, however, has the Olivier, the Lyttleton and the Cottesloe at the South Bank Centre.

FRINGE THEATRE
Fringe theatre in Britain enables the staging of new and avant-garde productions that are unlikely to find a home in the traditional, West End theatres. Diverse productions range from comedy to political protests. Prices are considerably lower than those in the West End.

The capital has about 80 fringe theatres. Many are situated away from the city centre where there is more available space at a cheaper rate. Civic centres in the suburbs of London and the south east also stage a good range of fringe events. Venues are usually quite small and are often found in converted warehouses or factories, in basements or pubs. The atmosphere is usually informal and less comfortable than in a traditional theatre.

- Until the mid-1800s it was possible to purchase seats on the stage as well as in front of it.
- In 1870, London music hall the Alhambra lost its licence because its manager presented 'an indecent dance' called the can-can.
- The American equivalent of British music hall is vaudeville.

THE LONDON PALLADIUM
The Palladium is one of London's biggest and most impressive theatres. It was built in 1910 on the site of an old circus and originally specialised in variety acts. Gradually, revues replaced variety performances and the Palladium enjoyed a considerable degree of success until 1928, when it was briefly turned into a cinema.

The 1930s saw a return

Advertising a show at the London Palladium.

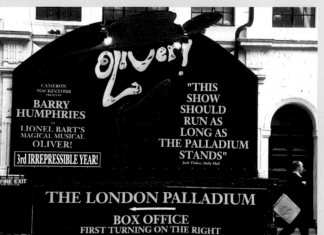

to plays and revues and in 1934, the building was officially renamed the London Palladium. Over the years, the London Palladium has become synonymous with light entertainment and laughter. Well known musicals such as *Singin' In the Rain*, *The King and I* and *Oliver* have all run at the theatre. In addition to this, the Palladium has been used more than any other as the host venue for the Royal Variety Show.

THEATRE ROYAL, DRURY LANE

One of the most historic theatres in London, the current Theatre Royal, Drury Lane is the fourth to be built on the site. The first theatre was built in 1662 and is rumoured to be the venue for Nell Gwynn's stage début at the age of 15. After closing during the plague outbreak of 1665 and the Great Fire of London in 1666, the theatre burnt down in 1672. A new theatre, purportedly designed by Sir Christopher Wren, opened in 1674 and was rebuilt in 1791. The third Drury Lane theatre opened in 1794 but survived for only 15 years before being destroyed by fire in 1809.

The current Theatre Royal was built using funds that were raised by the brewer

The Theatre Royal.

Andrew Lloyd Webber and Bill Kenwright's production of *The Wizard of Oz*.

Samuel Whitbread. The theatre opened in 1812 with a performance of Shakespeare's Hamlet. The theatre was witness to a royal upset when George III had a public argument with his eldest son, the Prince of Wales, in the foyer. The management decided it would be wise to keep the antagonists apart in future, which is why the theatre has a Prince of Wales box as well as a Monarch's box; one entrance to the auditorium is labelled 'King's Side' and the other 'Prince's Side'.

The theatre has hosted many memorable performances, not least by the 'man in grey', a ghost dressed in a long riding cloak, boots and a tricorn hat who is said to haunt the upper circle, particularly during matinees.

ANDREW LLOYD WEBBER

Andrew Lloyd Webber was born in 1948 in London. He showed an extraordinary talent for music from an early age and was reputedly writing his own pieces from the age of six. Following school, Lloyd Webber continued his studies at Oxford University and the Royal College of Music, where he began collaborating with Tim Rice on various works, with Rice writing the lyrics to Lloyd Webber's music.

In 1968, Lloyd Webber and Rice enjoyed their first success with the children's oratorio *Joseph and the Amazing Technicolour Dreamcoat*. This was followed in 1971 with the controversial rock opera *Jesus Christ Superstar*. Rice and Lloyd Webber continued to work together until the late 1970s; their last

major collaboration was *Evita* in 1978.

Following the split from Tim Rice, Lloyd Webber began work on *Cats*, a musical based on a children's verse by TS Eliot. The show premiered in 1981 and went on to become one of the longest running musicals in the history of British theatre.

Following this success, Lloyd Webber went on to write a succession of hugely popular musicals including *The Phantom of the Opera*, *Starlight Express* and *Aspects of Love*. In 1992, his contribution to British theatre earned him a knighthood.

MUSIC HALL

The origins of music hall and variety can be traced back to the 'taproom concerts' that took place in taverns during the eighteenth and nineteenth centuries. These concerts, organised by landlords in an attempt to attract more custom, were noisy, boisterous affairs where the inebriated audience heckled and sang along with the performers.

Throughout the nineteenth century, London experienced a massive population explosion and the demand for light entertainment grew. Landlords sought increasingly larger and more elaborate venues and by the 1880s music hall had become the television of its era.

English music hall began in earnest when Charles Morton built Morton's Canterbury Hall in London in 1852. The programme included classics combined with popular music and performances by Lillie Langtry (the mistress of Edward VII), Gracie Fields, Dan Leno and the male impersonator, Vesta Tilley. A typical show consisted of six to eight acts, possibly including a comedy routine, juggling, magic, mime, acrobats, dancing, singing and even sometimes a one-act play.

By the 1880s there were literally hundreds of music halls throughout London and many people visited them every week. However, by the early twentieth century, stricter licensing and building regulations made it difficult to continue the music hall tradition and it evolved into the less boisterous variety. Music hall's final death knell was sounded in the late 1920s with the advent of cinema. Some theatres attempted to keep the genre alive but few dedicated music halls survived after the 1940s.

Wilton's in the East End is the world's largest surviving Grand Music Hall, and now offers a range of entertainment including theatre, music, comedy, cinema and cabaret. Today, music hall continues to be performed, particularly in some of London's fringe venues, while the musical *Me and My Girl* revived many popular cockney songs.

- It is rumoured that Stravinsky wrote a string quartet in honour of music hall performer Little Tich, a diminutive singer who wore shoes 1.2 metres (4 ft) long.
- Ballet has not always been considered a high art form. When Diaghilev's ballet performed at the Coliseum in 1918, they had to share the programme with comedians and jugglers.
- The Lyric is the oldest of all the Shaftesbury Avenue theatres.

- One of the shortest theatre runs ever occurred at the Duchess Theatre in 1930, when the audience walked out before the end of the first performance of *The Intimate Revue*.
- The actor's union Equity was founded in the Duke of York's Theatre in 1920.
- The Shaftesbury Theatre was forced to close in 1973 when part of the auditorium roof fell in just as the musical *Hair* was about to celebrate its 2000th performance.
- The great actress Sarah Bernhardt made her final London appearance at the Shaftesbury Theatre.
- In the early eighteenth century, 'aquatic drama' became very popular in London theatres. Stages were replaced by large water tanks and famous nautical battles, shipwrecks and sea storms were re-enacted.
- 'Madame', the ghost of the first owner's wife, supposedly haunts the Duke of York's Theatre. She is suspected of slamming a door every night at around 10 o'clock.
- In the early 1900s, the Garrick Theatre's lessee had an apartment above the stage. His ghost is said to sometimes descend the stairs to give actors a goodluck pat on the shoulder.

LONDON DRAMA SCHOOLS

In addition to training tomorrow's actors, London's main drama schools also regularly stage productions that are open to the public (usually for a small fee).

The main schools are:
- Central School of Speech and Drama;
- Guildhall School of Music and Drama;
- London Academy of Music and Dramatic Art;
- Royal Academy of Dramatic Art.

OPEN AIR THEATRE

In the summer, there are many open-air performances in London parks, including Regents Park and Holland Park. Shakespeare plays are staged as well as ballet, concerts, Gilbert and Sullivan operas and shows for children such as *The Wind in the Willows*.

PROMENADE CONCERTS

Henry J. Wood launched London's promenade concerts (popularly called 'The Proms') in August 1895. They continued to be held every year and are now staged at the Royal Albert Hall. The last night at the Proms is hugely popular with a young, boisterous audience.

THE GIELGUD THEATRE

This classical Edwardian domed building, designed by W. G. R. Sprague, was built for an actor, Seymour Hicks, and the American Impressario Charles Frohman who went down with the *Lusitania*. Opened in 1906

The Gielgud Theatre.

as The Hicks Theatre, but was renamed the Globe in 1909. It was here the first actress appeared in pyjamas on stage.

The Gielgud Theatre was given its present name in 1995 in honour of Sir John Gielgud who first appeared there in 1939 as director and star of *The Importance of Being Earnest*.

NOEL COWARD

Coward was born in Teddington, near London in 1899. Like many others connected with the theatre, he began working in the profession from an early age, making his first acting appearance in 1911.

By the early 1920s Coward had begun writing plays in between his acting assignments, some of which were controversial due to the characters' sexual sophistication. Coward established his reputation as a playwright with *The Vortex* in 1924, which was particularly successful in London. He went on to write a number of memorable plays, some of which have stood the test of time and are still revived today, for example, *Private Lives*.

Noel Coward.

Noel Coward was an extremely versatile artist who could turn his hand to almost every function in the theatre. In addition to writing and acting, he also directed, danced, sang and wrote songs. His most memorable compositions

include 'Mad Dogs and Englishmen', 'Some Day I'll Find You' and 'Marvellous Party'.

Coward's services to the performing arts were recognised in 1970 when he was knighted. He spent the majority of his final years in Switzerland and the Caribbean and died in 1973.

THE MOUSETRAP

The Mousetrap, a 'whodunnit' by Agatha Christie, is the world's longest running play. It celebrated its 60th year in 2012, in which year it reached 24,000 performances. More than 10 million people have seen the play. In 1952 it started playing at the Ambassadors

The Mousetrap **is the longest running show in the world, in performance since 1952.**

Theatre, where it had its last performance on Saturday 23 March, 1974. It then moved next door to the St Martin's Theatre, to open on 25 March, 1974, where it has been running ever since. There is a cast of eight and many hundreds of actors have taken part in the play. An armchair and clock are the original props used in every single performance.

SHAKESPEARE'S GLOBE

The original Globe Theatre opened in 1599 in the notorious entertainment area of Southwark, just south of the River Thames. At this time, Southwark was a rough, rowdy area, full of theatres, taverns,

bear baiting and prostitutes. The original theatre burnt down in 1613 during a performance of Henry VII, when canon spark set fire to the roof. There was only one minor casualty, that being a gentleman whose breeches were set on fire. The theatre was rebuilt, but only survived until the Puritans closed it in 1642. Throughout the following centuries, various architects and historians tried to recreate the Globe, but no accurate records existed. In 1970, director Sam Wanamaker became so determined to rebuild the Globe that he established the Globe Playhouse Trust.

Work finally began on the project in 1988 only 200 yards from the site of the original Globe theatre on Bankside. Craftsmen skilled in traditional building methods were employed to build the theatre from authentic clay brick, green English oak, thatch and lime plaster. By the time it was officially inaugurated by the Queen in 1997, the Globe theatre had once again become a major London attraction. Every summer, the Globe stages plays by Shakespeare and his contemporaries on the type of stage for which they were written. The theatre is the first building in Central London to have a thatched roof since the Great Fire of London in 1666.

Elizabethan theatre has been re-instated in London in a reconstructed building sited (as it later turned out) just 180 metres (200 yards) from where the original Globe stood in Shakespeare's day.

The Barbican Centre.

THE ROYAL SHAKESPEARE COMPANY

Based in Shakespeare's home town of Stratford-upon-Avon, in 1961 the company embarked on an ambitious programme that included establishing a permanent base in London to stage modern plays and non-Shakespearian classics – as well as transfers of popular Shakespearian productions from Stratford-upon-Avon.

In 1977, the RSC opened the Warehouse in London's West End to promote less well-known plays, many by new writers. In 1982, the company moved to the Barbican Centre, which houses both the Barbican Theatre and the Pit, the successor to the Warehouse. Seating 1,200, the Barbican theatre was specially built with help from the Corporation of the City of London. The architecture is an adaptation of a traditional theatre incorporating excellent sightlines and a high standard of comfort. The Pit, an intimate, 200-seat studio, acquired its unusual name from its basement location.

After 20 years the RSC moved out of the Barbican, and the company now performs in various West End venues, matching the venue to suit the play.

THE NATIONAL THEATRE, SOUTH BANK

The movement for a National Theatre began as early as 1848 but it was not until 1963, that the Company was finally founded under the directorship of Laurence Olivier. For the first 13 years, the National was based at the Old Vic Theatre, while waiting for the new building on the South Bank to be completed. The new complex finally opened in 1976, next to the Southbank Centre. The National is home to three theatres under one roof: the Olivier, seating 1,200, the Lyttleton, seating nearly 900 and the Cottesloe, which seats up to 400. Plays are presented in repertoire, so that several different productions can be seen each week. The building is also a social centre, designed to look incomplete when it is not full of people. In addition to the three auditoriums, the foyers, river terraces and Theatre Square play host to a wide programme of events and activities, free exhibitions and live music, theatre tours, bookshops and places to eat and drink.

The National Theatre also takes productions beyond the South Bank, touring throughout the UK and abroad.

National Theatre banners on the South Bank.

CLASSICAL MUSIC

London has long been a renowned venue for classical music performance and training, with more orchestras than any other city in the world. Handel lived here for most of his life and the city inspired him to write his famous *Water Music* for King George I. Mozart played the organ and harpsichord at Ranelagh at the age of eight. Gilbert and Sullivan established their English operettas here in the late 1800s.

Enthusiasts today are well served with multiple venues for music, opera and ballet that include the Barbican, the Coliseum, Royal Festival Hall, the Royal Opera House at Covent Garden, Sadler's Wells, the Southbank Centre (Europe's largest arts centre), and Wigmore Hall. The BBC Proms at the Royal Albert Hall is a popular annual series of concerts.

WHOLESALE MARKETS

Sheep, cattle and pigs are no longer driven to market through the streets

- **The feeding of the population of a great city like London has since the Middle Ages been controlled by the Crown and local authorities. To ensure a good supply of fish, meat and vegetables wholesale markets were established in which weights and measures could be checked and quality assured.**

The produce might be shipped in from nearby nursery gardens or from the fisheries on the river and the North Sea, or from abroad. The costs of running a market were defrayed by charges made on merchants and in turn existing markets were given protection from competition. When the City Corporation was granted control of the markets for London it decreed that no rivals selling the same produce could set up within seven miles of those which had become established. That was judged to be the distance a merchant could walk to and from market in a day. In this way, London's oldest wholesale markets at Covent Garden, Smithfield, Billingsgate, Borough and Spitalfields were protected and survived for centuries, though not necessarily on their original sites.

SMITHFIELD

Originally a horse market and a large open space where dissenters were burned at the stake and rebels and traitors executed, Smithfield had become the largest and best known meat market in the country by the late Middle Ages. As there was no means of preserving meat, livestock was driven through the streets to be slaughtered on the spot at the market, with the huge herds causing traffic chaos. For example, in 1790 104,000 cattle and 750,000 sheep arrived on the hoof from various parts of the country. When a rival livestock market opened in Islington (then an open area) in 1834 a Royal Commission decided that the Smithfield cattle and sheep should be sold there, and the Smithfield Market Removal Act of 1852 confirmed the transfer to Copenhagen Fields in Islington.

That might have been the end of Smithfield but the City Corporation lobbied to keep a market for butchered meat. To house the stalls of the traders and meat stores a new building was designed by the City Architect Sir Horace Jones, the first two main parts of which were opened in 1868. These East and West Buildings cost £993,816 and were built above newly constructed railway lines that enabled meat to be delivered directly to the market.

A Poultry Market opened at Smithfield in 1875, although this building was subsequently destroyed by fire in 1958 and was replaced by the current building in 1962. Further buildings were added to the market in later years, the General Market in 1883 and the Annexe Market in 1888.

Now a Grade II listed building, Smithfield Market was refurbished at a cost of £70 million, though its functioning and working practices remain essentially Victorian, apart, that is, from vastly improved refrigeration. The area around Smithfield has now become very fashionable with a vibrant mix of clubs and restaurants.

Left: Smithfield in 1979 and (above) today.

COVENT GARDEN

This market grew up on land which was once agricultural and included the garden of the Convent of St. Peter of Westminster, a religious institution handed to the Duke of Somerset at the Dissolution of the Monasteries in the time of Henry VIII. When John Russell, 4th Earl of Bedford, became the owner he had a piazza built here designed by the architect Inigo Jones. In 1649 a small market became established

Fruit and vegetables on offer to traders at Covent Garden.

in the piazza, and it grew rapidly after the Great Fire of 1666 which destroyed food markets in the City. In 1670 Charles II put the market on a legal footing and it came to fill the whole of the piazza, by then known as Covent Garden (a corruption of Convent Garden), with wooden stalls and sheds. Permanent buildings were put up from the 1830s, with a flower market built in 1872.

Covent Garden became a by-word for fruit and vegetables, as well as for opera, with a theatre adjoining the Piazza. The congestion caused by the traffic to and from the market led to its removal to a site in Vauxhall, south of the Thames, in 1974. The Royal Opera House was then

Below and right: Billingsgate, where hundreds of tons of fish and seafood are sold daily.

renovated and took over some of the market land, and the old market buildings were converted into a vibrant tourist attraction.

BILLINGSGATE

The old Billingsgate market was established right on the Thames and originally handled all kinds of produce. It was not until the sixteenth century that it became London's wholesale fish market in charge of the laws relating to price and quality. Then Billingsgate held such a firm grip on the trade that fish might be sent up from the coast to be sold and returned to the port in which they had been caught. Fish came to the market via river, including Dutch eel boats which were given the privilege of being able to by-pass the market in return for their help feeding London after the Great Fire.

One of the first places in London to experiment with electric arc lamps

– the traders did not like the way they illuminated the fish – the old Billingsgate Market with its permafrost basement was judged unsuitable for a modernising City. In 1982 it was relocated to the former West India Docks on the Isle of Dogs. It took a good deal of its old customs with it, though the traditional job of fish porter, a prized cockney occupation, ended in 2012.

BOROUGH MARKET

Before the arrival of the Romans in 43AD, it is thought there was some kind of market here just to the south of where London Bridge was later erected. After the building of Old London Bridge, the market grew until it became a problem for traffic. It moved a short way and remained open as a wholesale market for fruit and vegetables. Though it is now not a wholesale market, it has become a hugely popular retail market for all kinds of food of high quality and high prices, with many restaurants also established in the market area.

SPITALFIELDS

In 1682 Charles II gave a silk thrower, John Balch, a charter to sell fruit and vegetables here on Thursdays and Saturdays. Most of the produce was grown locally. Later it became a market supplying the ever expanding population of London. It was a ramshackle place until a former market porter, Robert Horner, who had prospered as a potato wholesaler, bought the lease and had an architect design the buildings that are there today. Completed in 1887, the Market was designed in the Arts and Crafts style by George Sherrin.

Like Covent Garden and Billingsgate, Spitalfields was eventually judged too disruptive to modern traffic, and in 1991 the fruit and vegetable trade was moved out to Leyton in East London. The buildings have since been colonised by a variety of shops and stall holders.

STREET MARKETS

An integral part of the London scene

- **In Victorian London there were thousands of street sellers whose lives were colourfully documented in a series of articles written by the journalist Henry Mayhew for the newspaper** *The Morning Chronicle.*

Many of these interviews and descriptions of long-lost trades are collected in several volumes with the title *London Labour and the London Poor.* The streets are less lively now, but London remains rich in local markets which sell everything from food to furniture. In fact there has been a revival of street markets in recent years and a vogue for 'farmers' markets' in which producers of meat, cheeses, vegetables and other foodstuffs sell direct to the public (in theory, at least). Most markets have a range of goods though they might be better known for some than for others.

FLOWER, VEGETABLE AND FRUIT MARKETS

Whitechapel Market

This was a thriving market in Victorian times selling clothes and flowers and with a section for hay when London's transport was horse-drawn. It was dominated for a long while by local Jewish traders but more recently has developed an Eastern flavour as the local community has become predominantly Bangladeshi. Today a wide range of goods is sold here and it is close to Brick Lane, well known for its inexpensive curry restaurants.

Leather Lane Market

Despite its name, this is not a market for leather goods or shoes, but more of a bargain hunter's mecca selling cheap clothes, toiletries, electrical goods and some food.

Borough Market

This is one of the most popular food markets in London and is packed on Fridays and Saturdays when all the stalls, most selling fresh food, are open. In Southwark, just to the south of London Bridge, it has a history going back to the twelfth century. In 1755 it was closed down because the crowds who came to shop here obstructed the traffic going to and from the bridge, but money was raised locally to move it to a more convenient site where it survives today. It is a wholesale as well as a retail market, and as well as the stalls there is a host of restaurants and wine bars in the market.

Berwick Street Market

This once lively market has been in sad decline in recent years as Soho has lost many of its food shops and much of the area has been redeveloped. There are still some food stalls, however, and it is regaining the vibrant reputation it once had.

Berwick Street.

Columbia Road Flower Market

This charming Sunday market for flowers and garden plants has a most unusual history. It takes its name from a Victorian philanthropic enterprise which failed.

Colourful stalls at Columbia Road flower market.

Baroness Angela Burdett-Coutts had had built in this part of the East End some model dwellings for the working classes and she wanted to them to have access to reasonably priced food. She wanted to provide market space for free, and had a fine building put up which was opened in 1869. This was the original Columbia Market, the name taken from a Bishopric Burdett-Coutts had established in

British Columbia. Most of her charitable endeavours were successful, but the market was not, as the stallholders preferred to stay on the streets. After a long and unhappy history the building was demolished in 1958, but along Columbia Road the new flower market took root and has flourished.

Shepherd's Bush Market
Originally opened in railway arches around 1914, this lively market is currently the subject of a huge battle between the traders and developers who want to knock it down and put up a development which would contain apartments while the existing tenants would be rehoused in the new building. There is also a New Shepherd's Bush Market to the west along the Uxbridge Road.

Chapel Market, Islington
There is a wide range of goods from fish and vegetables to clothing sold in this popular market which now has, on Sundays, a lively farmers' market selling venison (in season) as well as meat and fish and vegetables, cheeses, bread, and dairy produce.

Brixton Market
The original Brixton market began in the 1870s on Atlantic Road when this formerly very salubrious suburb was being transformed by the arrival of the steam railway. It thrived and expanded, moving into Electric Avenue in the 1880s, when the stalls were lit with electric arc lamps. A road widening scheme to relieve traffic congestion forced traders off the street and, to accommodate them three arcades were built in the 1920s and 1930s: the Reliance Arcade (1924), Market Row (1928) and Brixton Village (formerly Granville Arcade, 1937). These are now listed buildings after an attempt by a developer to have them demolished. This extensive series of markets sells just

about everything and it has themes for Saturdays which includes a flea market once a month. There is now a farmers' market on Sundays, and Brixton Village

Portobello Road.

has become a hugely popular centre of small, high quality restaurants and cafes.

Portobello Road Market
Portobello Road Market is known the world over as a bustling antique market on Saturdays, its fame fanned by its popularity as a location in films such as *Notting Hill*. It takes its name from a farm that was built on the site in the mid-eighteenth century when this was still a rural area providing hay for London's horse-drawn vehicles. Porto Bello farm celebrated a victory by a sea captain in a war with the Spanish and is named after the town Portobello in Panama. Portobello Road is Victorian and was originally a food market. The antique traders only arrived in the mid-twentieth century. During the week there are still stalls selling fruit and vegetables and other foods.

CLOTHES

Petticoat Lane Market
Petticoat Lane was re-named Middlesex Street in 1830, but the popular name stuck – as is highly appropriate since this has long been a place to buy and sell second hand clothes. It was once an area populated by Huguenots, French Protestant refugees in the eighteenth century, and later Jewish immigrants. Today the largest influence is from the Asian community.

Roman Road Market
This well-established East End market specialises in fashions, fabrics, fruit and vegetables. In true East End tradition, there are numerous pie and mash shops close by.

Brick Lane
Originally the place where farmers sold their livestock and produce, Brick Lane market in E1 has become something of an East End institution. Today's market offers leather goods, cheap jewellery, second hand goods, bric-a-brac, furniture and toys. It even features a jellied eel stand for those shoppers who enjoy such things!

Goods piled high at Brick Lane.

Leadenhall Market

Leadenhall Market in the City has changed its character almost entirely in the last 20 years. It was known for its poultry, game and fish shops housed in a fine, nineteenth-century iron-framed building. Today there is just one butcher's shop and a cheese shop alongside cafes and restaurants and a variety of clothes shops and other retail outlets. However, the market has been revived with stalls set out Monday to Friday in the walkways between 11AM and 4PM.

Camden Lock Market

Camden Lock is one of the best known and most popular destinations for tourists in London. It is not strictly a street market, though there are stalls in places.

Camden Lock Market is picturesquely situated next to a lock of the Regent's Canal.

Much of it is housed in old factories, stables and warehousing that adjoin the Regent's Canal which is still used by canal boats. It is a vast, sprawling area of shops selling cheap clothing, restaurants and bars. It is certainly not 'up market'. The fact that it exists at all was the result of a vigorous campaign to prevent developers demolishing the old buildings that house its warren of shops.

Covent Garden Market

Covent Garden has been known for a very long time for two things: opera and vegetables. The Opera is still there, but the wholesale vegetable market was closed down in the mid-1970s and moved to Vauxhall on the other side of the Thames. As with so many now-famous London attractions, there were plans to demolish the nineteenth-century market buildings, but these were thwarted by a campaign

Covent Garden market has popular cafes and bars as well as shops.

to preserve the area (and by a timely dip in the economy). It is now a very popular destination in central London with shops and restaurants as well as street performers and buskers, some of whom perform outside the wonderful church of St. Paul's, built to the design of Inigo Jones in 1633.

Shepherd Market today.

Shepherd Market, Mayfair

This is no longer a market as such but a charming enclave within wealthy Mayfair built in the mid-eighteenth century when the area was being developed by Edward Shepherd. So it has nothing to do with sheep, although, before the district was developed, cattle were traded at the annual May Fair which was on the site of Shepherd Market.

Bermondsey Antiques Market

This market was originally in Islington, North London in the Caledonian Market which was closed down in the 1950s. It then moved to Bermondsey Square on the site of what was formerly the quadrangle of Bermondsey Abbey. It is an antique market which, until quite recently, had a special privilege as a *Marché Ouvert* which meant that stolen goods could

be sold at certain times without fear of prosecution. Only in 1995 did a baffled Parliament legislate to end this licence to sell 'dodgy goods'.

Chelsea Antiques Market

Open every day except Sundays, Chelsea antiques market is the place to go if you

are seeking unusual items. A particular strength is books, which account for about one-third of the space in the market.

Camden Passage

Confusingly, this market for antiques and collectable goods is not in the borough of Camden, but in Islington. There is a charming pedestrianised alleyway and a forbidding-looking brick building which is a former tram shed built by the London County Council. There are street stalls, but it is more an upmarket place for boutique shops and, as an 'antiques village', it does not have much of a 'market' feel today.

Spitalfields Market

Now one of the liveliest areas in London, Spitalfields has a long and venerable history and a very fine church designed by Nicholas Hawksmoor. Until 1991 it was an 'East End Covent Garden', selling fruit and vegetables wholesale. When that market moved further east to Leyton there was some doubt over the future of the abandoned buildings. However they have been developed into a thriving complex of markets, community spaces and restaurants.

Spitalfields Market.

PARKS AND GARDENS

Contrasts: from bustling markets to green parks

- For such a busy urban centre with a huge population, London is
- surprisingly green. The rush of traffic and press of people are quickly
- distanced once one steps into these lovely parks and gardens.

BATTERSEA PARK

With lakes hosting a range of bird species, and nooks and crannies where gardens have spread out, this extensive south London park was also home to London's funfair for many years.

BUSHY PARK

One of London's eight royal parks, this green space in the borough of Richmond was created between 1500 and 1537 when Cardinal Wolsey and Henry VIII enclosed ploughed farmland. Bushy Park was set up as part of a deer park.

CHELSEA PHYSIC GARDEN

Established by the Apothecaries Company in 1673, this garden was used to grow plants for research, and was accessible only to apothecaries for over 300 years.

It houses the earliest rock garden in the British Isles which was made from basaltic lava (brought from Iceland by Joseph Banks) and old building stone from the Tower of London. In 1681 the first heated greenhouse in England was built here. In 1734 cotton seeds from the Physic Garden were sent to a botanic garden in Georgia. It is from these original seeds that so many cotton fortunes in the Deep South were made. There is a herb garden with both historic and modern medicinal and culinary plants as well as many exotic trees, plants and shrubs. The garden was opened to the public in 1983.

CHISWICK HOUSE

Originally a country villa, this was modelled on Palladio's Villa Rotunda at Vicenza, Italy. The 5th Duke of Devonshire kept deer in the grounds. Apparently they were so savage that his son would not venture into the grounds unless armed with a sword. The gardens broke with the prevailing tradition of Dutch formality. There are many follies – an Ionic Temple, a Doric Column, two obelisks, statues of Caesar, Pompey and Cicero which came from Hadrian's Villa at Tivoli,

Chelsea Physic Garden, used by apothecaries since 1673.

an Inigo Jones gateway and a cascade. Avenues with tall hedges radiate out from the house and at the end of these are miniature buildings, which create a false perspective – the grounds appear much larger than they really are. In the nineteenth century an Italian garden was created together with a conservatory. An amphitheatre overlooking a lake is now used as an open-air theatre in the summer.

CRYSTAL PALACE PARK

This Victorian pleasure ground contains life-size models of dinosaurs and other extinct animals.

GREENWICH PARK

In 1426 Humphrey, Duke of Gloucester, built a house on the river. This was the forerunner of Greenwich Palace. In 1433 Henry VI gave him permission to enclose 200 acres, which has become the area of the present park. From 1515 deer have been kept in the park. This was the first Royal Park to be enclosed. In 1675, Christopher Wren built the Royal Observatory on the site of Humphrey's original house, and it was here that John Flamsteed developed the system of longitude and latitude. The zero meridian line of longitude passes through Flamsteed's house and is marked by a metal strip. Greenwich Mean Time is shown on a clock on an outside wall. There are around 23 tumuli in the park, some of which were opened in 1784 and were found to contain human hair, beads and fragments of cloth – but who is buried there still remains a mystery. Queen Elizabeth's oak was planted in the twelfth century. This enormous tree became hollow and a door and window were made in the trunk. Park offenders were locked inside it as a punishment. It died around 1880, but the magnificent trunk remains, covered by ivy.

HAMPSTEAD HEATH

Hampstead Heath covers about 800 acres (324 hectares). The wealth of plant life includes chamomile, cowslip, marsh forget-me-not, and dog's mercury – and it is probably one of England's most important conservation areas. There is a huge variation of habitat – bog land, heathland, woodland and grassland. It acts as green lung for central London, and consequently is often used as a welcome stopover by migrating birds such as swifts, blackcaps, and reed warblers. In winter, particularly, sea gulls and cormorants make their way inland to feast on the heath's well-stocked ponds. Resident birds include nuthatches, jays, tawny owls, woodpeckers, blue tits and treecreepers.

Wild life is abundant. Early risers may spot the occasional tiny muntjac deer. Also resident are foxes, voles, grass snakes

Light filters through trees at Kenwood House beside Hampstead Heath.

and weasels. Badgers visit the heath but no longer live there since badger baiters destroyed their last set. There are three bathing ponds but human swimmers have to share space with ducks and fish: there is the mixed pond (crayfish have been spotted here), the ladies' pond, where ladies may sunbathe topless, and the men's bathing pond. There is also a large summer lido. Stalwart swimmers continue to take a dip throughout winter, and some have a Christmas morning swim! Constable, who lived in Hampstead, painted many of his fine skies on Hampstead Heath.

HOLLAND PARK

Set between Kensington High Street and Holland Park Avenue, these formal gardens and a large woodland area came into public ownership after Holland House had been bombed during the Second World War. There is a fine avenue of lime trees, water features, statues, and a Japanese Garden that opened in 1991.

KENSINGTON GARDENS

The 275 acres of Kensington Gardens were formed from land taken from Hyde Park in 1689, after William and Mary moved into Nottingham House, now Kensington Palace. This is the only park in London in which royalty reside. William IV opened the gardens to the public all year round. Queen Caroline, wife of George II, created the present style of the gardens. She oversaw the planting of the enormous avenues of trees and the creation of the Round Pond and Long Water, which is a continuation of the Serpentine. There are some rare tree species here such as yellow oak and Montpelier maple. The park includes a pet cemetery containing cats, dogs, and even monkeys. The first burial was in 1880 when the Duke of Cambridge (the park's ranger) buried his wife's dog there. The final pet burial was in 1915.

Peter Pan's statue in Kensington Gardens epitomises the joy of childhood.

Next to the Long Water is the famous statue of Peter Pan surrounded by rabbits, mice and squirrels. Being stroked by generations of children's hands has worn these charming animals almost smooth. Also by the Long Water is Henry Moore's 19-foot high sculpture, carved from Roman Travertine marble. Victorian features such as the Italian Gardens and the Albert Memorial are now part of the 'ethos' of the gardens.

PRIMROSE HILL

Strictly speaking a part of Regent's Park, Primrose Hill, is 206 feet (62.8) high at the summit from where St. Paul's and Westminster Abbey can be seen, and, if visibility is good, the Surrey and Kent hills. Originally forest, it is now virtually all grassland and no longer has the primroses that were so abundant in the 1400s.

HYDE PARK

This area of 615 acres (249 hectares) was once the manor of Hyde, part of Westminster Abbey property. It became

a deer park under Henry VIII when large number of deer and wild boar were roaming there. Charles I opened Hyde Park to the public, providing a drive for people to show off their stylish horses and carriages.

During the Great Plague of 1665, many of London's citizens fled the crowded city to camp in Hyde Park.

Above: An early morning ride along Rotten Row in Hyde Park.
Right: A graceful statue by the Serpentine, Hyde Park.

By William III and Mary's reign, the pathway to St. James's Palace in the park had become notorious for footpads and thieves so William had the Row lit with 300 oil lamps. This was the first artificially lit public highway in England and became known as the new Carriage Road, or 'Route du Roi' (Route of Kings). The English pronounced this as Rotten Row, and so it is now known!

The Diana, Princess of Wales Memorial

The Serpentine in Hyde Park.

Fountain takes the form of an oval stream, with steps, curves and ripples, that flows into a tranquil pool; it was opened on 26 July, 2004.

The Serpentine is created

George II's wife, Queen Caroline, commissioned the creation of the Serpentine from the waters of the Westbourne in the 1730s. Named for its snaking shape, the Serpentine measures 28 acres (11.3 hectares).

unobserved by others.

The park is home to London Zoo, the Regent's Park's Open Air Theatre, and the Regent's Park mosque.

RICHMOND PARK

In 1637 Richmond Park was enclosed by Charles I for use as a royal hunting ground. Public rights of way were gained in the reign of George II. Richmond Park still contains herds of both fallow and red deer, as well as numerous bird species and many small mammals. Its semi-natural landscape of grassland, bog and bracken, wetland, woodland and ancient parkland trees, has made it a 'Site of Special Scientific Interest' and in 2000 it was designated as a National Nature Reserve.

Richmond Park began as a Royal hunting ground for Charles I and still has herds of red and fallow deer.

TRADESCANT GARDEN

This tiny quarter-acre garden in the churchyard of St. Mary's at Lambeth is a recreation of a seventeenth-century garden with a knot garden and several unusual species.

VAUXHALL GARDENS

Vauxhall Gardens (originally called Spring Gardens) were laid out a short distance east of Vauxhall Bridge. They were to prove an incredibly popular setting for

Celebrations and death

Public executions were performed at the north east corner of the park on Tyburn Tree. Up to eight people at a time could be pushed off the ladders and hanged.

In 1814, the spendthrift Prince Regent, the future George IV, organised a fair with festivities and fireworks to mark the end of the Napoleonic wars. The highlight was a re-enactment on the Serpentine of one of Lord Nelson's naval battles. Later, at his Coronation, elephants were ridden by oriental slaves on rafts disguised as chariots, towed by rowing boats down the length of the Serpentine.

The Great Exhibition

Hyde Park was the site of the Great Exhibition in 1851, spearheaded by Prince Albert as a celebration of art and invention. It was housed in the Crystal Palace, specially designed by Sir Joseph Paxton. At the end of the exhibition the building was moved to Sydenham but burnt down in 1936.

Public speaking

Near Marble Arch is the site of Speaker's Corner where, every Sunday, orators can stand on a soap box to air their views.

REGENT'S PARK

Originally part of the Forest of Middlesex, in 1539 some 554 acres (224 hectares) were reserved as a hunting park. In 1811 it was decided to hold a competition to design the space. John Nash, the architect friend of the Prince Regent, won the competition, producing a design based on two eccentric circles – the Inner Circle and the Outer Circle. The Inner Circle contains gardens while Nash placed town houses – beautiful terraces and villas – into a cunningly constructed urban landscape in the Outer Circle. The park is named after the Prince Regent who was Nash's greatest defender against his critics. The buildings survived almost unscathed until the Second World War when a combination of neglect and bombs lead to massive deterioration. But they are now restored to their former glory.

In 1841 the park was opened to the public. The Inner Circle now contains the Queen Mary's Rose Garden as well as a lake. There is a sculpture garden on the south east corner of the park. There is also a Secret Marienbad Garden – if discovered it reveals statues and ornamental urns, a fountain and a leafy bower in which the lucky visitor may sit music and entertainment from Charles II's time to the end of the nineteenth century. Initially, admission was free and the gardens could be reached only by a sixpenny boat ride. But in 1732 Vauxhall became fashionable and a grand reopening took place before Frederick, Prince of Wales. Most of the company wore masks, dominoes or legal robes. Admission fees were charged, and the gardens were transformed with more than 100 supper boxes, paintings, statues, arches, cascades, a music room, Chinese Pavilion and Gothic orchestra.

Supper was served in the arbours where the attraction, for some, was the company of masked ladies of somewhat dubious repute. Other entertainments included theatre, ballet, a Cascade, and battle enactments. By1859 the gardens' popularity had declined and they opened for the last time on 25 July.

ST. JAMES'S PARK AND GREEN PARK

Acquired by Henry VIII in the early 16th century, these parks act as a green backdrop to the many ceremonies that take place on The Mall, the processional route between the Palace and Whitehall and Horse Guards Parade. St. James's Park is famous for its views, ponds, waterfowl and its flower displays.

Left and below: St. James's Park with Buckingham Palace beyond the lake.

VICTORIA EMBANKMENT GARDENS

Sir Joseph Bazalgette, who designed London's sewerage system in the 1860s, also had the Victoria, Albert and Chelsea Embankments built, reclaiming over 52 acres from the river.

VICTORIA PARK HACKNEY

The East End of London was lacking a public park until in 1842, some 290 acres were purchased and the park laid out in 1845, with the lakes excavated in 1846.

WEST SMITHFIELD

West Smithfield is a quaint little square not far from Smithfield Market. It is the site of the original 'Smoothfield', an area used for jousts, tournaments, executions and Barts Fair.

BUCKINGHAM PALACE GARDENS

Buckingham Palace has the largest private garden in London with some 39 acres (16 hectares) set behind the massive palace frontage. On the north edge of the

West Smithfield.

garden is the herbaceous border, its plan conceived by King George VI. Today it is mulched with manure from the adjacent horse stables at the Royal Mews. There are many fine specimens of trees, including alder, arbutus, catalpa, lime, mulberry, oak, silver birch and sycamore. More than 350 types of wild flower grow, such as adder's tongue, cloverpink, coralroot, dog violet, hare's foot, heath bedstraw, marsh pennywort and water-speedwell. About 200 holly trees are evergreen and support a population of Holly Blue butterflies.

Overall, there are more than 400 species of natural and naturalised plants, and about 30 different bird species are residents or regular visitors to the lake, Within the gardens, one lake on its own measures 3 acres (1.2 hectares), and there are 20 acares of ornamental grass.

In 1961, the Queen added a curving avenue of Indian horse chestnut trees at the northwest corner of the palace. There are more than 200 mature trees in the garden as well as a rose garden. The grounds also contain a tennis court, summer house and the famous Waterloo Vase: this is a 15ft-stone urn, carved from a single vast block of Carrara marble by Sir Richard Westmacott. It was originally commissioned by Napoleon in anticipation of victory over Europe, but in the event the French king presented it to George IV to commemorate the British victory over Napoleon at Waterloo – an ironic twist.

Approximately ten gardeners (with one head gardener) tend the garden, including 29 acres (12 hectares) of lawn to mow. The centrepiece is the camomile lawn, the largest cut lawn in Britain; it takes a week to mow.

When the Hilton Hotel was built in the 1960s, a belt of chestnut trees had to be planted to prevent top-floor guests having a view straight into the Queen's gardens. Now the slightly higher temperatures in the city centre and the palace's high encircling walls have given the garden an almost tropical protection.

Commemorative Trees

The palace garden is full of beautiful specimens of trees. Ever since 10,000 mulberry trees were planted by James I there to feed silkworms, many other trees have been planted to mark some special association or occasion for the Royal Family.

- 1902: Copper beech. This, the oldest

The Waterloo Vase, a garden ornament in Buckingham Palace Gardens. This is a 4.5 metre (15 feet) stone urn, carved from a single vast block of Carrara marble by Sir Richard Westmacott.

commemorative tree in the park, was planted by King Edward VII and Queen Alexandra to mark his accession to the throne.

- 1913: London plane. Planted by King George V and Queen Mary to mark their 20th wedding anniversary.
- 1918: Caucasian lime. Planted for the Silver Wedding of King George V and Queen Mary.
- 1935: Indian chestnuts. Some of these were planted by King George V and Queen Mary to honour the Silver Jubilee.
- 1937: George VI's trees. Princess Elizabeth and King George VI planted trees to mark the king's coronation.
- 1948: English oak. A tree was planted to mark the birth of Prince Charles.
- 1987: In the wake of the Great Storm, the International Dendrology Society presented an oak to the Queen.
- 1969: Cut-leaf beech. Planted by Prince Charles on his 21st birthday. 1977: Silver lime. Given by the Royal Horticultural Society to mark the Silver Jubilee.

Open to the Public

The gardens of Buckingham Palace are open to visitors during August and September. In addition, the Queen hosts at least three garden parties each year, for about 30,000 guests.

COMMONS

As well as formally laid out parks and gardens, London contains a number of extensive open areas known as commons, usually once land set aside for common use by villagers. These include Barnes, Blackheath, Clapham, Merton, Streatham, Wandsworth and Wimbledon Commons.

BUILDINGS AND MONUMENTS
A skyline of towers and pinnacles

- **Every city conjures up images of buildings and skylines –**
- **silhouettes of form and pattern. This section reveals the stories**
- **behind a few of these edifices.**

ADMIRALTY ARCH
At the end of The Mall, this was built in 1910 to the design of Sir Aston Webb as part of the Queen Victoria Memorial.

ALBERT MEMORIAL
The Albert Memorial in Kensington Gardens, opposite the Royal Albert Hall, honours Prince Albert, husband of Queen Victoria, who died in 1861.

ALEXANDRA PALACE
Built in 1873 at the top of Muswell Hill and marketed as the 'People's Palace', this building seemed doomed from the outset. Days after its official opening, it mysteriously burnt down and despite being rebuilt quickly, was a commercial failure. Today, 'Ally Pally' remains something of a white elephant but is occasionally used for exhibitions, concerts and wedding receptions.

ARCHWAY BRIDGE
Along the Archway Road close to the Whittington Hospital is this cast-iron structure with the unhappy reputation of being a favourite spot for suicides.

APSLEY HOUSE AND ACHILLES
Apsley House at Hyde Park Corner, the home of the Duke of Wellington, opened to the public as a museum in 1952. At the back of the house is a statue of Achilles, erected in 1822 to commemorate the Duke of Wellington's achievements. Part of the building is set aside for residential use of the Duke's descendants.

BANK OF ENGLAND
William III founded the Bank of England, also known as the 'Old Lady of Threadneedle Street', but the bank did not occupy the site until 1734.

BARBICAN CENTRE
This complex of apartments, shops, theatres and restaurants was built in 1982 in a previously derelict area of Cripplegate.

BATTERSEA POWER STATION
Giles Gilbert Scott designed this industrial landmark in 1929. The power station ceased operation in 1989 and since then, the structure has stood empty. Several plans for redevelopment have come and gone.

Battersea Power Station.

Big Ben.

BIG BEN
Housed in St. Stephen's Tower at the northern end of the Houses of Parliament, the clock's name, Big Ben, is alleged to allude to Sir Benjamin Hall, the original commissioner of works. When it was installed in 1859, the name applied solely to the bell. However, it has now come to signify both bell and clock. The hands of Big Ben are 2.7 x 4.3m (9 x 14ft) long and the tower is 98m (320ft) high. The bell was cast by the Whitechapel Bell Foundry and was so heavy that it was taken to Westminster on a cart pulled by 16 horses. Shortly after its installation, the bell developed a crack and was out of service until 1862.

BOUDICCA'S MOUNT
To the northwest of Parliament Hill lies a tumulus known as Boudicca's Mount. Legend has it that the warrior queen was buried here after being killed in battle.

However another story claims that she was buried between platforms 9 and 10 in King's Cross Station. There is no evidence for either belief.

BROADCASTING HOUSE
The headquarters of the BBC is situated at the top of Regent Street. It has opened its doors to the public with behind-the-scenes tours of the building.

BRUNEL'S ENGINE HOUSE
This marks the site of the world's first under-river tunnel in Tunnel Street, Rotherhithe.

BT TOWER
Commonly known as the Post Office Tower, the BT Tower in Fitzrovia was once the tallest building in London. Designed in the 1960s, it featured a revolving restaurant high up the tower, which commanded excellent views. Sadly, bomb scares in the 1970s forced the tower to close to the public.

The BT Tower.

BUSINESS DESIGN CENTRE
The Royal Agricultural Hall, commonly known as the 'Aggy', was built on Upper Street, Islington in 1862. It held agricultural and livestock shows and gradually evolved into an exhibition hall known today as the Business Design Centre.

CENOTAPH
This takes its name from the Greek kenotaphion meaning 'empty tomb.' It was built in 1919–20 by Edwin Lutyens to commemorate those who lost their lives in the Great War.

The Cenotaph.

CENTREPOINT
On the corner of Charing Cross Road and New Oxford Street is an imposing skyscraper, now a listed building, built on the site of a slum called St. Giles.

CHARING CROSS
Outside Charing Cross Station stands a Victorian replica of the Charing Cross, one of 12 memorial 'Eleanor Crosses' erected by Edward I to mark the resting places of the funeral cortege of his wife Eleanor of Castile as it brought her body down to London from Nottingham. The original Charing Cross was pulled down by the anti-monarchist Roundheads during the Civil War.

CHARLTON HOUSE
The best example of a Jacobean mansion in London is Charlton House, near Woolwich, built in 1612.

CHILD'S BANK
Sited in Fleet Street, this is the oldest bank in Britain, dating from 1559.

CLEOPATRA'S NEEDLE
London's oldest monument has no known connection with the Egyptian queen and was originally erected in Heliopolis around 1475 BC. The Turkish viceroy of Egypt presented it to Britain in 1819 but 60 years passed before it arrived. Buried underneath it is a time capsule from 1887 containing objects such as a newspaper, a railway timetable and a box of hairpins.

COMMONWEALTH INSTITUTE
This 1962 building in Kensington High Street originally housed art and artefacts from the diverse cultures of members of the British Commonwealth. It is considered by English Heritage to be the second most important modern building in London after the Royal Festival Hall. With the charitable successor to the Commonwealth Institute moving to New Zealand House, the building is to be the new home of the Design Museum.

CONSTITUTION ARCH
This stands in the centre of Hyde Park Corner and was designed by Decimus Burton in 1828 to commemorate Britain's victories in the Napoleonic Wars. The Arch was originally a gateway into the grounds of Buckingham Palace.

DUKE OF YORK'S COLUMN
Overlooking St. James's Park, this was erected in 1833 – funded by docking soldiers' pay.

EROS

Commonly known as Eros, the cherub-like statue at Piccadilly Circus is officially entitled 'The Angel of Christian Charity' and was erected in 1893 as a memorial to the 7th Earl of Shaftesbury, a noted social and industrial reformer.

FREEMASON'S HALL

In Great Queen Street, this was built as a memorial to all the masons who died in the Great War. Parts of the building including the impressive Grand Temple are open to the public at certain times.

THE GUILDHALL

The administrative centre for the City of London, the first Guildhall was built on the same site in the early fifteenth century, but was virtually destroyed by the Great Fire of 1666. The present Guildhall was built in 1673 and enlarged after damage in the 1940s. Today the Guildhall's vast Great Hall serves as a meeting place for the Court of Common Council of the City of London.

GUILDHALL LIBRARY

Built in 1828, this contains an extensive collection of historical papers, maps and documents. It also houses the Guildhall Library Clock Room, which exhibits the London Clockmakers Company's collection of timepieces. In 1987, the remains of a Roman amphitheatre were found close to the Guildhall.

HIGHGATE CEMETERY

This is London's most famous graveyard. After it opened in 1839, it rapidly became the final resting place for many of London's rich and famous. The poet Christina Rossetti, novelist Radclyffe Hall, scientist Michael Faraday and political philosopher Karl Marx are all buried here.

The Terrace Catacombs provided inspiration for Bram Stoker's novel *Dracula* and were also at the centre of the bizarre 'Highgate Vampire' affair in the 1970s. Convinced that a vampire was at large, an occult society attempted to seek it out, destroying graves and scattering cadavers in the process.

HOGARTH'S HOUSE

This building in Great West Road, Chiswick, features a permanent exhibition of the artist's work.

HOUSES OF PARLIAMENT

The world-famous Houses of Parliament, also known as the Palace of Westminster, stand on the left bank of the Thames, the site of a royal palace for a thousand years. The first recorded building was a palace for Edward the Confessor in the eleventh century. By 1550 the palace was being used by the House of Commons and the House of Lords, but in 1834 was devastated by fire. The present buildings were completed in 1860.

KENWOOD HOUSE

Situated on Hampstead Heath, the house was originally built in the 1600s, but was remodelled by Robert Adam. One owner, the Earl of Mansfield, was the Attorney General in the late eighteenth century.

The Houses of Parliament.

During the Gordon Riots of 1780, a mob, believing that many of his prisoners were wrongly convicted, ransacked his home, Bloomsbury House, and then set off for Kenwood House. They were waylaid by the owner of the Spaniards Inn tavern on Hampstead Heath, who plied them with free drink until the army arrived to disperse them. The house now forms part of the Iveagh Bequest to the nation, along with some valuable paintings and books. It also serves as the venue for a series of outdoor classical concerts every summer.

LLOYD'S BUILDING

One of the city's most striking office blocks is the Lloyd's Building in Leadenhall Street. Constructed in 1984 and designed by Richard Rogers, this is the headquarters for insurers Lloyd's of London. Services such as pipes, stairs, and its glass lifts, are all placed on the outside of the building, so it is sometimes called the 'Inside-Out Building'. Its highly contemporary architecture contrasts with the surrounding classical buildings.

LONDON ARK

Right next door to the Hammersmith flyover stands the London Ark, quite literally an ark-shaped office block, designed by Ralph Erskine.

THE LONDON STONE

This block of limestone, located outside an office block in Cannon Street, is an ancient monolith of uncertain historical significance. During the Peasant's Revolt of 1450, the rebel Jack Cade struck it as he declared himself Lord of the City.

MANSION HOUSE

Standing opposite the Bank of England in the City, this is the official residence of the Lord Mayor of London.

MARBLE ARCH

This marks the western tip of the shopper's paradise Oxford Street. It was the site of the notorious Middlesex Gallows at Tyburn, the city's main place of execution from around 1300 to 1783.

MARLBOROUGH HOUSE

Built on land given to the Duchess of Marlborough by Queen Anne in 1709, this was a private house until 1953. It is now used as offices by the Commonwealth Secretariat.

THE MONUMENT

Designed by Sir Christopher Wren, this was erected to commemorate the Great Fire of London. Completed in 1676, it is 202 feet (62 metres) high.

The Monument.

OLD ROYAL OBSERVATORY

Set in Greenwich, this is London's oldest scientific institution. It was built in 1675 for Charles II's Astronomer Royal and today houses a permanent exhibition on the history of astronomy.

OLYMPIA EXHIBITION HALL

Starting life as the National Agricultural Hall in 1884, this became a circus venue before being established as an exhibition centre.

OSTERLEY PARK HOUSE

First built in the 1500s, this house is set in gardens that are now a large public park.

The Oxo building.

THE OXO TOWER

Originally part of the OXO company's headquarters, this building on the South Bank of the Thames now houses a range of fashionable restaurants and shops.

QUEEN'S HOUSE

There are two notable buildings in London with this name. One stands on Tower Green and was originally used as a prison. Three English queens were incarcerated there: Catherine Howard, Anne Boleyn and Lady Jane Gray.

Queen's House in Greenwich has a happier history. Built by the famous architect Inigo Jones in 1617, it is one of the best examples of Renaissance architecture in Britain.

ROYAL INSTITUTE OF BRITISH ARCHITECTS

Unsurprisingly, this is housed in one of London's most attractive buildings in Portland Place.

SEVEN DIALS

Between Covent Garden and Shaftesbury Avenue is the curiously named Seven Dials area, named after a Doric pillar topped by a seven-faced clock, erected at the junction of several roads in 1694. It became a regular meeting place for local villains, so the original pillar was removed in 1773. A new column was erected in 1989.

SOMERSET HOUSE

Edward Seymour 'Protector Somerset' built the first Somerset House in 1547. After the Civil War, it was occupied by the army. Following his death, Oliver Cromwell's body was stored there. By the beginning of the 18th century, Somerset House had fallen into disrepair and was rebuilt in 1809.

Once used by the civil service, the building opened to the public in 2000 and contains museums, restaurant, cafes and shops, and a winter skating rink.

Somerset House.

SOUTH BANK ARTS CENTRE

Covering two acres of land along the South Bank near Waterloo, this complex includes the Royal Festival Hall, the Queen Elizabeth Hall, the Purcell Room, the Hayward Gallery, the National Film Theatre, the Saison Poetry Library and the National Theatre. Built as part of the Festival of Britain in 1951, today it is one of London's premier art centres.

STRAWBERRY HILL

In 1747, the prime minister's youngest son, Horace Walpole, bought Strawberry Hill house in Twickenham. Walpole set about creating a spectacular 'gothick' fantasy in the house and grounds. The house was so besieged by visitors that he had to sell admittance tickets. After a period of restoration, the house re-opened to the public in 2010.

SYON HOUSE, BRENTFORD

Originally the home of the Dukes of Northumberland, this stately home is now open to the public. Its fine grounds are often used for exhibitions and a Butterfly House is set within them.

THAMES BARRIER

One of the most spectacular sights on the River, the Thames Barrier stretches between Silvertown on the north bank and Woolwich on the south. Completed in 1982 at a cost of £500 million, it is the world's largest moveable flood barrier. A series of enormous steel gates between concrete piers house the hydraulic lifting machinery. Normally the gates lie in the riverbed so that shipping can pass above them, but to protect London from flooding, the Barrier's gates can be raised, turning the gates through 90 degrees so that they stand 52 feet (15.8 metres) above the riverbed – approximately the height of a five-storey building.

When raised, each of the four main gates holds back the flow of water upstream. The Barrier has been raised many times, particularly to protect the city from a 'surge tide' from the North Sea. The Barrier can be closed as quickly as 15 minutes, although 3 hours is usual.

TOWER OF LONDON

The building of this began shortly after William the Conqueror's successful invasion of England in 1066. Since then, it has been used as a palace, a prison, an arsenal, a royal mint, a place of execution, a menagerie and a public records office. The oldest part of the structure is the White Tower, which was completed around 1078. Elizabeth I was imprisoned here before she became queen. Among those executed at the Tower were Henry VIII's wife, Anne Boleyn in 1536, and Lady Jane Grey and her husband in 1554. In 1483, Edward V and his brother (the Princes in the Tower) were last seen here before they disappeared, presumed murdered.

Yeoman Warders or 'Beefeaters' live within the Tower grounds and, among other duties, are responsible for organising the millions of tourists that visit the Tower each year. They also keep an eye on the

A weather vane on the Tower of London.

resident ravens that have nested at the Tower since the 1600s. Traditions states that the nation will fall should the ravens ever leave the Tower.

Nelson's Column in Trafalgar Square.

TRAFALGAR SQUARE

This is probably the most famous of all London squares. It was constructed on the site of the King's former mews and took 20 years to complete. The square commemorates Britain's naval victory at the Battle of Trafalgar and its main feature is Nelson's Column, named after Horatio Nelson, the admiral in charge of the British fleet. Nelson's Column is 185ft (56m) high and a 17ft (5m) effigy of Admiral Nelson surveys London from the top. Four lions sculpted by Landseer guard the base. There are also four plinths in the square, one at each corner, carrying sculptures of King George IV and generals Charles James Napier and Henry Havelock. In the mid-nineteenth century the square's designers ran out of money, so were unable to erect the final planned sculpture of William IV. Instead, the fourth plinth remained empty until it began to be used for temporary exhibits from 1999.

THE TROCADERO

This is at Piccadilly Circus and was originally a music hall. Today it houses an electronic games complex, shops, an IMEX cinema and a traditional cinema.

VICTORIA MEMORIAL

Edward VII commissioned this to stand outside Buckingham Palace as a tribute to his mother. At the centre is a sculpture of the Queen, surrounded by allegorical figures representing Victorian values such as courage, constancy and truth.

WHITTINGTON STONE

At the bottom of Highgate Hill is the Whittington Stone that allegedly marks the spot where Dick Whittington heard church bells calling him back to London to become mayor.

NEWER BUILDINGS IN CENTRAL LONDON

ArcelorMittal Orbit

Britain's largest piece of public art, this 377ft (115-metre-high) steel sculpture is also an observation tower allowing visitors to view the entire Olympic Park in which it is based in Stratford, east London. The spiral walkway for visitors is part of the artistic sculpture. Designed by Anish Kapoor and Cecil Balmond, the Orbit tower will remain part of the 2012 Olympics legacy to London.

Britain's richest man, the steel tycoon Lakshmi Mittal, chairman of steel company ArcelorMittal, contributed the bulk of the £19.1 million cost. The remainder came from the London Development Agency.

Canary Wharf

The name derives from earlier dockland days, when many imports came from the Canary Islands. Construction work began in 1988 to include office buildings, multilevel indoor shopping centres, the Docklands Light Railway, a conference and banqueting centre, and car parks.

The tower at One Canada Square (often wrongly called 'Canary Wharf' itself) has 50 floors and is 800ft (243m) high. From 1991 to 2010 it was the tallest building in Britain before being overtaken by the Shard London Bridge.

It takes the lifts 40 seconds to travel up from the lobby to the 50th floor, and the building is designed to sway nearly 14 inches (35 cm) in the strongest winds.

An aircraft warning light at the top of the pyramid-shaped roof flashes 40 times a minute – 457,600 times a day.

Some 7,000 people work in the building.

City Hall

Another modern landmark, designed by Foster and Partners, is the new City Hall. Since 2002 it has been home to the Mayor of London, the London Assembly and the GLA. This geometrically modified sphere of glass stands on the south bank of the Thames near Tower Bridge. The main feature of the interior is a spiral ramp and staircase that curves right up to the top.

The 'Gherkin'

30 St Mary Axe (formerly the Swiss Re Tower) has been nicknamed the 'Gherkin' from its beginning. This 41-storey, round, tapered building was designed by Lord Foster. Its 24,000 square metres (28,700 square yards or five football pitches) are covered in glass, over 10,000 tons of structural steel.

London Eye

This was constructed to celebrate the new Millennium. It is the largest observation wheel in the western hemisphere, standing 443 feet (135 metres) high – nearly three times the height of Tower Bridge. Its 80 'spokes' contain 3.7miles (6 km) of cable: laid flat this would run from Trafalgar Square to Canary Wharf. Some 1,700 tons of steel were used in its construction. Its total weight is 2,100 tons and it took over a week to lift it from a horizontal place to a vertical one.

The Eye turns continuously at one quarter of walking speed 10.25 inches (26cm) per second. Each revolution takes about 30 minutes and the Eye rotates an average of 6,000 times a year. Its 32 passenger capsules can each carry 25 people, meaning 15,000 visitors can ride the Eye every day. It is the highest public viewing platform in London, and passengers can see over 25 miles (40km) in each direction, even as far as Windsor Castle.

The O2

Originally the Millennium Dome, this has the biggest roof in London, measuring 20 acres (8 hectares). Its enclosed volume is 2.1 million cubic metres – equivalent to 3.8 billion pints or 12.8 million barrels of beer.

City Hall.

The O2 Arena.

The area the Dome covers is:
- 100 times larger than Stonehenge
- 6 acres (2.4 hectares) larger than the Great Pyramids of Egypt
- 3 times larger than the Coliseum of Rome
- 25 times larger than India's Taj Mahal
- and would hold 1,100 Olympic-size swimming pools or 80,000 double-decker buses
- The O2 is the world's largest fabric construction with 92,000 square metres (1 million square feet) of fabric. It is also the strongest fabric building in the world: the roof would support the weight of a jumbo jet. If it was inverted and put under Niagara Falls it would take ten minutes to fill.
- Exterior masts lean at three times the angle of the Leaning Tower of Pisa and are 40 metres (1,341 ft) taller.

Shard, London Bridge

Topped out in 2012 at 309.7 metres (1,016 ft), it is the tallest building in the European Union, and dominates the skyline of the south bank. The viewing gallery in this crystalline-faced tower offers the highest 360° views of London.

The Shard, London Bridge.

Strata SE1

Commonly called the Razor, this 43-storey skyscraper in the Elephant and Castle, south London, is 148 metres high (486 feet) and is primarily residential. There is a 'Sky Lobby' or viewing corridor on the 39th floor, and the summit houses a luxury penthouse flat. The Strata is notable for its sustainability efforts. It is one of the first buildings in the world to incorporate wind turbines, which generate enough electricity to cover usage in the common areas and more, and there is provision for rainwater to be collected for reuse.

ST. PAUL'S CATHEDRAL, WESTMINSTER ABBEY AND OTHER CHURCHES

London has always been an amalgam of different peoples and creeds, with some rulers tolerant of different religions and others, such as Henry VIII and Bloody Mary, torturing or killing many who resisted the chosen faith of the day.

The city's major religious buildings include:

The Chapel Royal, St. James's Palace

Here Charles I took Holy Communion before his execution and the Chapel hosted the marriages of William and Mary, George III and Queen Charlotte, Victoria and Albert, George V and Queen Mary.

Christ Church, Spitalfields

Designed by Nicholas Hawksmoor with a high, broached spire, the church was circled by Victorian prostitutes plying their trade. Aware that they would be arrested if caught standing still at the roadside, they paraded around the church until they picked up a punter.

St. Bride's, Fleet Street

This is the journalists' and printers' church, built on the site of an old printing press. Its tiered spire has also given us the shape of modern wedding cakes.

St. George's, Mayfair

A fashionable church for weddings: among those who have tied the knot here are Theodore Roosevelt, Benjamin Disraeli and George Elliot.

St. Margaret's Church

The official church of the House of Commons since 1614. Samuel Pepys, John Milton and Winston Churchill are some of the many who have married here.

St. Martin-in-the-Fields

This stands on the corner of Trafalgar Square in an area once surrounded by fields. Charles II was christened here. The current church was built in 1726 and has been a refuge for the homeless since the First World War. The churchyard, only 60 metres (200 feet) square, is thought to hold the remains of up to 70,000 people!

St. Paul's Cathedral

A cathedral dedicated to St. Paul has stood on the Ludgate Hill site for more than 1,400 years. Printing in England was started by William Caxton in what is now the courtyard. The medieval church was destroyed in the Great Fire of 1666.

Designed by Sir Christopher Wren, the new St. Paul's was completed in 1710. Wren's masterpiece is also his burial place. The famous dome – one of the largest in the world – is made of three shells: an outer dome, a concealed brick cone for structural support, and an inner dome. Above the Whispering Gallery is the Stone Gallery which gives a view over the city; even higher up is the Golden Gallery, 85 metres (280 feet) above the ground. The cross on the top is set 112 metres (366 feet) high. Including the Western Steps, the cathedral is 170 metres (555 feet) long.

The crypt, the largest in Europe, houses more than 200 tombs including Wellington's (plus the 19-ton carriage that took his body to the cathedral in 1852), and that of Lord Nelson.

St. Sepulchre-Without-Newgate

Set opposite the Old Bailey, the churchyard was once so popular with grave robbers that the families of the deceased paid night watchmen to keep an eye on the graves from a specially constructed tower that still stands today.

Southwark Cathedral

The Harvard Chapel here is named after John Harvard, founder of the famous university in the USA. Harvard was born in Southwark and baptised at the church in 1607.

Westminster Abbey

The Abbey stands near the Houses of Parliament, on the grounds of a former Benedictine Monastery. Legend has it that Saberht, the last Christian king of the East Saxons, founded a church here; certainly monks were living and working here by about AD 785.

Edward the Confessor built a new church on the site in 1065 but in 1245 Henry III pulled this down – bar the nave – and replaced it with the current Abbey. Since William the Conqueror, every British sovereign (except Edward V and Edward VIII) has been crowned here. Kings and queens from Edward the Confessor to George II are buried here.

Poets' Corner includes the tombs of Geoffrey Chaucer, Robert Browning and Ben Jonson amongst others. The last person buried in there was the actor Laurence Olivier in 1989. The Grave of the Unknown Warrior, whose remains were brought from Flanders after the First World War, is in the centre of the nave.

Westminster Cathedral

This Victorian Roman Catholic Cathedral was built with more than 12 million bricks. Its nave is the widest in the country and the campanile rises to more than 82 metres (270 feet).

Churchyard, Old St. Pancras, King's Cross

The design of the old British red telephone box may have been inspired by a mausoleum here. Also here, 16-year-old Mary Godwin and the poet Shelley declared their undying love over Mary's mother's grave and then eloped to Italy.

Westminster Abbey.

THE DARK SIDE
From Gloomy Macabre to Joyful Festivities: Brides in the bath and poisoned umbrellas

- **While the London scene has many glories – splendid buildings,**
- **proud historic moments, and worthy characters – it has its darker**
- **side, too, and this can be equally fascinating to explore.**

AD 61 Boudicca
Queen of the British Iceni tribe, Boudicca, angered by the treatment of herself and her daughters by the Romans, led an army which destroyed the newly created town of Londinium, slaughtered all those who could not flee, and razed it to the ground. Her army was defeated shortly afterwards and Roman London was rebuilt.

842 Vikings
More than four centuries after the Romans abandoned London, the Anglo-Saxon settlement, Lundenwic, was attacked by Vikings and partially destroyed.

1066 Leprosy
Leprosy was rampant and special hospitals called Leprosaria were built on the outskirts of London. St. James's Palace and the church of St. Giles-in-the-Fields near Tottenham Court Road were built on the site of leprosaria. (St Giles is the patron saint of lepers.)

1189 Pogrom
In one of a spate of pogroms in England, the citizens of London turned on Jews, burning their houses and killing many.

1212 Fire and water
A disaster began with a fire on the south side of London Bridge. While a crowd tried to put it out, burning embers set fire to the north side, trapping them. To escape they jumped into boats, overloading them so that they sank. Many people who were not consumed by the fire were drowned. However, a figure of 3,000 dead is regarded as an exaggeration.

1305 William Wallace
Scottish hero William Wallace was hanged, disemboweled, beheaded, and quartered at Smithfield on the orders of King Edward I. His head was boiled and preserved with tar, and was the first to be displayed on London Bridge. The last time a criminal's head was displayed there was in 1678.

1348–50 Black Death
Bubonic Plague reached London in November 1348 and inflicted a horrible death on at least 20,000 Londoners of

Newgate Prison.

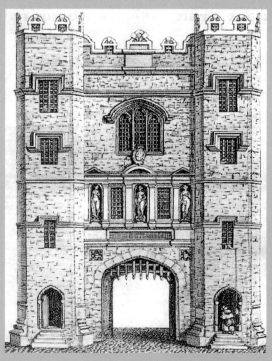

the next two years. The epidemic became known as the Black Death because the buboes or swellings the disease caused turned dark purple or black.

1381 Peasants' Revolt
Watt Tyler, a leader in the Peasants' Revolt. clashed with Richard II and the Mayor of London. Accounts vary, but most agree that Tyler was wounded and taken to St. Bartholomew's Hospital which adjoins Smithfield. He was dragged from his bed, probably already mortally wounded, and beheaded. The City Militia then arrived and surrounded the rebels whose pleas for mercy were granted by the King.

1381–1747 Tower Hill
Tower Hill was the place for the execution of upper class and important people by beheading when decapitation was regarded as more humane than hanging. The last beheading on Tower Hill was in 1747.

1417 Oldcastle's execution
On 14 December John Oldcastle, a soldier and Lollard heretic, was executed by hanging over a fire in St. Giles in the Fields. Elizabethan plays were written about him and some believe he is the inspiration for Shakespeare's Falstaff.

1450 Jack Cade's revolt
Jack Cade was one of those rebel leaders who emerge from obscurity, earn themselves some notoriety, and then die: in his case, beheaded after he was already dead. Cade, who also went by the name John Mortimer, led an assault on London with protesters who demanded the

removal of corrupt government officials and were angry with Henry VI's losses of English territory in France. A £1,000 reward was put on Cade's head, and he was tracked down in Sussex and mortally wounded, dying on the way back to Southwark. He was beheaded and quartered at Newgate, his body parts sent on a tour of the rebel areas to prove he was dead and his head displayed on London Bridge.

1483 Princes in the Tower

When Edward IV died suddenly on 9 April his elder son was proclaimed Edward V, but as he was only 12 years old his uncle, his father's brother, Richard, Duke of Gloucester was made protector. The Tower of London was then still a Royal Palace and Edward and his younger brother, Richard were sent to live there. The duke had the princes declared illegitimate and was crowned as King Richard III. The princes were not seen again. What happened to them is a mystery though most people believe they must have been murdered.

1531 Boiling

Richard Rose (Roose), a cook working in the house of Bishop Fisher of Rochester allegedly attempted to poison his master. The bishop survived but others died. The poisoner was said to have been boiled alive in Smithfield. Some historians suggest it was Anne Boleyn who should have been in the pot as she was the more likely culprit.

1538 Roasting

An atrocity was committed by Henry VIII when he became angered that Franciscan monks would not recognise him as head of the Church and opposed the dissolution of his marriage to Catherine of Aragon. Father Forest, Catherine's confessor, who was in his sixties, was suspended over a fire in Smithfield and was roasted to death.

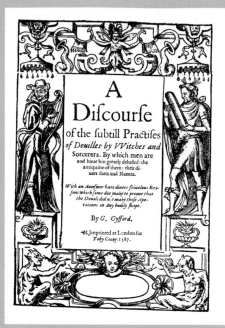

A 1587 pamphlet about witches.

Women were ducked to discover if they were witches.

1541 Witches

A Witchcraft Act was passed making the crime of sorcery (however defined) a felony rather than a heresy, giving jurisdiction to the civil rather than ecclesiastical courts. The majority of those accused of witchcraft were women, who were regarded as especially susceptible to the influence of evil forces.

Conviction for witchcraft, after 'tests' by ducking, carried the death penalty. When fears of sorcery abated the old laws were repealed and an Act of 1735 made it an offence to pretend to be a witch.

1555–58 'Bloody Mary'

During the reign of Queen Mary 300 Protestant martyrs were burned at the stake for refusing to convert to Catholicism. Many were Londoners, martyred in Smithfield.

1586 Elizabethan barbarities

When Anthony Babington and his Catholic conspirators who planned to assassinate Queen Elizabeth I were discovered they were sentenced to be hung, drawn and quartered. On a specially erected scaffold near Holborn, Babington and six others were hanged but were cut down before they were dead, then they were castrated and disemboweled. When the Queen learned of their fate she ordered that the remaining conspirators should not be mutilated until they were dead.

30 January 1649 Royal execution

After the Civil War, King Charles I was beheaded outside Banqueting House at Whitehall.

1661 Cromwell exhumed

By the time of the restoration of the monarchy in 1660, three of the ringleaders who had ordered the beheading of Charles I (Cromwell, Henry Ireton and John Bradshaw) had all died of natural causes. However, a decision was made to hang them anyway, and their bodies were exhumed and taken to Tyburn where their lifeless corpses were duly strung up and quartered, and their heads were chopped off. There is a persistent rumour that Cromwell's family somehow managed to exchange his body with another and the macabre ritual was not inflicted on him at all. It was supposedly his head which was impaled on a spike at the south end of Westminster hall for 20 years or so before it was taken down. One tradition has it that this gruesome relic became a fairground attraction.

1665 The Great Plague

Unlike earlier plagues, this epidemic hit the poorer suburbs of London harder than the wealthy city centre. At its height, records suggest that 7,000 people were being buried a week.

September 1665: each day 1,000 corpses were buried in communal graves.

1666 Who started the Great Fire?

There were suspicions that the fire which destroyed so much of London in 1666 must have been started deliberately, and sure enough a French watchmaker, 25-year-old Robert Hubert, was apprehended apparently trying to leave the country shortly after the fire had burned out. Hubert immediately confessed to starting a fire in Whitehall, clearly ignorant of the fact that the fire did not reach there. He then described putting fireballs into the bakery in Pudding Lane in the City where the fire began. Nobody believed him and thought him a little 'destracted'. But somehow he was able to find the ruins of the bakery when asked to identify it. He was hanged. Shortly afterwards the captain of a Swedish ship which Hubert had taken to England testified that he could not have started the fire as he had not gone ashore until two days after it had started. The conclusion in the end was that the fire was an Act of God and punishment for the sins of Londoners. On the Monument designed by Wren to commemorate the fire there was for a long time the inscription 'the most dreadful Burning of this City; begun and carried on by the treachery and malice of the Popish faction'.

On the corner of Giltspur Street and Cock Lane in Smithfield, there is a small statue called The Golden Boy of Pye Corner which bears the following inscription: 'This Boy is in Memmory Put up for the late FIRE of LONDON Occasion'd by the Sin of Gluttony'.

1685 Beheading

Although beheading was regarded as a relatively humane form of execution, some heads rolled more readily than others. It took several blows – reports range from five to seven – for the executioner Jack Ketch to sever the head of the Duke of Monmouth, member of a plot to dethrone Charles II. There is a legend that, as there was no portrait of him, his head was sewn back on so that one could be painted. In reality the National Portrait Gallery has a portrait of him which was painted two years before his death.

1705 John 'Half-Hanged' Smith

There are tales of people surviving the death penalty, the most famous of which is that of John 'Half-hanged' Smith. Convicted of robbery, Smith was taken to Tyburn on Christmas Eve 1705 to be hanged. Whereas hangmen in the latter days of capital punishment made sure the victim had their neck broken and died fairly quickly, this was not the case in the eighteenth century. Smith had been hanging for 15 minutes when the crowd heard there had been a reprieve and he was cut down still alive. Asked about his near-death experience he reportedly said that there had been 'a great blaze or glaring light ... and then I lost all sense of pain ... After I was cut down, I began to come to myself and the blood and spirits forcing themselves into their former channels put me by a prickling or shooting into such intolerable pain that I could have wished those hanged who cut me down'. Smith continued in a life of crime but appears to have escaped a second trip to Tyburn.

1746 The 45

One of those who had taken part in 1745 in Bonnie Prince Charlie's failed attempt to return a Stuart to the throne was James 'Jemmy Dawson' who, along with 16 other members of 'The 45' was hanged on Kennington Common. Their bodies were mutilated and a young woman who was attached to Dawson was said to have swooned and died of a broken heart.

1782 Resurrection of a thief

Although only the bodies of convicted murderers were available to the medical profession for dissection at the time, the body of John Haynes, a thief and housebreaker, was handed over to a doctor when he was cut down from the scaffold at Tyburn. The doctor, Sir William Blizard, noticed signs of life. Haynes recovered and was able to tell Sir William what he had experienced: 'The last thing I recollect was going up Holborn Hill in a cart. I thought then that I was in a beautiful green field; and that is all I remember till I found myself in your honour's dissecting-room'.

It was customary for the condemned to have a drink or two on the way to Tyburn which perhaps explains the memory loss.

2–5 June 1780 The Gordon Riots

After three days of rioting, in which many buildings were torched, the Riot Act was read and troops were brought in to subdue the 60,000-strong band of men led

The hanging of Jack Sheppard, thief, was watched by 200,000 people.

by Lord George Gordon protesting at a law offering leniency to Catholics. Though they were outnumbered, the 10,000 troops were armed and were ordered to fire on the crowds. It is thought 285 rioters died from the hail of bullets. Another 25 were hanged. Remarkably, despite the attacks on Catholic property, no Catholics appeared to have been killed.

December 1811 Ratcliffe Highway

The Ratcliffe Highway in London's 'sailor town' was notorious for violence but the murders that took place here in 1811 caused a sensation for their brutality and the fact that they were committed in the homes of the victims. The first attack was on a young couple and their infant son. The second was on the publican of the Kings Arms, his wife and a woman servant. A lodger in the Pear Tree public house, John Williams, was the prime suspect but he hanged himself in prison before he was tried. His body was buried with a stake through his heart at the junction of Commercial Road and Cannon Street.

11 May 1812 Assassination of a Prime Minister

When Spencer Perceval stepped into the lobby of the House of Commons one evening in 1812 he was confronted by a man who drew two pistols and shot him in the chest. He died shortly afterwards. His assailant was just a man with a grudge, a merchant called John Bellingham who felt he had not been well treated by the government. Bellingham was hanged.

1820 Cato Street Conspirators

Angered by the Combination Act passed in 1799 which forbade working men to gather together for a common purpose, a group of radicals met secretly in London and plotted to assassinate the prime minister and the entire cabinet. Their last hide-out was in Cato Street near the Edgware Road. When their plot was discovered the police raided the hideout and one officer was killed. Four conspirators were sentenced to be hung, drawn and quartered while seven were sentenced to transportation. The sentences of the four who were hanged were amended so that they were beheaded but not otherwise mutilated.

July 1840 Hanging of Courvoisier

When Francois Courvoisier, the valet of Lord William Russell, was hanged outside Newgate Prison for robbing his employer and slitting his throat there were some famous people in the crowd of 40,000 witnessing the execution. Charles Dickens was there and William Makepeace Thackeray, author of an essay *On Going to see a Man Hanged*. 'I feel myself shamed and degraded at the brutal curiosity that took me to that spot,' he wrote.

1849 A husband and wife hanged

When Marie Manning, a Swiss maid, and her husband Frederick, a publican, were hanged at Horsemonger Lane Gaol for murdering a wealthy friend, Charles Dickens rented a room overlooking the scene so that he could observe the behaviour of the crowd that gathered from the night before the execution. It was the first time in 150 years that a husband and wife had been hanged together. Dickens was horrified by the gallows humour of the crowd and its boorish behaviour and wrote a letter to the *Times* to express his disgust. '... thieves, low prostitutes, ruffians, and vagabonds of every kind, flocked on to the ground, with every variety of offensive and foul behaviour. Fightings, faintings, whistlings, imitations of Punch, brutal jokes, tumultuous demonstrations of indecent delight when swooning women were dragged out of the crowd ... gave a new zest to the general entertainment.'

1864 Britain's first railway murder

One of the most thrilling murder enquiries followed the discovery of a badly injured man, aged 70, on the railway line near Hackney Wick station in north London. He died the next day, and evidence pointed to a young German, Franz Muller. Muller took a sailing ship to America, but police overtook him on a steamship, arriving three weeks before him. He was found guilty and hanged. It was the first railway murder and had two consequences. First, a regulation that passengers should have some way of communicating with the guard, and a revulsion at the behaviour of crowds at a public hanging.

1888 Jack the Ripper

A series of five brutal murders of women in Whitechapel in London's East End caused widespread fears that a crazed killer was stalking the streets at night. The victims had their throats cut and organs were removed from three of them. A letter claiming to be from the killer was signed Jack the Ripper. The letter is generally thought to be a hoax but the name captured the popular imagination and for ever after the search for the real Ripper has continued.

1903 Was this man Jack the Ripper?
Severin Klosowski was born in Poland where he studied medicine and trained as a surgeon. In 1887, when he was 22 years old, he emigrated to London where he worked as a hairdresser and opened his own barber's shop. He was convicted of poisoning three women who

Jack the Ripper killed and mutilated at least five victims but was never caught.

had lived with him as wives. The fact that he was a cold-hearted killer, had been a surgeon and had lived in the East End at the time of the Jack the Ripper murders has made him a plausible candidate for the serial killer of Whitechapel.

1910 Dr. Crippen
When the wife of American Hawley Harvey Crippen went missing her friends worried that some accident had befallen her. They noticed he had a new lover who was wearing his wife's jewellery and clothing. He said his wife had gone to America and

died there. But then he changed his story. Police found Crippen charming and helpful until he suddenly disappeared. A search of Crippen's house at Hilldrop Crescent in north London found body parts buried under floorboards. Warrants for Crippen's arrest were issued. The captain of a ship sailing to Canada became suspicious of two of his passengers, apparently a man and a young boy (who looked very like a young woman) and using his wireless telegraph got a message to Scotland Yard. A police inspector took a faster ship to Canada and arrested Crippen before he could go ashore.

The use of wireless to capture a criminal excited the world.

1914–18

39 Hilldrop Crescent, Islington, Dr. Crippen's house.

During the First World War convicted German spies were executed by firing squad at the Tower of London.

1915–17 First Air Raids on London
For the first time London was bombed from the air when a German Zeppelin appeared over north London on 31 May 1915. In that first raid 28 people were killed and more than 80 injured. The Zeppelin raids were not as destructive as the raids by Gotha Bombers which are thought to have killed 835 people in London and on the south coast of England.

1940 The Blitz and rocket attacks
From September 1940 until the end of the Second World War in May 1945 there were 1,224 air raid warnings in London and the wail of the sirens were a constant source of anxiety, especially during the Blitz, the months of the heaviest bombing raids. There were 354 bombing raids overall and in the final months of the war nearly 3,000 rocket attacks, first the V1s or 'doodlebugs' then the more destructive V2 rockets which made no sound before they exploded. The death toll is usually put at 29,890 with 50,000 badly injured.

1942 A new Jack the Ripper?
Four women were killed and mutilated in February, and their murderer was found by chance. An RAF cadet, George Cummins, was arrested for assault, and the murdered women's handbags were found in his lodgings. He was hanged on 25 June.

1953 Serial killer John Christie
When John Christie was finally convicted in 1953 of killing eight women, murders he had committed over a period of about ten years, it became clear that another man, Timothy Evans, had been wrongly accused of killing his own wife and daughter for which he had been hanged in 1950. The case of 10 Rillington Place, Christie's home in Notting Hill, caused a national

scandal, partly because of the horrors of the crimes in which he had usually gassed his victims before strangling them, partly because of the failure of the police to catch him earlier, and partly because of the miscarriage of justice. Evans had been Christie's lodger and Christie was a witness against him. Evans was given a posthumous pardon for the murder of his daughter, but not of his wife. Christie was hanged at Pentonville Prison.

2 October 1952 Railway disaster
A commuter train at Harrow station was hit by an express train and another express ploughed into the wreckage. The local train was built largely of wood and broke into pieces. 122 people died.

13 July 1955 Ruth Ellis
The last woman executed in the UK.

1957 Lewisham railway disaster
87 people died in an accident caused by heavy smog.

1960s The Krays
The Kray twins, imprisoned in 1968, ran London's major criminal gang during the '60s. In March 1966, Ronnie shot dead a rival gang member in The Blind Beggar pub, Whitechapel Road. A would-be informer is rumoured to be buried in the concrete of the Hammersmith flyover.

1970 Babes in the Wood murders
The murderer of two children found in Epping Forest was only convicted in 2000.

November 1974 Lord Lucan
Lord Lucan disappeared after the family's nanny was found battered to death in his home at 46 Lower Belgrave Street, SW1.

February 1975 Moorgate tube crash
41 killed and 74 injured when a tube train failed to stop and rammed into a dead-end tunnel.

A rival gang member was shot dead by Ronnie Kray in The Blind Beggar pub in Mile End Road.

September 1978 Poisoned umbrella
On Waterloo Bridge, Bulgarian exile Georgi Markov was pricked by a hypodermic needle disguised in an umbrella. He died.

30 April 1980 Iranian Embassy Siege
Iranian separatists held staff and journalists hostage in the Embassy at 16 Prince's Gate, killing one man and throwing his body outside the door. SAS troops stormed the building, killing five terrorists. One hostage also died.

1981–83 Muswell Hill murders
Workmen clearing drains in 23 Cranley Gardens, N10, discovered a blockage caused by human remains. Dennis Nilsen, who had lived there since 1981, had killed at least three men. As the bodies decomposed, he buried parts, threw some away and flushed some down the drains.

15 June 1982 'God's Banker' dies
Italian banker Roberto Calvi, involved with the Vatican in fraud, was found hanging under Blackfriars Bridge. At first this was thought to be suicide, but later was believed to be murder.

1987 King's Cross tube station
31 people died in a fire.

August 1989 Tragedy on the River
57 party-goers died when dredger *Bowbelle* rammed the *Marchioness* pleasure boat.

1979–96 IRA bombs:
- 30 March 1979
- MP Airey Neave was killed by a car bomb as he drove out of Parliament.
- 20 July 1982
- Four horse-guards in Hyde Park and seven bandsmen in Regent's Park killed.
- 10 April 1992
- At the Baltic Exchange, in St. Mary Axe, a bomb killed three people.
- 24 April 1993
- Bomb killed one person in Bishopsgate, shaking the entire City.
- 9 February 1996
- Canary Wharf bomb killed two people.
- 18 February 1996
- IRA member Edward O'Brien died with four passengers when his bomb exploded prematurely on a bus at Aldwych.

5 October 1999 Paddington
Two trains collided near Paddington, killing 31 people and badly burning many others

7 July 2005 Terrorist attack
In a carefully planned attack on London, four young Islamist terrorists blew themselves up killing 52 people. As commuters packed the Underground in the morning each of the suicide bombers headed for a different line. Three made it onto trains as planned but one was delayed and boarded a No 30 bus which had been diverted in the aftermath of the first explosions. The bus was destroyed when he detonated his homemade bomb.

CRIME AND PUNISHMENT
From highwaymen patrols and Bow Street Runners to the modern constabulary

- **London had no 'police force' as such until the creation of the Thames Police in 1798 to patrol the docks. But efforts to keep public order and to detect and combat crime did evolve earlier on, with 'policing' a social responsibility of the citizens, in much the same way as fire prevention was regarded as general social duty. But pursuing thieves and other law-breakers was, however, the responsibility of the victims of crime.**

Overseeing this archaic system of policing were the dignitaries of the City, mostly wealthy merchants and tradesmen who were elected to various bodies as aldermen and councillors.

In theory, anyone accused of stealing could be sent for trial by jury, the evidence against them presented to the courts by the victims and their witnesses. In practice, by the early eighteenth century many petty offenders were simply committed to the House of Correction at Bridewell or the workhouse at the discretion of City dignitaries who were serving as magistrates. The governors of Bridewell determined the punishments.

A great many of the cases sent to the Old Bailey were to do with theft, particularly by servants or 'shop lifters'. The prosecutors were as a rule shopkeepers, tradesmen and merchants. A Grand Jury sifted the evidence, another jury passed judgement. Trials were summary: the Old Bailey juries took them in batches handling 20 or 30 a day.

Between 1770 and 1851 the way in which crime was policed and criminals were dealt with underwent fundamental changes, probably in response to the new problems presented by the great growth of towns which accompanied rapid industrial change. Punishments of convicted criminals now ranged from hanging to branding on the thumb and/or a spell in the pillory (head and arms secured) or the stocks (legs only secured). Whipping and various forms of public humiliation were practised until the early 1800s, but there was still no real concept of the 'prison sentence' as punishment.

Old-fashioned blue lanterns can still be found outside some police stations.

Looming over all criminal proceedings was Tyburn, where the notorious triangular gallows had been established since at least the fourteenth century. As there were something like 200 offences for which a person could be hanged, the numbers heading for the gallows would have been absurdly high if there had not been some adjustments to the 'Bloody Code'. A ritual arose in which those condemned to death were taken from Newgate Prison on a three-mile route to Tyburn in a cart or tumbril, followed by crowds.

The hanging tree was considered to be essential to London's policing: a gruesome deterrent that did away with the need for a 'continental' style police force which was regarded as potentially oppressive. Of those hanged in the eighteenth century it is thought the great majority were men under the age of 21 and that the most common offences were highway robbery, theft, or counterfeiting of coinage. The majority of those convicted of capital offences after 1750 did not hang: it was a Royal prerogative to issue pardons and transmute hanging to transportation, a discretion exercised often by judges themselves.

The transportation of criminals to the colonies had been practised since the founding of Virginia in the seventeenth century. For those condemned to death then reprieved, sentences of transportation to the colonies for anything from seven years to life were customary. Until the American War of Independence (1776–83) criminals were sent to the east coast counties of America, then from 1788 transportation was to Australia.

Outside the City, new courts were established by magistrates, the first at Bow Street in 1740. It was here, under the Fielding brothers, that a semi-professional thief-taker was established, a prototype police force of the mid-eighteenth century.

As London grew in size policing became more and more a paid occupation rather than a social duty, while daily newspapers that were circulated in coffee houses transmitted news of crimes and appeals for the apprehension of alleged criminals. The prevalence of crime in the capital was a constant concern but the hangings at Tyburn and, from 1783, Newgate, were not directed for the most part to stamping out acts of violence. They targeted mainly crimes against property.

By the early nineteenth century it was clear that the old criminal system was not workable. The first modern, salaried police force was established in London by Sir Robert Peel in 1829 (the 'Peelers' and 'Bobbies'). Between 1829 and the mid-1850s the number of offences for which people could be hanged was drastically reduced, and although public hangings continued until 1868, their numbers were tiny compared with 50 years earlier. Transportation was curtailed after 1853 (though it continued until the 1870s) and a programme of prison building began.

THE CITY OF LONDON POLICE FORCE

When the Metropolitan Police (the Met) was founded in 1829 the City of London, which had had its own system of policing, steadfastly refused to be absorbed into the new organisation. Parliament bowed to the wishes of the Corporation, and the City of London Police Act of 1839 put the policing of the Square Mile on a firm footing. The City Police has the same ranks, works to the same regulations, and carries out the same policing services as the Metropolitan Police. The only difference is that it is accountable to the Corporation of London, not a police authority.

WOMEN POLICE OFFICERS

There were no women police officers when the Metropolitan Police were formed in 1829 and it was not until 1973 that they fully integrated into the force. However, a Women Police Service had been founded in 1914 with the specific task of discouraging women from going in to prostitution.

THE ROYAL PARKS CONSTABULARY

A force of Royal Park Keepers with the powers of police constables within the parks was created in 1872. In 1974 they became the Royal Parks Constabulary, and in 2004 the Metropolitan Police took over.

SCOTLAND YARD AND THE SPECIAL BRANCH

Between 1883 and 1885, an Irish nationalist terrorist group called the Fenians held a bombing campaign in London and blew up the Met's headquarters, Scotland Yard. The Fenians' activities led to the formation of the Special Branch as the first, specialist subdivision of the Met's Criminal Investigations Department. Meanwhile, the Fenians' aims were effectively taken over by the IRA (Irish Republican Army) from 1916. New Scotland Yard, the current headquarters of the Metropolitan Police, opened in 1890.

THE OLD BAILEY

The Old Bailey courthouse was named after the street in which it was located, next to Newgate Prison in the western part of the City of London. It was destroyed in the 1666 Fire of London and rebuilt in 1674, with the court open to the weather to prevent the spread of disease. It was roofed over in 1734. In 1834 it was designated the Central Criminal Court, trying cases not just from London but of major crimes from around the country. The building itself is owned by the City of London and the one that exists today was officially opened in 1907. On the dome

The Statue of Justice on top of the Old Bailey.

above the court is a bronze statue of Lady Justice holding a sword in her right hand and weighing scales in her left. There are now 18 courts in all.

ROYAL COURTS OF JUSTICE

This complex deals mainly with civil litigation through the sessions of the Court of Appeal, the High Court of Justice, and the Crown Court. It was completed in 1882 but its design emulates thirteenth-century building styles. Here are the courts of admiralty, divorce, probate, chancery, appeals, and the Queen's Bench.

The Victorian Gothic buildings of the Royal Courts of Justice on the Strand.

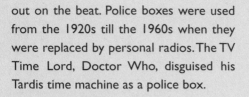

THE FLYING SQUAD

Starting out in 1919 as the 'Mobile Patrol Experiment', 12 detectives from New Scotland Yard were given the authority to operate anywhere within London. They had motor cars, which was novel in those days, and a horse-drawn Great Western Railway van with holes cut in the side for surveillance. The experiment was judged a success and in 1921 this new branch of the force was given the name the Flying Squad. They are also known as the Heavy Mob and the Sweeney (from cockney rhyming slang: Sweeney Todd = Flying Squad).

AIR SUPPORT UNIT

The Met's Air Support Unit was formed in 1980 with a single helicopter. It now has three working round the clock and a staff of 18 constables, three sergeants, and a police inspector. Their main task is to help search for suspects who are hiding from police on the ground, following vehicles that police are chasing, providing a high-level view of crowds and helping to police crime generally.

MOUNTED POLICE

The Mounted Branch of the Metropolitan Police has a longer history than any other element of the force, for it can trace its origins to 1760 when the Bow Street magistrate Sir John Fielding set up patrols to combat highway robberies on the roads leading out of London. Starting with just eight men, the Bow Street Horse Patrol policed the main roads within 20 miles of Charing Cross. In 1805 the force was increased to 50. The coming of the railways did away with most highway robbery but the horse patrols always found a new job to do. For a while they patrolled the rural fringes of London to deter the theft of livestock, armed sometimes with pistol and sword. Then they were used to carry messages, a job that became redundant with the electric telegraph and telephone. From that time on they became a useful force in controlling crowds.

One of the best-known examples is Billy, the White Horse of Wembley, ridden by PC George Scorey who helped hold back the crowd which got out of hand and spread onto the pitch when the first Cup Final was played there in 1923. The Mounted Branch now has 140 officers, women as well as men since 1971, and 120 horses.

POLICE BOXES

These large, blue kiosks, topped with a flashing light, were once a common sight in London. They were linked to the local police station and allowed officers to communicate with their colleagues while out on the beat. Police boxes were used from the 1920s till the 1960s when they were replaced by personal radios. The TV Time Lord, Doctor Who, disguised his Tardis time machine as a police box.

DIALLING 999

The 999 telephone emergency service was first introduced in 1937.

LONDON'S PRISONS

In the early eighteenth century there were 22 public gaols in London and many more 'houses of correction'. Most of the prisons were run commercially with the gaoler taking fees from the inmates and charging for various services. Until the early decades of the nineteenth century prisons were chiefly places to hold convicted men and women before they were hanged, sentenced to transportation or pardoned. When death sentences were at their height between the 1770s and the 1830s not all those condemned were actually executed. Petitions for mercy were successful in more than half the cases at some periods, with the death sentence commuted to transportation. With the decline in crimes which carried the death penalty and the end of transportation in the late 1800s, London's prisons took on their modern function of holding those convicted for periods of time in which it is hoped they might be reformed. The city's prisons include:

THE CLINK

Built in Southwark in 1144 for the Bishop of Winchester to hold those convicted for religious misdemeanours, the Clink was one of the earliest prisons and remains a nickname for all gaols.

The Mounted Branch was originally formed to deal with highwaymen.

Wormwood Scrubs prison was built entirely by prison labour.

NEWGATE

The first Newgate was built into the western wall of the City of London in 1188 in the reign of Henry II. It became the principal prison for holding those accused of the most serious crimes, with both men and women kept in irons. There were frequent outbreaks of what was called 'gaol fever' and in 1750 the disease spread to the Old Bailey courthouse next door leading to 60 deaths, including that of the Lord Mayor. Following this a windmill was placed on top of the prison to power a ventilation system devised by the clergyman inventor Stephen Hales who believed 'gaol fever' was caused by bad air. Gaol fever was later identified as typhus, which is spread by lice. When hanging at Tyburn was stopped the gallows were set up outside Newgate. The Old Bailey is built on the site.

HOLLOWAY

One of the most famous prisoners sent here on remand was Oscar Wilde. Known locally as 'Camden Castle', as it was architecturally like a turreted fortress, it became a prison exclusively for women in 1903. It was where the Suffragettes convicted of various offences committed in their campaign for votes for women were imprisoned. There were executions at Holloway with five women hanged between 1903 and 1955. In 1955 Ruth Ellis, who had shot her boyfriend, was the last woman to be executed in Britain.

PENTONVILLE

Completed in 1842, Pentonville Prison in north London was designed on principles recommended by Jeremy Bentham, the reformer, with five wings radiating from a central hall. It became the model for new prisons built around the country from the mid-nineteenth century. It became a teaching prison for those who applied to the Home Office to be put on the list of executioners. The method of hanging, calculating the weight of the prisoner and the length of the 'drop', was illustrated with a dummy. Between 1902 and 1961, 120 men were hanged at Pentonville, including Hawley Harvey Crippen in 1911.

WORMWOOD SCRUBS

'The Scrubs' was designed in 1870s as a national long-term penitentiary, modelled on Sing Sing gaol in America. Its bricks were all made on the site in East Acton by convict labour. Today Wormwood Scrubbs provides lower security accommodation for remand and short-term prisoners.

FLEET PRISON

The original building of this infamous debtors' prison, by the Fleet River which then ran open to the Thames, dated from 1197. In its early days it held some political prisoners, but by the eighteenth century it housed debtors and bankrupts who might live there with their families. Prisoners had to pay fees and there was a grill in the wall of the Fleet to allow them to beg money from those passing in the street outside. Rules in the prison were often lax, though the office of warden could be bought and sold and in 1728 Thomas Bambridge ran the Fleet with such cruelty he was himself committed to Newgate. Destroyed in the Gordon Riots, the Fleet was rebuilt and continued to be a debtors' prison until it was closed in 1844. The Fleet Prison features in a number of stories set in London, including *The Pickwick Papers* written by the young Charles Dickens.

EXECUTION DOCK

A mile downriver from the Tower of London was a gallows where those condemned to death by the Admiralty courts were hung. These were pirates, mutineers and men who had committed murder at sea. The Thames is tidal at Wapping, rising and falling every six hours or so, and Execution Dock would be set up at low tide so that the hanged men would be washed over by three flood tides before their bodies were cut down. Captain Kidd was executed here.

ELIZABETH FRY

In 1813 Elizabeth Fry, a Quaker, learned about the appalling conditions in which women were kept in Newgate Prison. Her campaign to improve conditions in gaols led to an 1823 Gaols Act which brought in paid gaolers, visits from chaplains and women warders in charge of female inmates.

SIEGE IN ST JAMES'S

In 1984, WPC Yvonne Fletcher was gunned down outside the besieged Libyan People's Bureau. The siege proved to be one of the most politically tense events for London in the 1980s and was eventually ended by drastic army action.

THE CRIME MUSEUM

This museum in Scotland Yard is the oldest museum of its kind in the world.

EVENTS AND FESTIVALS
London's year

- There is always some colourful, exciting event to see in London – whether traditional pageantry such as the daily **Changing of the Guard at Buckingham Palace** or a festival of modern music such as the **Notting Hill Carnival in August.**

DAILY: ALL YEAR ROUND

Changing the Guard
At Buckingham Palace at 11.30AM.

Ceremony of the Keys, Tower of London
The official handing over of the keys of the Tower of London has taken place nightly for 700 years. Begins at 10PM.

A large dragon plays its part in Chinese New Year celebrations in London's Chinatown.

JANUARY AND FEBRUARY

New Year's Day Parade
1 January
Bands, floats, and carriages process from Westminster to Mayfair.

Charles I Commemoration
Last Sunday in January
Anniversary of the execution of King Charles I. Cavaliers march through central London in seventeenth-century dress; prayers are said at the Banqueting House, Whitehall.

Great Spitalfields Pancake Race
Last day before Lent (based on the lunar calendar)
Traditionally, on Shrove Tuesday or Pancake Day, pancakes were made to use up butter and eggs before Lent fasting. Teams dress up to race in relays, flipping pancakes. Held at noon or thereabouts, Old Spitalfields Market.

Chinese New Year
January/February
Dragon and lion dances, processions and street entertainment take place in Chinatown near Leicester Square on the Sunday following the lunar Chinese New Year.

MARCH AND APRIL

St. David's Day presentation
1 March (or nearest Sunday)

A member of the Royal Family usually presents the Welsh Guards with the principality's national emblem, a leek.

Oranges and Lemons Service
3rd Thursday in March
Children are presented with the fruits during a special service in St. Clement Danes Church in the Strand, and the church bells ring out the nursery rhyme at 9AM, noon, 3PM and 6PM.

Hot Cross Bun Ceremony
Easter Friday
A sailor adds a hot cross bun to the collection in the Widow's Son pub in Bromley-by-Bow, east London. This is in honour of a widow who baked a bun every year for her only son who died at sea.

Easter Parade
Easter Sunday
Around Battersea Park. Brightly coloured floats and marching bands; a full day of activities.

Harness Horse Parade
Easter Monday
Morning parade of heavy working horses in gleaming brass harnesses and plumes, at Battersea Park.

The Queen's Birthday
21 April
This is celebrated with 21-gun salutes in Hyde Park and on Tower Hill at noon by troops in parade dress.

National Gardens Scheme
Late April or early May to October
Private gardens in Greater London are open to the public on set days.

MAY

May Fayre and Puppet Festival
Second Sunday in May
Covent Garden: procession at 10am. Service at St. Paul's Church, Covent Garden at 11:30AM, and then Punch and Judy shows until 6PM where Pepys watched England's first Punch and Judy show in 1662.

Pearly Kings and Queens Service
Third Sunday in May
Memorial service held at St. Martin's in the Field.

Chelsea Flower Show
Last week in May
Plant and flower displays in grounds of Chelsea Royal Hospital. Tickets only available in advance.

JUNE

Beating the Retreat
Early June
The Retreat is beaten on drums by mounted regiments; a very colourful ceremony.

Trooping the Colour.

Last Night of the Proms at the Royal Albert Hall.

Royal Academy's Summer Exhibition
Early June to mid-August
Founded in 1768 with Sir Joshua Reynolds as president and Thomas Gainsborough as a member, the Academy has sponsored summer exhibitions of living painters for over 200 years. Visitors can browse and purchase. Exhibitions are presented daily at Burlington House, Piccadilly.

Trooping the Colour
A designated day in June
To mark the 'official' birthday of the Queen, she inspects her regiments and takes their salute as they parade their colours (flags) before her in Horse Guards Parade, Whitehall. It was essential in battle for troops to recognise their flags as a rallying point, and the first such ceremony was held in Charles II's reign. The young men under the bearskins have been known to pass out from the heat.

Also known as the Queen's Birthday Parade, the pageant extends from Buckingham Palace along the Mall.

City of London Festival
June and July
Annual arts festival throughout the City. Classical concerts venues, include St. Paul's Cathedral.

JULY

Hampton Court Palace Flower Show
Early July
A five-day international event at East Molesey, Surrey. Visitors can purchase the exhibits.

Kenwood Lakeside Concerts
Every Saturday in summer, early July to early September
Annual concerts on the north side of Hampstead Heath. Firework displays and laser shows enliven the premier performances as music drifts from a performance shell across the lake.

The Proms
Mid-July to mid-September
The Henry Wood Promenade Concerts at the Royal Albert Hall attract huge international crowds. The Last Night of the Proms is particularly popular.

AUGUST

Notting Hill Carnival
For two days, usually the Bank Holiday weekend on the last Sunday and Monday in August, one of the largest street festivals in Europe takes place. Colourful processions combine with live music and Caribbean food.

SEPTEMBER

Mayor's Thames Festival
Early September
Weekend of processions, events and stalls along the river around Waterloo down to London Bridge.

Open House
Mid-September
Weekend event: general public can visit buildings of architectural significance that are normally closed.

Raising of the Thames Barrier
September – October
Once a year in a full test is done on this miracle of modern engineering; all ten of the massive steel gates are raised against the high tide.

OCTOBER

Costermongers Pearly Harvest Festival
Harvest thanksgiving service attended by Pearly kings and queens at St. Martin's in the Fields, Trafalgar Square.

The Thames barrier, the world's largest moveable flood barrier.

The traditional pageantry of the State Opening of Parliament.

State Opening of Parliament
First Monday in October
Ever since the seventeenth century, when the English executed Charles I, the British monarch has had no right to enter the House of Commons. Instead, the Queen opens Parliament in the House of Lords, riding from Buckingham Palace to Westminster in a royal coach with the Yeomen of the Guard and the Household Cavalry.

In the Royal Robing Room at the Palace of Westminster the monarch puts on ceremonial robes and the crown.

The Strangers' Gallery is open to spectators on a first-come, first-served basis.

Judges Service
First Monday in October
The judiciary attends a service in Westminster Abbey to mark the opening of the law term. Then, in full regalia and wigs, the procession walks to the House of Lords for the 'Annual Breakfast'. A great view can be had from behind the Abbey.

Quit Rents Ceremony
Late October
An official at the Royal Courts of Justice receives token rents on behalf of the Queen; includes ceremonial splitting of sticks and counting horseshoes.

NOVEMBER

London to Brighton Veteran Run
Over 300 veteran cars compete in this race that starts in Hyde Park and goes through south London on its way to the south coast town of Brighton.

Guy Fawkes' Night
5 November and near Saturdays
Commemorating the anniversary of the discovery of the Gunpowder Plot, an attempt to blow up King James I and his Parliament. Bonfires are lit and Guy Fawkes, the most famous conspirator, is burned in effigy. Firework displays nowadays mostly replace the bonfires.

Christmas lights
Early November to the New Year
Switched on by a celebrity, bright lights decorate Oxford Street, Regent Street and many other shopping areas.

Wreaths laid at the Cenotaph in Whitehall for Remembrance Sunday.

Remembrance Sunday
Nearest Sunday to 11 November
To remember those who died in war, the Queen, the prime minister and other dignitaries lay wreaths and observe a minute's silence at the Cenotaph. Red poppies are worn.

Lord Mayor's Procession & Show
Second Saturday in November
The procession, with some two miles of colourful floats, goes from the Guildhall to the Royal Courts of Justice in the City. This marks the inauguration of the new lord mayor and his presentation to the monarch, who must ask permission to enter the City square mile – a right jealously guarded by London merchants since the 1600s.

DECEMBER

Caroling under the Norwegian Christmas Tree
Most evenings in Trafalgar Square.

Watch Night
31 December: New Year's Eve
Thousands gather in Trafalgar Square to celebrate the New Year while at St. Paul's Cathedral, a New Year's Eve service takes place at 11:30PM.

Pearly Kings and Queens
The London tradition of the Pearly Kings and Queens began in 1875, inspired by a young lad, Henry Croft. Born in 1862 and raised in an orphanage, at 13 Henry became a municipal road sweeper and ratcatcher in the local market. He worked hard and soon made many friends – including the costermongers, a tough set of fruit sellers who looked after each other and collected money to help any fellow sellers in need. Costermongers wore 'Flash Boy Outfits' to distinguish themselves from the other traders, decorating the seam of their trousers with a row of pearl buttons that they found in the markets. Fascinated by this, Henry decided to help the unfortunate and the children back at the orphanage. He adopted a costermonger's 'flash boy outfit' and totally covered this with tiny pearl buttons. After many hours sewing, Henry appeared in his suit at a local carnival.

An instant attraction, he was able to raise money – and was soon approached by many fund-raising hospitals and churches. Henry asked the costermongers to help and

soon there was a Pearly Family for every London borough: the Pearly monarchy had begun. When he died in 1930, Henry had collected over £5,000 (equivalent to £200,000 today). His spectacular funeral was filmed by Pathe News. All four hundred Pearlies attended and followed the coffin to Finchley Cemetery. A statue was erected over the grave, showing Henry wearing his famous buttoned suit.

The Pearly tradition has continued and some 40 families still collect at fundraising events for charity. Some can be traced back to the original Pearlies, including Henry's great-granddaughter. Their motto is: 'One Never Knows'. In 1975 the original Pearly Kings and Queens Association agreed to meet every month in the crypt in St. Martins in the Field, Trafalgar Square. Dedicated to helping the church, the Pearlies all attend the Harvest Festival Service there and a Memorial Service in May (the month of Henry Croft's birthday) for past Pearlies. Both of these services are spectacular events as they are attended by all the Pearlies and their children – Pearly Princes and Princesses – dressed in their buttoned suits.

A Pearly family ensures the tradition will not be lost.

SPORT
Opportunities to watch or play

- As the capital of a nation renowned for its enthusiasm for both playing and watching sport, London provides many sporting possibilities for both watching and participating in a wide variety of sporting activities. Here are details of just a few.

SPORTS FACILITIES

More than three fifths of adult Londoners take part in sporting or physical activity every month. Sports halls and swimming pools abound, even in Inner London – despite the fact that less than 40 per cent of the region's population live there. So many city workers and commuters can use these facilities on the way home from work or during lunch breaks.

There are ice skating rinks in Bayswater, Brixton and Broadgate and several climbing walls in the Inner London area. Other more specialised facilities, such as indoor tennis and bowling centres, are more plentiful in Outer London. The Thames, reservoirs and the regenerated Docklands area provide the opportunity for water sports including canoeing, rowing, sailing and windsurfing. Also available are pool and snooker in pubs and clubs, horse riding in Hyde Park, Hampstead Heath or Wimbledon Common, and tennis courts in many local parks.

FOOTBALL

One of the most popular pastimes for Londoners is football – whether playing or watching the sport. London is home to 12 teams playing in the professional league, with six London teams in the FA Premier League. Arsenal's Emirates Stadium has a capacity of 60,432, while Chelsea's capacity is 42,055 and Tottenham Hotspur's is 36,310.

FOOTBALL ORIGINS

Modern English football has its formal origins in 1863 when the Football Association was founded. The Challenge Cup (later the FA Cup) was launched in 1871. The world's first international match was played on 3 November 1872 between England and Scotland. Soon fixtures between the major clubs led to the formation of the Football League in 1888. By 1914, football had become the British national sport. London teams are now world famous.

WEMBLEY STADIUM

Wembley is a famous stadium with a long tradition as a venue for sport and entertainment. It was originally part of a much larger complex built for the 1924 British Empire Exhibition. It became the main venue for the 1948 Olympic Games, the 1966 World Cup and 1996's European Football Championships. It was also the venue for the Live Aid concert in 1985. Wembley's famous twin towers were not included in the original structure, but were

The new Wembley stadium with its iconic arch.

added in 1963 as part of the celebrations of the 100th Anniversary of the Football League.

The new Wembley Stadium, with an iconic arch, opened in 2007 as part of a massive redevelopment.

LONDON MARATHON – FACTS AND FIGURES

This is London's largest sports event, involving 40,000 people and is the biggest

The six London Premiership teams

Name	Founded	Nickname	Stadium
Arsenal	1886	The Gunners	Emirates Stadium
Chelsea	1905	The Blues	Stamford Bridge
Fulham	1879	The Cottagers	Craven Cottage
QPR	1882	The Superhoops	Loftus Road
Tottenham	1882	Spurs	White Hart Lane
West Ham Utd	1895	The Hammers	Boleyn Ground

Weary runners approach the finish line of the London marathon.

one-day fund-raising event in Britain: more than £47 million was raised in 2010 (latest available figures).

In its inaugural race in 1981, only 7,055 competitors took part. With places for 35,000 runners in 2013, the vast majority of those will expect to finish the course from Greenwich Park to Buckingham Palace. During the race they will get through about 2,000 sticking plasters and 100 pounds of Vaseline.

CRICKET

The origins of cricket are obscure. One theory is that the game was invented by shepherds to help them pass long hours spent in the fields. Another theory suggests that it developed from an ancient game called club-ball. The first recorded cricket match took place at Coxheath in Kent in 1646, where the players used 'battes' which resembled straightened hockey sticks. These were swung like clubs while the balls were simply stones or any other convenient missile! Today, balls are made from cork, covered with red leather. The modern cricket bat was invented in the 1850s.

Test matches are the most popular events. These international competitions are played every summer: two are held in London; the second match is always played

The Oval cricket ground – once the site of a market garden.
Marylebone Cricket Club (MCC) insignia.

at Lord's Cricket Ground in St John's Wood and the final match is always played at the Oval, in Kennington south of the river. The 'London' clubs are Middlesex, who play at Lords and Surrey, who play at the Oval. When the Montpelier Club was homeless in 1844, the search was on for a new ground. One member secured a lease on the Kennington Oval, a market garden then owned by the Prince of Wales. Hoping to attract new members from all over the county, the Club renamed itself the Surrey County Cricket Club and moved into its new premises in 1845. The Club remains at the Oval to this day.

The Middlesex County Cricket Club has various grounds all over London but its most famous ground is Lord's, home of the Club since 1877. Thomas Lord, a member of the Marylebone Cricket Club (or MCC) founded Lord's. In the eighteenth century, cricket was traditionally played by the gentry but as the game became increasingly popular and attracted large, boisterous audiences, the players decided

The grass courts of the Wimbledon Tennis Championship.

to look for a more exclusive venue. Thomas Lord found suitable land on a rural site in St John's Wood, situated in the Parish of Marylebone, giving rise to the name of the Marylebone Cricket Club. The site was named after him.

RUGBY

The name 'rugby' is derived from Rugby School, where the game was invented in the nineteenth century. In the UK, two types of rugby are played. Rugby Union has 15 a side and only became a professional sport in 1995, whereas Rugby League has 13 a side and has long been a professional game. In London, the bigger Rugby Union teams are Harlequins and Wasps, but other clubs include London Irish, Richmond and Saracens. The Rugby Union cup final is played at Twickenham, where international matches are also held.

Harlequins began life as Hampstead Football Club in 1866. Membership had ceased to be purely local by 1870, so a new name was needed. As the Club wished to retain their 'HFC' monogram, they wished the new name to begin with the letter 'H'. 'Harlequin' was chosen

by popular consensus – but half of Hampstead Football Club left to form a new team – the Wasps.

Wasps RUFC was originally formed in 1867 at the Eton and Middlesex Tavern in north London. Its name reflects the Victorian fashion of naming clubs after insects, birds or animals. Wasps were invited to be founders of the Rugby Football Union in 1871. However, the team turned up on the wrong day for the inauguration ceremony, thus forfeiting their right to be classed as founders!

THE WIMBLEDON LAWN TENNIS CHAMPIONSHIPS

The All England Lawn Tennis Club, which developed from an earlier croquet association, hosts this famous tennis tournament, the world's most historic tennis event. The Championships last a fortnight, running from the last week in June to the first week in July. It is the only Grand Slam tennis tournament still played on grass. Around half a million spectators visit Wimbledon each year.

When it all began in 1877, the only event in the Lawn Tennis Championship

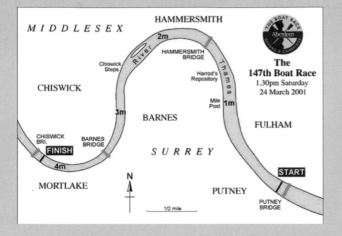

THE OXFORD AND CAMBRIDGE BOAT RACE

An event unique to London is this annual race between the two oldest universities in England. Dating from 1829, it takes place in late March or early April over 4 1/4 miles from Putney to Mortlake – three times the length of an Olympic course. The Boat Race was begun by Charles Merival, a student at Cambridge, and his Harrow schoolfriend, Charles Wordsworth (nephew of the poet William Wordsworth) who was studying at Oxford. On 12 March 1829, Cambridge sent a challenge to Oxford and thus the tradition was born. The first race took place at Henley-on-Thames in Oxfordshire and newspapers reported that crowds of 20,000 came to watch. It was such a success that the townspeople organised a regatta of their own which became Henley Royal Regatta.

After that first year, the early boat races took place at Westminster but, by 1845, had become too crowded, so the race moved up-stream to Putney. At first, the crews wore no distinguishing colours. Then, in 1836, Oxford raced in dark blue – the colour of their stroke-man's college (Christ Church). Cambridge adopted the duck egg blue of Eton.

There has been only one dead heat, in 1877. The judge on the finish ('Honest' John Phelps) was asleep under a bush as the crews raced past. Awakened and asked the result he said, 'Dead heat to Oxford by four feet'!

In 1912 both boats sank and the race was re-run the next day, but the race has never been cancelled due to bad weather.

CRYSTAL PALACE

Crystal Palace National Sports Centre in Sydenham Hill is a centre for athletics. It provides indoor and outdoor facilities for over 100 different sporting activities, including swimming, football and martial arts, as well as catering for specialist activities such as scuba diving, canoeing, skiing and fencing. The stadium seats 12,000 spectators and the Sports Hall accommodates 2,000.

2012 OLYMPICS LEGACY

From swimming at the Aquatics Centre, cycling on new paths, or watching world-class athletics or other sporting events at the main stadium, the Olympic Park in east London has transformed the sporting opportunities in the capital. Designed from the beginning to offer a sustainable legacy to the city, the specially built Olympic venues will encourage sporting participation for years to come.

- There have been six sinkings in the Oxford and Cambridge Boat Race.
- 710,000 bottles of water are drunk during the London marathon.
- In 1877, spectators paid just one shilling to watch the Wimbledon final.
- Some believe that cricket was invented by shepherds to pass the time in the fields.

was the Gentlemen's Singles. In 1884, the Ladies' Singles was launched. The Wimbledon tennis tournament has had royal associations since 1907 when the Prince of Wales and Queen Mary were spectators. Today it is still attended by enthusiastic members of the Royal Family.

THE STELLA ARTOIS TOURNAMENT

This tennis championship in Hammersmith finishes a week before Wimbledon begins. The tournament is popular with players as it provides a good opportunity for them to acclimatise to playing on grass courts.

The Crystal Palace arena.

LONDON 2012: THE OLYMPICS
The city goes for gold.

- In 2012 London became the first city in the
- world to host three Olympic Games (after
- 1908 and 1948). The Olympics bring the world
- together through sport, and the overall
- message of the spectacular Opening Ceremony
- was 'This is for everyone'.

Athletes parade around the stadium during the Opening Ceremony.

The Opening Ceremony featured thousands of volunteer performers recreating scenes from Britain's past and present. Here giant chimneys erupt from the ground as a pastoral scene gives way to the pandemonium of the Industrial Revolution.

The Olympic torch in the innovative form of a Cauldron of 'petals', which come together to form the Flame of Unity.

Fireworks complete the Opening Ceremony and announce the beginning of the Games.

In one of the Opening Ceremony's most exciting sections, the Olympic Rings rise high above the stadium and come together in what seems to be a shower of sparks.

The Velodrome. During competitions the temperature was maintained at 28°C to provide optimal conditions for the cyclists.

The Aquatic Centre used more than 180,000 tiles to line the pools.

The Olympic Park, which covered 2.5 square kilometres (nearly one square mile), the size of 357 football pitches. After the games it was renamed the Queen Elizabeth Olympic Park.

The Olympic Stadium seated 80,000 spectators during the games.

American Michael Phelps becomes the most decorated Olympian of all time with 22 medals.

GB's Bradley Wiggins wins the men's cycling time trial.

Great Britain's Jessica Ennis does a lap of honour after winning the women's heptathlon.

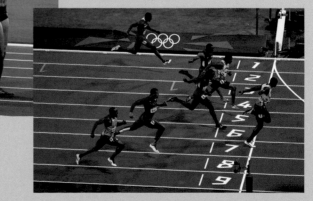

Usain Bolt of Jamaica wins gold in the men's 100 metres and sets a new Olympic record of 9.63 seconds.

BIBLIOGRAPHY

Ackroyd, Peter
London, the Biography
Chatto & Windus, 2000

Alton, G.A.
Contemporary Accounts of the Great Plague
Tressell Publications, 1985

Alton, G.A.
The Great Fire of London
Tressell Publications, 1987

Baker, Michael H. C.
London Transport 1933–1962
Ian Allan Publishing, 1996

Baker, Michael H. C.
London Transport since 1963
Ian Allan Publishing, 1997

Baker, Richard
Richard Baker's London
Jarrold Colour Publications, 1989

Barman, Christian
The Man who Built London Transport: A Biography of Frank Pick
David & Charles, 1979

Barker, T. and M. Robbins
A History of London Transport Vol. 1: The Nineteenth Century
Allen & Unwin 1975

Barker, T. and M. Robbins
A History of London Transport Vol. 2: The Twentieth Century
Allen & Unwin, 1974

Barnett, Isobel
Exploring London
Ebury Press, 1985

Bateman, Nick
Gladiators at the Guildhall
Museum of London Archaeological Service, 2000

Black, J. Anderson, Owen North and Holly North
Crimes and Punishment
Blitz Editions, 1998

Booth, Charles
Life and Labour of the People in London (17 vols)
Macmillan, 1902

Briggs, Asa
A Social History of England
Penguin, 1999

Brown, R. Douglas
The Port of London
Lavenham Press, 1978

Church, Richard
London's Parks: An Appreciation
HMSO, 1993

Clout, Hugh
The Times History of London
Times Books, 1991

Cox, Jane
Hatred Pursued Beyond the Grave
HMSO, 1993

Cox, Jane
London's East End: Life and Traditions
Weidenfeld and Nicolson, 1993

Davies, Andrew
The Map of London: From 1746 to the Present Day
B T Batsford, 1987

Davies, Gill
The Timechart History of Medicine
Worth Press, 1999

Duncan, Andrew
Secret London
New Holland Publishers, 1995

Duncan, Andrew
Walking London
New Holland Publishers, 1999

Fletcher, Geoffrey
The London Nobody Knows
Penguin, 1962

Haliday, Stephen
The Great Stink of London
Button Publishing, 1999

Hawkes, Jason
London from the Air
Ebury Press, 1992

Hawkes, Jason
London Landmarks from the Air
Ebury Press, 1996

Hobhouse, Hermione
A History of Regent Street
Macdonald & Janes, 1975

Hobley, Brian
Roman and Saxon London: A reappraisal
Museum of London, 1986

Hollis, Leo
Cadogan Book of Historic London Walks
Cadogan Books, 2005

Hornak, Angelo
London from the Thames
Little, Brown & Co, 1999

Hudson, Sarah
AA All-in-One Guide
AA Publishing, 1998

Inwood, Stephen
A History of London
Macmillan, 1998

Jackson, Alan
Rails Through the Clay: A History of London's Tube Railways
Allen & Unwin, 1962

Jackson, Alan
Semi-Detached London: Suburban Development, Life and Transport 1900–39
Allen & Unwin, 1973

Jenkins, Alan
The Book of the Thames
Macmillan, 1983

Jones, Richard
Walking Haunted London
New Holland Publishers, 1999

Kynaston, David
The City of London (4 vols)
Chatto & Windus 1994–2000

Lejeune, Anthony and Malcolm Lewis
The Gentlemen's Clubs of London
Bracken Books, 1984

London's Royal Parks
The Royal Parks, 1993

Milne, Gustav
The Port of Roman London
Batsford, 1985

Nelles Guide: London, England and Wales
Nelles Verlag GmbH, 1996

Olsen, D.
Town Planning in London in the Eighteenth and Nineteenth Centuries
New Haven, 1964

Olsen, D.
The Growth of Victorian London
Peregrine Books, 1979

Organ, Kenneth O.
The Oxford Illustrated History of Britain
Oxford University Press, 1984

Parsons, Tom
100 Treasures of Buckingham Palace
Royal Collection Enterprises 2000

Plowden, Alison
Elizabethan England
The Reader's Digest Association, 1982

Porter, Roy
London, A Social History
Hamish Hamilton, 1994

Porter, Stephen
The Great Fire of London
Sutton Publishing, 1996

Rennison, Nick
London Writing
Waterstone's Booksellers, 1999

Richardson, John
The Annals of London
Cassell & Co, 2000

Ross, Cathy and John Clark
London: the Illustrated History
Penguin/Museum of London, 2011

Sheppard, Francis
London: A History
Oxford University Press, 1999

Spencer, Herbert
London's Canal
Putman & Co, 1961

Thorold, Peter
The London Rich
Penguin, 1999

Time Out Guide: London
Penguin, 1989

Travers, Tony
The Politics of London, Governing an Ungovernable City
Palgrave Mamillan, 2004

Waller, Maureen
1700: Scenes from London Life
Hodder & Stoughton, 2000

Weightman, Gavin
London River, The Thames Story
Collins & Brown, 1990

Weightman, Gavin
Bright Lights, Big City, London Entertained 1830–1950
Collins & Brown, 1992

Weightman, Gavin and Steve Humphries
The Making of Modern London: A people's history of the capital from 1815 to the present day
Ebury, 2007

Weinrab, Ben, Christopher Hibbert, John and Julia Keay
The London Encyclopedia, 3rd edition
Pan Macmillan, 2011

White, Jerry
London: The Story of a Great City
Andre Deutsch/Museum of London, 2010

Yap, Nick and Rupert Tenison
London – The Secrets and the Splendour
Könemann, 1999

IMAGE CREDITS

Images are public domain/out of copyright or private collection unless otherwise credited.

front cover Getty Images; 2–3 Corbis; 4 Getty Images; 8 Corbis; 9–11 map Oxford Cartographers; 12–14 maps Mike Taylor (SGA Suffolk), images Corbis; 16–17 longships, Thinkstock/Dorling Kindersley Royalty Free; Alfred, Edward, William, Thinkstock/© Getty Images Credit: Photos.com; 18–19 Henry, DAG Publications; Magna Carta, Thinkstock/© Getty Images Credit: Photos.com; Tower of London, Thinkstock/iStockphoto; 20–21 Charing Cross, Wikimedia Commons Author Adam Bishop, licensed under the Creative Commons Attribution-Share Alike license; Edward, Thinkstock/© Getty Images Credit: Photos.com; Wallace, Corbis; Black Death, Wikimedia creative commons/Susan Boyd Lees; 22–23 Whittington, Thinkstock/© Getty Images Credit: Photos.com; Humphrey, Alamy; Agincourt, Caxton, Roses, Corbis; 24–25 Bosworth, Corbis; Drapers, Alamy; Queen's House, Thinkstock/ Ingram Publishing; Anne, ship Thinkstock/© Getty Images Credit: Photos.com; Jane, Thinkstock/iStockphoto; 26–27 modern Globe, David Playne; 30–31 Billingsgate, Thinkstock/iStockphoto; Turpin, bridge Thinkstock/© Getty Images Credit: Photos.com; Gin Lane, Thinkstock/iStockphoto; 34–35 Montague House, docks, Corbis; Regent Street, Bedford Square, Roy Williams; Benjamin, Getty Images; 36–37 Moorfields, Alamy; Regent's Canal, Southwark Bridge, Corbis; 38–39 Marble Arch, Roy Williams; Cato Street, Corbis; 40–41 Nelson's Column, Thinkstock/ Polka Dot/ Jupiterimages; Exhibition, Big Ben, sewers, Corbis; 42–43 Needle, streetscape, Thinkstock/© Getty Images Credit: Photos.com; Albert Bridge, Greenwich, Putney Bridge, Thinkstock/iStockphoto; 44–45 Savoy, Eros, Tate, Ritz, Chelsea, Coliseum, Roy Williams; Baden-Powell, Corbis; 46–47 Geological Museum, Roy Williams; Baird, Science Picture Library; 48–49 Festival, World Cup, Corbis; 50–51 street party, Shard, river pageant, Roy Williams; Olympic flame, wedding, Corbis; 52–53 Father Thames, Kew Bridge, Eye, Blackfriars, police, M16, Cutty Sark, David Playne; Old London Bridge, Playne Photographic Library; Tower Bridge, Thinkstock/iStockphoto; race, Battersea, barrier, Rupert Tenison; 54–55 World History Archive/Alamy; 56 Corbis; 58 North Wind Picture Archive/ Alamy; 59 Hilary Morgan/Alamy; 60–61 Eros, Bruno Zarri; Berkeley Square, Regent Street, David Playne; Princes, Chinatown, David Playne; Soho, Alan Copson; Carnaby, Brian Gibbs; 64–65 view, David Playne; Exchange, Monument,

Ben Yates; 66 David Playne; 68 Corbis; 70–71 foundry, Whitechapel Foundry; Docklands, Ben Yates; 72–73 conversions, Alex McCarren; Canada Square, Bruno Zarri; 74 Bruno Zarri; 76–77 Yeoman, Historic Royal Palaces; Downing Street, M16, David Playne; 78–79 procession, Jeremy Hemming; St. James's, David Playne; Buckingham, Brian Gibbs; 80–81 Kensington, Brian Gibbs; coach, David Playne; Banqueting House, Historic Royal Palaces; horse, Jeremy Hemming; 82–83 Corbis; 86–87 Derek Littlewood; 88–89 sewer, Thames Water; Cabinet War Rooms, Derek Littlewood; 90–91 excavating, Jane Cox; 93 Down Street, Derek Littlewood; bus, David Playne; 94–95 tram, Transport Museum; taxi, David Playne; Little Venice, Roy Williams; 96–97 BM, British Museum; Clink, IWM, Ben Yates; Aquarium, Jolyon Phillips; 98–99 NHM, David Playne; armour, crown, Royal Armouries; 100 David Playne; 101 Blood Brothers, Jolyon Phillips; Palladium, Rupert Tenison; 102–3 Oz, Corbis; Theatre Royal, Theatre Royal; Gielgud, David Playne; 104–5 Mousetrap, Globe, South Bank, David Playne; Barbican, Barbican Theatre; 106–7 Smithfield, Billingsgate, Corporation of London; 108–9 Berwick, David Playne; Columbia, Brick Lane, Rupert Tenison; Portobello, Chris Linnett; 110–11 Camden, Shepherd, David Playne; Covent Garden, Rupert Tenison; Spitalfields, Corbis; 112–13 Chelsea, Chelsea Physic Garden; Kenwood, Alex McCarren; Pan, Brian Gibbs; 114–15 ride, David Playne; statue, Sue Cunningham; rowing, Rupert Tenison; deer, Viv Mullett; 116–17 chairs, Alex McCarren; lake, Brian Gibbs; Smithfield, Ben Yates; Waterloo Vase, The Royal Collection © 2001 Her Majesty Queen Elizabeth II; 118–19 Battersea, BT Tower, Cenotaph, Rupert Tenison; 120–21 Monument, David Playne; Somerset, OXO, Rupert Tenison; 122–23 Tower, Brian Gibbs; Nelson, Rupert Tenison; City Hall, David Playne; 124–26 Shard, Roy Williams; Westminster, David Playne; 126–29 Playne Photographic Library; 130–31 paper, Crippen, Playne Photographic Library; Blind Beggar, Rupert Tenison; 132–33 Justice, Chris Parker; 134–35 Corbis; 137 Proms, Robbie Jack; 138–39 Parliament, Cenotaph, Corbis; Pearlies, Brian Gibbs; 141 Marathon, Jeremy Hemming; 143 Crystal Palace, Marion Bull; 144 Corbis; 145 Velodrome, Park, Stadium, Alamy; Aquatic Centre, Phelps, Wiggins, Ennis, Bolt, Corbis; back cover Royal Barge, Olympic Rings, Corbis; Buckingham Palace, Getty Images.

While every effort has been made to trace copyright holders and seek permission to use illustrative material, the publishers wish to apologise for any inadvertent errors or omissions and would be glad to rectify these in future editions.

INDEX